The
Healthy
Life

To the JSHealth community.
Thank you for being by my side,
understanding me, supporting me and
being so passionate about healthy living.
We are in this journey together.
I am so proud of you.

The Healthy Life

JESSICA SEPEL

Contents

WELCOME TO THE HEALTHY LIFE

Are you ready to nourish your body with nutrition and heal your relationship with food? Put an end to diets and negative self-talk? Are you ready to clean up your eating habits and kickstart a healthy lifestyle? Are you ready to be the happiest, healthiest version of yourself? I know you are – and I'm so glad to come along for this ride. Thank you for making the decision to better your health and for letting me be your guide. Believe me when I say that your wellbeing has a ripple effect; it will have a huge, positive impact on your life and the lives of those around you.

I know this, because I've been there. Who I am now is very different from the person I was just a few years ago. I had a very turbulent relationship with food and my body after starting a diet – for fun – when I was sixteen. I wasn't particularly overweight, but losing weight excited me. So I dieted. And I felt AMAZING. People were commenting. I could wear a bikini with such confidence. *Wow … this is fun! I am on top of the world.* One thing led to the next, and I took it too far. I became obsessive. I am a typical Type-A personality and a perfectionist. I became a dieter. A fad dieter. A calorie counter. I dieted and dieted to the point of food restriction and became incredibly underweight. I began fearing food. I needed control over every mouthful of food and ounce of body weight. It was exhausting. And then, these restrictions led to binges. A vicious cycle, because after the binge I would restrict even further. If my diet wasn't perfect, my life felt out of control. So I used food to control my life.

Being thin felt good. It felt like I could control EVERYTHING. It's a very false sense of control, because you are not fixing the core issue. But in order to keep that feeling I had to keep my diet and weight under control. It took years of self-healing, therapy and study about health and the human body, but I have finally freed myself from the tormenting thoughts. Sometimes those old thoughts do pop up. This is because my mind tries to bring me back to patterns of the past. 'Jess, you don't look skinny enough in those pictures.' 'Jess, you are not good enough.' 'Jess, you did not eat perfectly today.' But now I am able to rein in those thoughts and say … 'Hang on a minute. Stop. Perfect does not exist. You are good enough. You are healthy.' This period nearly scarred my relationship with food for life.

Today, I can see that I chased love, happiness and approval in all of the wrong places. I used food to reward and punish myself. Since I could never maintain the 'perfect' diet or 'ideal' weight, I was caught in a toxic cycle. I felt I needed to be thin to be loved and appreciated. I constantly compared myself to others. I believe those negative thoughts only did more harm to my weight than good. I obsessed over food and my body and suffered as a result. On the outside, I 'had it all', but I just couldn't see it. I was distracted by the endless and futile pursuit to be perfect, and lost sight of the blessings in my life. For a while there, I lost my self-confidence and balance. I focused my uncertainty and self-hate on my body, and in turn, my body became my biggest burden. I feared scales, yet I couldn't stop jumping on them. The number that flashed up would make or break my mood for the day. Instead of focusing on my talents, strengths and blessings, all I could think about was the heaviness of my body. And I blamed everyone else for my problems – including my weight.

If I were to paint a portrait of my life then, it would look like this:

* sleep-deprived
* drowning in low self-esteem
* listless and lacking a zest for life
* putting on weight without understanding why
* crippled by anxiety
* suffering from hormonal havoc
* dependent on alcohol in social settings
* gulping down four 'calorie-free' black coffees a day
* abusing artificial sweeteners
* eating low-fat everything
* paranoid about getting sick
* calorie-counting and fad-dieting
* exercising intensely twice a day
* depriving myself of foods, which meant I ended up bingeing
* visiting every dietician in Sydney.

Oh, I was also surgically attached to my iPhone, obsessed with spray tans and completely, utterly out of touch with my own body. The scary thing is, I thought my lifestyle was normal. Healthy, even – and I was studying health! My mind was the master and my body was the slave. It. Was. Exhausting. And it's no way to live.

Fast forward a few years, and I'm a completely different person inside and out. I have taken control of my life and my thoughts. I now take a more gentle approach to nutrition, health and wellbeing. It's as simple as this: I listen to my body and give it exactly what it needs.

So what did I change? First, I committed myself to learning as much as I could about nutrition and how the body works. I also:

* built up my self-esteem and my relationship with food
* started seeing a good psychologist to tap into the roots of my pain and to manage stress
* gave up processed foods for wholefoods
* reduced my gluten and sugar intake
* drank less caffeine and alcohol
* drank more water
* added more greens into my diet
* cut out toxic scenes and relationships that did not serve me well
* made sleep a priority
* embraced natural skincare and cleaning products
* moved my body in ways that I loved.

I learnt to respect myself. I learnt that I am good enough, just as I am. Thanks to this shift, I am now able to say I love my body. It's taken me a long time to be able to call my body beautiful and doing so still brings tears to my eyes.

Now that I'm on the other side, I want to help anyone and everyone I can. I look around and see women constantly battling their bodies. I see them striving for perfection and beating themselves up when they perceive that they've failed. I see far too many gorgeous souls suffering from low self-esteem. I see the anxious, tired and overweight people who have no real sense of how to make things better. It breaks my heart to see people in the pain I remember so clearly. I'm here to tell you that it does get better. You can get off the guilt rollercoaster. You can stop fighting yourself. You can learn to love yourself and your body unconditionally. You can be imperfectly perfect.

Since releasing my first self-published ebook, *The Clean Life* my professional and personal health journeys have developed in ways I could have never imagined. *The Healthy Life* not only features recipes from my ebook but reflects more of what I've learnt about myself, nutrition and living a healthy lifestyle. I'm so excited to bring you new and delicious recipes and refined tips and tricks that I've picked up along the way.

I wrote this book to inspire people to feel more comfortable in their own skin. I am living proof that a gentle approach – one where you let go of self-criticism and focus on making small but positive changes – works. It really does. I'm not perfect. *No one is*. I'm still learning and I want nothing more than for you to join me, and to support others on the same path.

I hope this book provides guidance, comfort and freedom from the pointless pursuit of perfection. Because that's how I feel now: free from the obsessions, harsh thoughts and stress. Free from deprivation and diets. Free from everything that was holding me back.

It's a wonderful, euphoric feeling.

Let's do this!

Jess xo

HOW THIS BOOK CAN HELP YOU

There are so many conflicting messages about health, it can be hard to know who to listen to. In my opinion, we need to tune in to our own bodies and continue to educate ourselves. It's up to us to stay informed and to follow the methods and guidelines that suit our bodies and lifestyles best.

Do you:

* wake up tired?
* get bloated after eating?
* experience slumps at 11 am or 4 pm?
* catch yourself doing three things at once?
* find it hard to lose or maintain your weight?
* have a low sex drive?
* feel guilty after indulging?
* struggle to retain and remember information?
* get skin breakouts?
* suffer from debilitating PMS?
* feel angry at everyone and everything?
* desperately want to change something about yourself or life?

If you answered yes to any of these, you've found the right book. In here, I share a range of healthy habits to inspire you to live a more wholesome, happy life.

Before You Start...

I'd love for you to fill out this questionnaire. Then, when you're on the journey, you can come back to it and see just how far you've come. If you follow all aspects of The Healthy Life plan, I promise your answers will change dramatically in a matter of weeks.

1. How do you feel right now, emotionally and physically?.................................
....

2. What is your greatest health challenge?...
....

3. At what point in your life did you feel your best?.................................
....

4. What do you feel is stopping you from being your best right now?...............
....

5. What are your main health goals?...
....

6. How do you take care of yourself right now?..
....

7. Do you feel incredibly alive and present in your life?................................
....

Identifying a problem is the first step to solving it. If you can articulate what is holding you back or making you unhappy, you'll have a better chance of envisioning the path in front of you.

Use #thehealthylife and #jshealth on Instagram to let everyone know how your new and improved lifestyle is going. Remember, we're all in this together.

Commitment Contract

I promise to embark on this health journey with optimism.

I am dedicated to making health a priority – the number one priority – in my life.

I will be honest and patient, and continue to make small changes to have a big impact.

I promise to forgive myself for any choices or attitudes I had in the past, and look to a brighter, happier, healthier future.

I will remind myself daily that I am enough just as I am.

I relieve myself from the need and desire to look and be perfect.

And I will commend myself for putting in the effort to better my health.

Name: ....

Date: ....

10 Principles for a Healthier Life

The Endocrine Syst

Health is holistic

It doesn't matter how fit you are – if you don't eat right, all your hard work is going to waste. It doesn't matter if you eat like a nutritionist – if you don't move your body then it won't perform at its optimum. And it doesn't matter if you're a green-juice-drinking, TRX-loving yogi – if you're under a lot of stress and pressure, your health will suffer. That's why I advocate a holistic philosophy, one that pays attention to diet *and* lifestyle, and connects the mind, body and soul.

In this chapter, you'll discover my top ten guidelines to a healthy life. As soon as I addressed these issues, my body and mind responded in a huge way. I felt lighter and brighter, happier and healthier, and I've felt that way ever since.

The Healthy Life program homes in on the following:

1. good gut health
2. blood-sugar balance
3. detoxing the liver and your environment
4. keeping hormones in check
5. less stress, more rest
6. emotional eating and the power of self-love
7. movement
8. beauty from the inside out
9. sleep
10. weight loss.

This book will teach you how to eat, move and ultimately feel better; it's not about weight loss. If you follow the guidelines and start listening to your body, any extra weight you're holding on to will drop off. As I tell my clients, weight loss is one of the side-effects of healthy eating.

Once you've learnt about the ten principles, you'll be ready to put them into action.

PRINCIPLE 1. GOOD GUT HEALTH

You are not what you eat; you are what you digest and absorb. It's not the prettiest part of the body, but your gut is the key to sustaining good health. It deserves a lot of care and attention, and that's why it's my number one area to target. The digestive system turns the food you eat into fuel. When it's sluggish, your body will not absorb the nutrients it needs for optimal health. On the flipside, when the gut is functioning well, it boosts your energy and immune system, and prevents all sorts of diseases.

How does digestion work?

Digestion begins in the mouth. As we chew, our saliva coats the food and sends signals to the brain to prepare for the digestive process. Too many people inhale their food, which compromises the first step of digestion. Once the food enters the stomach, hydrochloric acid and enzymes work to break it down into small particles. Then those particles travel to the small intestine, allowing the nutrients to be absorbed into your blood. Lastly, the waste matter moves to the large intestine, ready to be excreted – and that's when you feel the urge to go to the bathroom. Many people have damaged microvilli (gut wall), which means they do not absorb all the nutrients they should. But don't panic! Most digestive dysfunctions can be easily treated.

What's all this talk about leaky gut?

When there are gaps in the gut lining, food fragments can escape into the bloodstream, leading the body to react with an immune response. This is usually caused by food allergies and known as 'leaky gut syndrome'. It usually rears its head with symptoms like bloating, gas, cravings and food sensitivities.

Healthy stool = healthy digestion

It is important to 'go' once or twice daily for the healthy release of toxins. If you've got a dysfunctional digestive system, you may experience constipation, diarrhoea, bloating, flatulence, reflux, skin disorders, abdominal discomfort, sluggish metabolism, hormonal imbalances, low energy, mood swings and poor immunity. Poor chewing, overeating, food allergies and frequent use of antibiotics can affect digestion.

Healthy gut = healthy mind

Believe it or not, our digestive system is closely connected to our mind. That's because we make serotonin (the 'feel-good' hormone) in our gut – which explains why people with digestive issues tend to experience low moods. Furthermore, 80 per cent of our immune system lies in the gut. Many people with autoimmune conditions usually suffer from gut dysfunction or poor gut health. Antibiotics destroy the good bacteria in the gut, which is why it's so important to repopulate your gut with the 'good' stuff by taking probiotics.

To give your gut some love, follow these tips.

* Drink filtered water between meals. Fluids help to remove excess toxins and keep the bowels healthy.
* Start an elimination diet, noting the foods that energise you, and those that set off bloating and tiredness. Cut those foods out for 1–2 weeks, then slowly reintroduce them to see if they make a difference to how you feel. Ask your nutritionist for help to detect food intolerances.
* Maintain good amounts of hydrochloric acid and digestive enzymes. The easiest way to do this is to enjoy one tablespoon of apple cider vinegar or lemon in warm water each morning. For bonus points, start each meal with something raw and bitter, such as rocket leaves with a drizzle of lemon juice.
* Chew your food well – 20 chews per mouthful should do it!
* Eat and drink prebiotic and probiotic foods, or take supplements to support the 'good' gut bacteria.

WHAT ARE PRE- AND PROBIOTICS?

Prebiotics support the growth of good bacteria, so eat onions, garlic, dandelion, greens, artichokes and bananas. Probiotics repopulate the gut with good bacteria. They're found in fermented veggies like kimchi. I recommend taking a multi-strain supplement (with 5–10 billion species) morning and night.

TOP TIPS FOR HEALING YOUR GUT:

- Eat less! Some digestive problems are simply the result of overeating.
- Add 1–2 tbsp slippery elm to water, oatmeal or smoothies daily to repair the gut lining.
- Take 2–4 g glutamine daily. Glutamine repairs the gut lining. It is usually found in powder form and is an ingredient in most gut-repairing formulas (found at most health-food stores). I add 1 tsp into my smoothies daily.
- Don't drink with meals. Liquids dilute the digestive juices.
- Avoid gluten and all grains for a 4–6 week trial period, as they can damage the gut lining.
- Drink 40 ml of aloe vera juice in the morning to soothe your gut.
- Cut down on sugar for 2–3 weeks. Sugar is inflammatory and feeds the bad bacteria in the gut.
- Eat less fruit and only eat it on an empty stomach. Eat 2 servings of low-fructose fruits such as berries each day. Find my favourite low-sugar fruits on page 95.
- Aim to eat your last meal 2–3 hours before bedtime.
- Sip on chamomile tea at night. It soothes and relaxes the bowel wall, and reduces the possibility of constipation.
- Load up on fibre. My favourite sources are wholegrains (like brown rice and quinoa), beans, legumes, fruit, vegetables, soaked chia seeds, ground flaxseed and psyllium husk. These foods get your bowels moving and help to eliminate excess toxins and hormones.
- Soak grains, nuts and seeds to aid digestion. Find out how on page 98.
- Reduce stressors in your life. The gut shuts down in times of stress.
- Eat peacefully and mindfully. When you sit down to a meal, it should be the only thing on your mind. Avoid talking on the phone, watching TV or reading emails. Focus on the taste and texture of the food and chew, chew, chew! This will curb overeating and improve your relationship with food.

JSHEALTH SIGNATURE STEP-BY-STEP GUIDE TO HEAL YOUR GUT

This three-month program is ideal if you suffer from bloating, frequent gas, stomach pains, nausea, reflux, constipation or diarrhoea, an autoimmune condition or a detected parasite.

PHASE 1: GUT CLEANSE
WEEKS 1–4

Day 1 – Before bed, take a colon-cleanse formula that contains magnesium oxide. Your physician or local health-food store can advise dosage. Alternatively, mix one tablespoon of Epsom salts in water and drink first thing in the morning to cleanse the colon.

Day 2 – Begin daily parasite cleanse for four weeks using an antimicrobial herb formula. These formulas can be found at health-food stores and are known to kill any unwanted bugs and parasites. They usually contain antimicrobial herbs such as garlic, lavender oil, oregano, thyme, wormwood and black walnut hulls. Take the dose before each main meal, three times a day. Continue for four weeks.

Dietary advice
1. Start the day with warm lemon water – add some fresh ginger or mint leaves for extra gut love.
2. Take 40 ml of aloe vera juice each morning.
3. Take 1 tbsp apple cider vinegar before each main meal – this increases stomach acid and digestive juices, helping you to digest and absorb the nutrients in your food.
4. Remove all cow dairy (milk, yoghurt, cheese, ice-cream) – for dairy alternatives see page 97.
5. Remove all gluten (bread, cereal, pasta, crackers – also gluten found in packaged foods and sauces like soy sauce) – for gluten-free swaps see page 21.
6. Remove all sugar (junk foods, chocolate, candy).
7. Remove all soft drinks – regular and diet.
8. Remove all alcohol.
9. Limit caffeine to 1 drink per day (black coffee or tea with nut/coconut milk). If you think coffee irritates your gut, cut it out completely during healing.
10. Minimise fructose consumption – no more than 2 servings of fruit per day and stick to berries and citrus fruits or papaya.
11. Other foods to abstain from:
    * packaged foods (gluten-free included)
    * bottled/tinned sauces
    * take-out food.

Note: you can skip this phase or reduce this phase to two weeks if your digestive symptoms are mild. However, most people seem to do really well with this sort of gut cleanse.

PHASE 2: REPAIR
WEEKS 5–8

Dietary advice

1. Continue on a dairy-free, gluten-free, sugar-free diet. See Heal Your Gut Meal Plan on page 23–23.
2. Other foods to abstain from:
   * alcohol – strictly remove in this phase
   * caffeine – limit to 1 caffeinated drink per day (black coffee or tea with nut/coconut milk)
   * fruit – no more than 2 servings of fruit per day, must be berries, citrus fruit or papaya, best early in the morning only
   * packaged foods (gluten-free included)
   * bottled/tinned sauces
   * take-out food
   * soft drink
3. Be strict with these supplement recommendations – they work magic! You can find them at most health-food stores. Some stock products with all-in-one formulas of the following ingredients:
   * glutamine: 4 g a day – add to smoothies or take in capsule form
   * slippery elm: 1 tbsp a day in smoothies or water
   * aloe vera juice: 40 ml upon waking each morning
   * fish oil: 2 g with food
   * zinc: 30 mg just before bed
   * turmeric: 500 mg with food
   * apple cider vinegar – 1 tbsp before each meal.

PHASE 3: REPOPULATE
WEEKS 9–12

Repopulate the gut with good bacteria via probiotic supplements and probiotic-rich foods.

Maintenance support

1. Probiotic to be taken 2 times per day on an empty stomach: multi-strain, 20–50 billion (1 in the morning before breakfast and 1 just before bed)
2. 1 digestive enzyme after each meal (found at most health-food stores – I use Doctor's Best, Best Digestive Enzymes, found on iherb.com)
3. 2 g glutamine powder daily: add to smoothies/water
4. 2 g fish oil daily with food

TOP TIP

Drink chamomile tea every night before bed. I usually soak 2 teabags in hot water – it acts as an amazing natural laxative.

Diet

1. Start the day with warm lemon water or a shot of apple cider vinegar.
2. Continue gluten-free long term.
3. Add 1–2 tbsp fermented vegetables at each main meal (found at most health-food stores, or make your own).
4. Include plenty of fibre: gluten-free wholegrains, legumes, nuts, seeds, fruits and vegetables.
5. Kombucha for added probiotic benefit to improve digestion (drink in moderation – it is a powerful laxative).
6. One daily serving of dairy for 2 weeks, then increase to 2 servings a day – best to stick with goat's cheese/yoghurt.
7. Enjoy low-fructose fruits and start adding other fruits of choice once a day.
8. Enjoy gut-cleansing foods such as ginger, garlic, dark leafy greens, psyllium husk, chia seeds, kefir, fermented veggies, fennel and peppermint.
9. Avoid chewing gum.
10. Consider avoiding the nightshade family (eggplant, tomato, capsicums/peppers and potatoes) if you have extreme gut issues. They can be inflammatory and worsen symptoms. Remove for a trial period.

TOP TIP

If you suffer from constipation, consider a magnesium supplement under the guidance of a health practitioner. I recommend 400–800 mg of magnesium citrate/dyglicinate just before bedtime – works like a charm!

WHAT TO EXPECT

As your body rids itself of toxins, you may feel less than fantastic in the first few days of your gut cleanse. That's completely normal! You may experience some of the following: headaches (especially if you are having coffee withdrawals), brain fog, heightened emotions, low energy/fatigue, irritability, nausea or a change in appetite.

IN YOUR WORDS

Thank you for your wonderful work and for sharing your ideas and recipes with people like me, who struggle day to day with my relationship with food. I live in England so I am about as far away from you as I can be, yet you continue to inspire me. – *Jen*

FLATULENCE? TRY MAKING THESE CHANGES

* Pop a digestive enzyme with each meal.
* Chew on raw fennel – it calms the stomach.
* Enjoy peppermint and ginger tea.
* Drink 1 tbsp apple cider vinegar in water 3 times a day.
* Try to work out what foods cause gas and eliminate them. Many people find the brassica veggies (broccoli, cauliflower, kale and cabbage) difficult to digest.

IN YOUR WORDS

I have always been health-conscious but for all the wrong reasons. I was introduced to your blog and it immediately resonated with me. It really helped me to change the way I think and feel about my body and it taught me about the true meaning of balance and how everything is interconnected. I have not only lost weight and toned my body over the last year, I have completely changed my thinking and am so aware of how certain foods make my body feel and how to pay attention to my body and its needs! There is no one like you out there with such spot-on perspectives, techniques and recipes! I still read your blog weekly and it never fails to inspire me!

Almost exactly one year after I made my booklet with your recipes and I started to follow your blog and make big changes in my life, I made the courageous decision to quit my comfortable office job and launch my business in the health and wellness industry! I am now working full time in my business and couldn't be happier! I am a wholesale distributor for a couple of brands and I also make my own organic dessert that I sell to cafés and health-food stores! – *Jessica Nagy*

GLUTEN-FREE SWAPS

Does it ever seem like the whole world is going gluten-free? You're not imagining it – the number of people who are adapting a gluten-free lifestyle is increasing exponentially. And most feel better without gluten.

The top benefits I hear from clients include less bloating and fewer gut issues, more energy, and finding fun alternatives to gluten-filled foods that are so much more nutritious. Experimenting with a diet change to benefit your health is exciting, but it can also be overwhelming. The great thing is there are so many new options (many of them natural, wholefoods) to replace them that I guarantee you won't miss the old.

Pasta

Love your creamy spaghetti at dinner? Try Prawn and Zucchini Noodles (see page 185), mung bean pasta, black bean pasta, brown rice pasta or konjac noodles. All can be found at most health-food stores or online. I jazz them up with Homemade Walnut Pesto (see page 252), olive oil and rock salt.

Bread

There's nothing like morning toast or a hearty slice of bread with warming soup. These options are satisfying and healthy: my Signature Gluten-free Loaf (see page 141), my Healthy Vegetable Bread (see page 169), gluten-free Ezekiel bread and brown rice cakes.

Cereal

A quick breakfast option or topping for yoghurt – all gluten-free AND sugar-free: organic rolled oats (certified gluten-free), buckwheat/quinoa porridge, 4-Step Granola (see page 164) and chia pudding.

Crackers

Try brown rice cakes, flaxseed crackers or Flats (a delicious new veggie cracker I've found in Sydney health-food stores).

Pizza

Try my must-make recipe for Cauliflower Pizza (see page 203), a pizza made in the style of an omelette and topped with your favourite veggies, rocket and goat's cheese or a gluten-free pizza crust, available at most health-food stores.

Condiments

So many condiments and sauces have hidden gluten, like soy sauce and tomato sauce. Instead, spice up your meals with tamari, olive oil, lemon juice, apple cider vinegar, Mrs Dash seasonings, rock salt, Dijon mustard and fresh herbs.

Heal Your Gut

LIMITING FRUCTOSE, GLUTEN, DAIRY AND REFINED SUGAR

Slow-cooked Lamb
Shoulder (see page 193)

LIQUID: Must drink 2 L filtered water daily + lots of herbal tea

	MONDAY	TUESDAY	WEDNESDAY
Pre-breakfast: lemon water + 1 probiotic capsule + 40 ml aloe vera juice **BREAKFAST**	Heal Your Gut Smoothie (see page 134)	Turmeric Omelette (see page 155) with a slice of my Signature Gluten-free Loaf (see page 141)	Heal Your Gut Smoothie (see page 134)
MID-MORNING SNACK Try to have a fresh green juice at this time or a green wholefood powder in water	Sliced raw fennel, carrot and cucumber with 2 tbsp tahini/hummus/nut butter	¼ cup mixed raw almonds and pumpkin seeds (preferably soaked overnight or activated) + a handful of blueberries	Fresh carrot, beetroot, ginger and green apple juice + a handful of raw nuts
Pre-lunch: 1 tbsp apple cider vinegar in water **LUNCH** **Tip:** add 1–2 tbsp fermented veggies – found at most health-food stores	150 g turmeric-spiced grilled chicken, avocado and rocket salad. Drizzle with lemon juice, olive oil and rock salt	150–200 g salmon + Homemade Walnut Pesto (see page 252) + salad with avocado and fresh baby spinach, drizzled with lemon juice/apple cider vinegar, olive oil and rock salt	Chicken Teriyaki Bowl (see page 186)
MID-AFTERNOON SNACK	¼ cup mixed nuts and seeds + celery sticks	2 JSHealth Sugar-free Protein Balls (see page 269)	Boiled egg + sliced carrot and fennel
Pre-dinner: 1 tbsp apple cider vinegar in water **DINNER** **Tip:** season main meals with olive oil, tamari, Celtic sea salt, fresh/dried herbs and spices and lemon juice. Use My Super Clean Dressing (see page 125)	150–200 g Herb and Almond-crusted Snapper (see page 178) with Cauliflower Mash (see page 229) + steamed greens	Stir-fry 150 g chicken or 100 g tempeh, basil, broccoli, bok choy and green beans, seasoned with fresh ginger, tamari and a little olive oil (see page 210)	Herb-crusted Salmon (see page 176) with steamed asparagus + mixed green salad
SUPPER	Chamomile tea + probiotic capsule	Dandelion root herbal tea + probiotic capsule	Rooibos chai tea + probiotic capsule
GUT SYMPTOMS – write down how your tummy is feeling today			

Kale, Fennel, Avocado and
Almond Salad (see page 219)

Signature Gluten-free
Loaf (see page 141)

Curried Barramundi
with Cavolo Nero
(see page 182)

THURSDAY	FRIDAY	SATURDAY	SUNDAY
2 poached/boiled eggs on my Signature Gluten-free Loaf (see page 141) or a good quality gluten-free loaf + ¼ avocado + sautéed greens (spinach, kale etc.)	⅓ cup gluten-free oats cooked in coconut milk and water. Add 2 tbsp LSA, a pinch of ground cinnamon and some fresh berries	Heal Your Gut Smoothie (see page 134)	Brekkie salad: 1 cup rocket/spinach leaves, ¼ sliced avocado, 1 sliced tomato, handful of sprouts and a sliced boiled egg. Add a squeeze of lemon juice, season with Himalayan salt and pepper
2 JSHealth Sugar-free Protein Balls (see page 269)	Sliced carrots smeared with 1 tbsp almond butter	1 sliced green apple smeared with 1 tbsp almond butter and a sprinkle of ground cinnamon	Sliced raw fennel, carrot and cucumber with 2 tbsp tahini/hummus/nut butter
Large mixed green salad with ¼ cup cooked sweet potato + 150 g chicken breast (or protein of choice), drizzled with lemon juice, olive oil and rock salt	1–2 poached/boiled eggs, avocado, broccoli and baby spinach salad, drizzled with My Super Clean Dressing (see page 125)	Large green salad with 1 tin wild salmon or tuna + ¼ avocado and roasted beetroot with a lemon juice, Dijon mustard and olive oil dressing	Kale, Fennel, Avocado and Almond Salad (see page 219) with 150 g sliced dukkah-spiced chicken breast/200 g grilled salmon, drizzled with lemon juice, olive oil and rock salt or use My Super Clean Dressing (see page 125)
100 g coyo (or organic Greek-style yoghurt, if tolerated) mixed with a handful of berries and nuts and a pinch of ground cinnamon	¼ cup raw nuts (preferably soaked overnight or activated) + a handful of berries	Sliced raw fennel, carrot and cucumber with 2 tbsp tahini/hummus/nut butter	Sliced raw fennel, carrot, cucumber and celery with 2 tbsp tahini/hummus/nut butter
Slow-cooked Lamb Shoulder (see page 193) with Broccoli Mash (see page 229) + steamed greens of choice drizzled with lemon juice and olive oil	Lettuce Burger (see page 190)	Curried Barramundi with Cavolo Nero (see page 182) + fresh green salad	Lettuce cups with 150 g chicken or 150–200 g fish. Simply fill cos/iceberg lettuce leaves with chopped veggies, Avocado Smash (see page 255) + tahini/mustard and lemon juice to dress
Chamomile tea + probiotic capsule	Lemon and ginger tea + probiotic capsule	Rooibos chai tea + probiotic capsule	Dandelion root herbal tea + probiotic capsule

Worksheet

Copy the worksheets throughout the book and stick them to your fridge or inspiration board.

Do you suffer from any digestive issues (bloating, constipation, etc.)?

....
....
....
....
....

What three changes will you make to start healing your digestion this week?

....
....
....
....

Is there anything you need to let go of emotionally? Consider family, relationships, work and financial issues.

....
....
....
....
....
....

PRINCIPLE 2. BLOOD-SUGAR BALANCE

A steady, even blood-sugar level is key to a healthy body. Unfortunately, many people ride the blood-sugar rollercoaster. They have a bowl of sugar-laden cereal, crave something sweet after lunch and are gagging for a sweet treat, like chocolate, when 3 pm rolls around. These constant energy lifts and crashes are signs of imbalance.

What does GI mean?

GI stands for Glycaemic Index. It's a measure of how quickly blood-sugar levels rise after eating certain foods. Low-GI foods release glucose slowly, keeping your energy and mood stable, and assisting weight loss along the way. Interestingly, carbs boost our 'feel good' brain chemicals, serotonin and endorphin. As humans, we instinctively know this; that's why we crave carbs when we're feeling tired or low. The trick is to choose the ones that will satisfy us for longer. To stay off the blood-sugar rollercoaster, always eat carbs along with some form of protein or fat.

How blood sugar works

When we ingest high-GI foods (like processed and refined carbohydrates), we release glucose, causing a rapid spike in our blood-sugar levels. Some of that glucose is used for energy; however, our body only needs a limited amount to function so the excess is stored as fat. After the glucose has been distributed (and after it spikes our blood sugar), we crash quickly, experiencing fatigue, hunger and irritation. It's a fast rise and an even faster come-down. When our energy is low, we crave carbohydrates, caffeine and sugar to pick us up. And then the cycle starts again.

What about insulin?

Insulin is secreted by the pancreas and is in charge of transporting glucose into cells for energy. The problem is, it's a fat storage hormone. So when you regularly have excessive glucose (from refined carbs), the insulin becomes 'deaf' to the glucose which means the insulin stops effectively transporting glucose to the cells. This leads to high glucose in the blood or high blood sugar which is the precursor to diabetes. Insulin also blocks the effects of the leptin hormone, which signals to our brain that we're full. That's why people with a high-sugar diet tend to overeat – they literally don't know when to stop.

Thanks to the rise of processed foods (and very clever marketing), there are record numbers of people with diabetes. That's why it's so important to keep your blood sugar in check. The benefits of a stable blood-sugar level include:

- ✳ increased energy
- ✳ stable mood
- ✳ improved concentration
- ✳ weight loss/stable weight
- ✳ reduced cravings
- ✳ hormonal balance
- ✳ minimised risk of disease.

THE BALANCING ACT

Some steps to help you balance your blood-sugar level and get off the rollercoaster for good.

* Eat protein with each meal.
* Enjoy low-GI foods (like veggies, protein, wholegrains, fruits and good fats) to allow for the slow release of energy.
* Eat regularly. Switch to 5–6 small meals a day.
* Add good fats such as avocado, tahini and olive oil to your meals, particularly lunch. This should reduce sugar cravings.
* Include a healthy, protein-rich snack in between meals.
* Eat breakfast within an hour of waking up and make sure it includes protein and a healthy fat.
* Avoid sugar and refined carbs (e.g. white bread, white pasta, lollies) – these are the worst offenders. See page 93 for carbs you can enjoy.
* Limit yourself to 2 portions of fruit a day. Berries are the best choice in my opinion.
* Avoid soft drink, fruit juice and artificial sweeteners.
* Manage your stress. Our stress hormones, adrenaline and cortisol, are directly linked to blood sugar. Stress does not do your body any favours.
* Reduce stimulants like alcohol, caffeine and nicotine.
* Have a teaspoon of ground cinnamon a day.

SUPPLEMENTS THAT HELP REGULATE BLOOD SUGAR

Support yourself with chromium, magnesium, cinnulin, vitamin B complex and vitamin C. Chat to your nutritionist or naturopath for more information and dosage.

CURBING YOUR SWEET TOOTH

To beat sugar cravings, follow the blood-sugar balancing tips in this chapter. When your blood sugar is stable, you automatically crave less sugar. Then start adding more dark leafy greens to your plate. Think kale, spinach, broccoli and rocket. This will trick your tastebuds into appreciating bitter foods over sweet ones. Greens are also loaded with magnesium, the nutrient that regulates blood sugar. Step it up a notch by squeezing lemon juice over rocket before your meals, and adding vanilla extract to smoothies and yoghurt.

Try to get to the root of your cravings. What are you really hungry for? Since sweet treats are associated with joy (like birthdays), many people crave sugar when they are unhappy about something. We think that a cookie is going to make us feel better, when it may make us feel worse. Whenever I crave something sweet, I either make myself a delicious and wholesome alternative (like bliss balls), or do something else that makes me happy, such as reading a magazine, chatting to my bestie or having a bath.

Worksheet

What are your most typical cravings?

....

....

What feelings do you associate with these cravings? Write them down. For example, when I'm sad, I crave chocolate. When I'm stressed, I feel like salty foods.

....

....

....

Keep a blood-sugar diary for a few days. Record how you feel when you wake up, mid-morning, lunch, mid-afternoon, evening and before bed. Can you identify any patterns?

....

....

....

....

What changes will you make to balance out your blood sugar?

....

....

TOP TIP

Love your fruit? Mix it with a handful of nuts and some Greek-style yoghurt for a low-GI snack.

PRINCIPLE 3. DETOXING THE LIVER & YOUR ENVIRONMENT

Not only is the liver the largest organ, but it does an astonishing amount of work to keep your body clean and healthy. A healthy liver maintains blood-sugar levels; metabolises carbohydrates, fats and proteins; eliminates toxins; synthesises and stores vitamins and minerals; and regulates hormones. It's the master of detoxification, but our environment and lifestyles often impede the process. Think about it: our world is full of plastics, pesticides and hormones, and many of us love alcohol and caffeine. These can lead to irritability, poor sleep, hormonal imbalance and acne, all signs that point to a sluggish liver.

The better our liver functions, the better the rest of our body can function. When it comes to wellbeing and weight loss, it is essential to give our liver some love. That's why detoxification is so important: it helps to take the load off our overworked livers and allows the body to heal.

The lowdown on liver function

The liver metabolises hormones and other substances in two phases: phase 1 prepares the toxins to be excreted, while phase 2 flushes them out of the body via urine, liver bile, perspiration and exhalation. Each phase requires important nutrients, most of which can be found in food.

Heal your liver now

Treat your liver (in the best way!) by trying the following for optimal function:

* eat plenty of dark leafy green veggies, especially broccoli, spinach, kale and rocket. Also cauliflower and cabbage.
* eat colourful fruits and veggies – citrus fruits, sweet potato, tomatoes, carrots and berries
* include onions, garlic and leeks in your meals
* add herbs and spices – especially turmeric and parsley
* eat sprouts
* include nuts and seeds – especially walnuts, Brazil nuts, almonds and chia seeds
* enjoy protein-rich foods such as lean chicken, oily fish, eggs, beans and legumes
* swap coffee for green tea or dandelion tea
* reduce alcohol intake
* cut way down on sugar, including fruit
* consider supplementing with a vitamin B complex, St Mary's thistle or Brassica sprout powder
* avoid processed and packaged foods.

Eat through the rainbow and you'll be on the right track to liver love! Main liver loaders are caffeine, alcohol, cow dairy, wheat/gluten, red meat and bad fats such as transfats found in vegetable oils, processed and fried foods. For step-by-step guidance, follow my Detox Plan on pages 30–31.

I love to serve kale chips when my guests arrive at dinner parties. Brassica veggies such as kale contain an enzyme that detoxes the liver.

Ensure half of your plate is made up of greens for every main meal. Don't be afraid to add greens to breakfast!

Eat antioxidant-rich foods such as pomegranate seeds and goji berries for glowing skin and a clean liver.

Keep meals simple and balanced. Good fats are great for extra liver love.

Detox Plan

Sweet Berry Omelette
(see page 145)

LIQUIDS
2 L of filtered water, unlimited herbal tea, Healthy Vitamin Water (see page 309), fresh green juices

Pre-breakfast: Warm water with lemon or cleansing tonic + probiotic

	MONDAY	TUESDAY	WEDNESDAY
BREAKFAST	Brekkie salad: 1 cup rocket/baby spinach leaves, ¼ avocado, 1 sliced tomato, a handful of sprouts and a sliced boiled egg. Add a drizzle of lemon juice, season with Himalayan salt and black pepper	2 boiled eggs rolled in turmeric/chopped parsley with sautéed onion, kale and spinach + ¼ avocado + 3 tbsp cooked quinoa (optional). Drizzle with lemon juice. Or JSHealth Protein Smoothie (see page 134)	Sweet Berry Omelette (see page 145) – 2 eggs beaten with a handful of fresh/frozen blueberries, stevia, 1 tbsp psyllium husk, ground cinnamon, 1 tbsp milk. Or JSHealth Protein Smoothie (see page 134)
MID-MORNING SNACK	Grated carrot with lemon juice and a pinch of Himalayan salt + ¼ cup raw almonds + 1 cup green tea	1 sliced green apple with almond butter + a sprinkle of ground cinnamon + dandelion tea with stevia and ground cinnamon to sweeten	Fresh carrot, ginger and beetroot juice + sliced celery sticks + lemon and ginger herbal tea
LUNCH	150–200 g grilled salmon + salad with asparagus, baby spinach, pumpkin seeds and quinoa with Tahini Lemon Dressing (see page 258)	Detox Salad (see page 225) with 150 g chicken breast or 150–200 g grilled salmon	Mixed bean and lentil salad (½ cup mixed beans and ½ cup lentils) with baby spinach, carrot and tomatoes + a sprinkle of pumpkin seeds
MID-AFTERNOON SNACK	Nori rolls (seaweed) filled and rolled with veggies and hummus + ¼ cup mixed nuts and seeds + celery sticks	Sliced raw carrot, cucumber, celery and fennel with 2 tbsp hummus/tahini/nut butter	Carrot slices smeared with almond butter and a sprinkle of ground cinnamon
DINNER	150–200 g grilled Cajun-spiced snapper with steamed broccoli and green beans (season with olive oil, fresh herbs, lemon juice and rock salt)	150–200 g Herb-crusted Salmon (see page 176) with lightly grilled/steamed asparagus and broccoli	Asian-style chicken (150 g) stir-fry with bok choy and broccoli (seasoned with ginger, leeks, garlic, tamari) or Tempeh (100 g) and vegetable quinoa sushi
SUPPER	Herbal tea of choice	Almond-milk rooibos chai (caffeine-free) with ground cinnamon and stevia	Peppermint tea

Zucchini and Mint
soup (see page 185)

3-Step Overnight
Pudding (see page 158)

Cleansing Chopped
Salad (see page 244)

THURSDAY	FRIDAY	SATURDAY	SUNDAY
2-egg turmeric omelette with spinach, tomatoes, fresh rocket + ¼ avocado. Drizzle with lemon juice.	Quinoa porridge: ⅓ cup oats or quinoa flakes made with coconut milk + a handful of berries + a handful of walnuts. A sprinkle of ground cinnamon, vanilla powder and stevia	JSHealth Protein Smoothie (see page 134)	3-Step Overnight Pudding (see page 158)
Celery sticks and carrot sticks with 2 tbsp hummus/tahini + 1 cup green tea	Green juice – kale, celery, cucumber, mint, lemon juice and spinach + ¼ cup raw walnuts	1 cup blueberries + ¼ cup pumpkin seeds + 1 cup green tea	Celery sticks and carrot sticks with 2 tbsp hummus/tahini + 1 cup green tea
150 g Moroccan-spiced chicken breast + salad with grilled zucchini, avocado, pomegranate and rocket with Tahini Lemon Dressing (see page 258)	Cleansing Chopped Salad (see page 244) with 150 g chicken breast + ½ cup cooked sweet potato + Super Clean Dressing (see page 215)	150–200 g grilled Salmon + kale, avocado and fennel salad with an Asian-style dressing (tamari, lemon juice, ginger, garlic). Optional: add 3 tbsp cooked quinoa	Detox Salad (see page 225) with 150 g chicken breast or 150–200 g grilled salmon
2 brown rice cakes with smashed avocado and fresh tomato	1–2 JSHealth Sugar-free Protein Balls (see page 269)	Nori rolls (seaweed) filled and rolled with veggies and hummus	Kale Chips (see page 270) with 2 tbsp hummus/tahini and lemon juice
Zucchini & Mint Soup (see page 185) + 150 g rosemary and lemon chicken breast on a bed of broccoli mash	Kale and spinach stir-fry with protein of choice (150–200 g chicken/fish/tempeh) sautéed in garlic, tamari, ginger and sesame oil	150–200 g Herb and Almond-crusted Snapper (see page 178) on a bed of Cauliflower Mash (see page 229) + green salad or Tomato & Basil Zucchini Pasta (see page 204) with protein of choice	Cleansing Chopped Salad (see page 244) with grilled chicken breast/salmon using My Super Clean Dressing (see page 215)
Almond-milk rooibos chai (caffeine-free) with ground cinnamon and stevia	Lemon and ginger tea	Chamomile tea	Lemon and ginger tea

For vegan and vegetarian protein replacements see page 114.

Worksheet

Do you suffer from any of the issues associated with sluggish liver function (e.g. irritability, acne, weight gain)? Write these down.

....

....

....

How do you feel after you drink coffee or alcohol? For example, does coffee give you energy or does it make your heart race? Do you experience nasty hangovers? Can you consider taking a two- to four-week break from the two stimulants?

....

....

....

How can you make your environment a happier, healthier place? Is there anything in your environment that doesn't serve you?

....

....

....

What changes will you make to give your liver a break?

....

....

....

TOP TIP

Drinking a green juice daily is the easiest way to give your liver a nutrient hit.

WHILE YOU'RE AT IT ...
DETOX YOUR ENVIRONMENT

Reduce stress and give your liver a break by making a few lifestyle changes.

* Invest in a high-quality water filter.
* Replace plastic water bottles with stainless steel ones.
* Buy organic produce. When that's not possible, always wash or peel fruit and veggies to remove pesticides.
* Opt for steaming and grilling over deep-frying.
* Minimise time spent in traffic.
* Try to pinpoint the underlying cause with the help of a nutritionist or holistic doctor.
* Switch to natural household cleaning products.
* Reduce your intake of meat, dairy and fatty food.
* Always choose organic grass-fed, grass-finished meat.
* Do not heat foods in plastic.
* Use paper bags and Mason jars to store food.
* Avoid all tinned foods. (Keep tinned tuna to twice a week.)
* Use an aluminium-free natural deodorant.
* Cut back on perfume. If you decide to use it, spray on your clothes rather than skin.
* Avoid fake tan.
* Choose natural skincare and make-up brands.
* Use natural sanitary products.

PRINCIPLE 4. KEEPING HORMONES IN CHECK

Happy, healthy hormones

Hormones are incredibly important when it comes to achieving optimal health. Thanks to our fast-paced lives and high-stress environments, many women suffer from hormonal imbalance. I was one of them just a few years back. It's becoming more and more common – but luckily, there are ways to get everything back on track.

The endocrine system

Think of the endocrine system as an orchestra: when one of the parts is out of tune, the rest go out of sync. As conductors, it's our job to make sure our hormonal systems are working harmoniously.

Adrenals

Adrenaline is our short-term stress hormone, responsible for the 'fight or flight' response. (So when you're in danger, that kicks in.) *Cortisol* is the long-term stress hormone. While cortisol is great for helping us get through a tough workout, too much of it is a problem. It stops fat burning, causes dysglycaemia (irregular blood sugar) and leads to oestrogen dominance. And it can pack fat onto your midsection – no thanks!

The stress–sex hormone connection

Everything in the body is interconnected, so stress hormones have an impact on sex hormones. The interplay between progesterone and cortisol is a good example. Progesterone is an anti-anxiety, anti-depressive hormone, responsible for burning fat and holding on to pregnancies. As Dr Libby (*Rushing Woman's Syndrome*) says, it's a hormone 'we all want bucket loads of forever'. But when cortisol competes with progesterone, cortisol will always win. This then causes low progesterone, which is counterbalanced by high oestrogen. That is why many women's systems become oestrogen-dominant, leading to PMS, endometriosis, polycystic ovarian syndrome and weight gain. It's not a pretty picture, is it?

Spotlight on the thyroid

High oestrogen and cortisol levels can suppress thyroid function. Located on your neck, the thyroid is a nifty gland in charge of secreting T4 and T3, which regulate the body's metabolism. You need a healthy thyroid in order for your body to function smoothly. If you want your body chemistry to remain in sync – and trust me, you do – it's important to **feed your thyroid with key nutrients such as iodine, selenium and iron**. Unfortunately, conventional diets often lack these nutrients. Iodine deficiency in particular is very common and has led to an increase in thyroid disorders. But

HOW TO KEEP YOUR THYROID (AND HORMONES) IN TIP-TOP SHAPE

Nutrition

- Eat protein with every meal.
- Include all brassica veggies – broccoli, cabbage, cauliflower and kale.
- Load up on omega-3s – chia seeds, flaxseed, walnuts and salmon.
- Increase your iron intake – eat red meat two to three times a week.
- Drink only filtered water.
- Add seaweed to soups and salads.
- Reduce gluten – bread, pasta, cereal, etc.
- Reduce inflammatory triggers like caffeine, sugar, alcohol and refined carbs.
- Use Dulse flakes in cooking – they're high in iodine.
- Eat 3–4 Brazil nuts daily – they're rich in selenium.
- Steer clear of soy products – these can disrupt the endocrine system.
- Test for food intolerances that can trigger an autoimmune response on the thyroid. If you have Hashimoto's, I recommend going fully gluten-free.
- Consider supplementing with iodine, selenium and iron under a nutritionist's guidance.

Lifestyle

- Stress can really impact the thyroid gland. Prioritise rest and deep belly breathing daily. I love popping my legs up against the wall for 10 minutes.
- Spend at least 15 minutes in the sun every day.
- Use a non fluoride–based toothpaste.
- Detox your environment to reduce your exposure to external oestrogens. (Find out how on page 28.)
- Do yoga, interval training and weights regularly to boost your metabolism and overall health.
- Indole 3 Carbinol and DIM (which is found in all cruciferous veggies) are supplements that help with clearing oestrogen via the liver.

too much iodine can also irritate the thyroid and lower its function. So never self-prescribe iodine and only supplement under professional guidance. Whenever my clients show symptoms of this deficiency, I refer them to a doctor for a urine iodine test. Thyroid issues present themselves in a variety of ways, but hypothyroidism (less thyroid hormones on tissues) and hyperthyroidism (excess hormones) are the most widespread. Hypothyroidism is often caused by an autoimmune disorder called Hashimoto's Thyroiditis, which is prevalent in women. The symptoms of an underactive thyroid can be subtle, but usually include depression, weight gain, fatigue and elevated cholesterol.

Are you always in a rush? Do you ever feel like you can't speak up? Do you try to do too many things at once?

According to Dr Christiane Northrup (*Women's Bodies, Women's Wisdom*), since the thyroid is located in the throat chakra, thyroid complications result from a belief that we can't voice how we really feel. Try these affirmations: 'I have time for everything' and 'I can express myself freely and creatively'.

The best hormone-balancing tips

Whenever my hormones go out of whack due to travelling or stress, I rely on these tried-and-tested methods. They work every time:

- ✳ support your liver (see page 28)
- ✳ detox your environment (see page 33)
- ✳ nourish your adrenals (see page 39)
- ✳ help your digestive system (see page 15).

Rest

I bang on about this a lot, but rest is so, so important for hormone health (and sanity!). Along with alone time, make restorative exercise a part of your life. You can't go past yoga.

Supplements

Under a nutritionist or naturopath's guidance, try magnesium, vitamin B complex (especially B6), zinc and fish oil. These supplements really help with hormonal balancing. Herbs can also be incredibly effective.

Fluid retention

When you're suffering from fluid retention, first consider the emotional factor. Is there something or someone in your life you need to let go of? If the answer is yes, work on releasing that issue. Poor circulation can cause fluid retention, so dry body brush (see page 65) in the mornings. Drinking 2 litres of water a day, sipping on dandelion root 'coffee' and following the tips in this hormone section should help clear out any excess fluid.

Worksheet

What are you willing to eliminate from and add to your diet for healthier hormones?

....
....
....
....
....
....

How will you incorporate more rest into your day?

....
....
....
....
....
....

Which good fats will you add to your plate?

....
....
....
....
....
....

PRINCIPLE 5. LESS STRESS, MORE REST

Do you often feel anxious, worried or irritable? Do you ever feel exhausted and overwhelmed? Do you tend to forget things? Do you suffer from stiff muscles and tension headaches? Do you have high blood pressure? Do you catch every cold that comes around? Do you have digestive and eating issues?

If you answered yes to one or more of these questions, you're probably overburdened by stress. You're not alone. I'm committed to exposing myself (and my body) to as little stress as possible. It has a huge impact on your body, as well as your mood, energy and happiness. It just won't get you anywhere. You can make all the healthiest choices in the world but if your body is stressed, your health will suffer.

I want you to have the same less-is-more attitude towards stress.

Let's talk about stress, baby

To some extent, stress is inevitable. Small bursts of stress are not only part of everyday life, but they're also healthy. They keep us motivated. However, we live in a society where we're expected to go, go, go. We're trying to be the best workers, friends, mothers, wives and girlfriends and in doing so, we put our health on the backburner. Our lives are so fast-paced and hectic, it's almost become a competition to see who's 'busiest'. Rest is considered indulgent and most people I meet feel guilty at the thought of taking ten minutes to themselves, just to chill out. That's ridiculous! I used to feel guilty too, I get you.

Stress is the root of most health conditions. Scary, isn't it? Although short- and long-term (and even chronic) stress manifests itself differently, it affects the whole body in a big, bad way. We'll talk about all the problems it can cause later, but for now, just note that we need to stress less. A lot less. Stress is environmentally induced (by living in polluted, busy cities), but it's exacerbated by lifestyle choices and habits. People add stress to their already stressed-out lives by saying, 'I need to run for an hour after work', 'I need to see this friend and that friend'. Mentally, they're internalising negativity and losing touch with their own body. They end up as the worst versions of themselves.

Luckily, this kind of 'extra' stress is the part you can control, before it develops any further and takes a toll on your health. Stress is a part of life, we just need to learn how to manage it. That's exactly what I did – but let me tell you, it wasn't easy. By sharing my story, I hope you'll learn the lessons I did a lot more quickly.

The stress response

Back in caveman days, we faced a fair few threats: tigers, lions, bears. When we were under attack, our adrenals and brain triggered a stress response, which flooded our body with adrenaline and cortisol. These hormones pumped blood to our heart, lungs, brain and muscles, helping us to fight or run away. Cortisol gave us a burst of energy. Have you ever heard the saying, 'run for your life'? That's where it comes from. In the past, stress was short-lived. Once we out-ran the animals, these chemical messengers returned to normal. The problem now is that our bodies still have this biological response to stress, but we have a lot more psychological stress in our lives: work, financial problems, relationships, the list goes on. For many people, the stress response never shuts off, which often results in chronic stress – which is best friends with high blood pressure, headaches, insomnia, irritable bowel syndrome, poor immunity and weight gain.

The goal is to find a healthy stress response, to find balance. If you can do this, you'll feel energised, strong and ready for whatever life throws at you, instead of feeling anxious or wired all the time. Sound good?

Adrenals in the spotlight

One of the most common stress side effects is adrenal exhaustion. As a nutritionist, I see it all the time. A typical sign of adrenal exhaustion is waking up tired but then you're energetic late at night and even crave salt. Our adrenal glands sit on top of the kidneys and they're chiefly responsible for releasing hormones in response to stress. They also regulate blood sugar, maintain the body's energy levels and produce numerous hormones – like adrenaline and cortisol, the 'fight or flight' hormones.

Ongoing stress – whether it be emotional, environmental or physical – is bad for the adrenals. Initially, it causes high cortisol levels, resulting in weight gain, especially around the midsection. Then, it can cause blood-sugar imbalances, memory loss and high blood pressure etc. Overworked adrenals eventually crash, leading to adrenal exhaustion. And then you can say hello to chronic fatigue, irritability, inability to concentrate, insomnia, anxiety, PMS, sugar cravings … and they also speed up the ageing process – hey, premature wrinkles!

I ended up with adrenal exhaustion a few years back and it was not fun. Unfortunately, it's far too common. Most women are dominated by their sympathetic nervous system these days, meaning their bodies are in hormonal havoc. You don't have to be one of them.

Work stress and workout stress

Your body can't tell the difference between work stress and workout stress. To adrenals, they're the same. So if you're feeling exhausted, you're better off ditching the gym for the beach. Exercise can relieve stress for some people but for most of my clients, it stresses them out more. Taking care of the adrenals is key to optimal health, happiness and weight management.

That leads me to my motto: Time to unwind. If I could teach you only one thing, it would be the importance of rest. Downtime is absolutely vital to your health. We all need to slow down and breathe and do so more often. In today's fast-paced society, we're constantly on the go. We forget to chew our food, laugh or greet people with a smile. We barely have time to pause and reflect, or to give ourselves a break. Or when we do take a break, we feel guilty. While it's fantastic to be successful and social, we need to stop rushing. **Slow down. Breathe. Take it all in.**

I'll be honest – I'm a busy bee too. But I want to be present. I want to have an energy and zest for life. And I want to feel connected to my own body. So when I feel like life is taking over, I stop, rest and rejuvenate. When we slow down and find stillness, we are better human beings. We're more productive, friendlier and more open. Our bodies can't cope with the constant go, go, go. They give us signs – like headaches and irritability – but we ignore them, or solve the problem by popping a few pills. **Where you are right here, right now, is all that matters.**

Taking the time to rest and recuperate will do wonders for your day-to-day life. It recharges you at a cellular level. It refreshes you so you can complete tasks and allows you to approach your relationships and health with more vigour and energy. If you're a business whiz, think about it this way: because it makes you more efficient, productive and happy, rest offers the best return on investment. Rest is one of the mind and body's essential building blocks. So if you take a nap after studying, you'll retain the information better. If you take rest days between tough training sessions, you'll get stronger and leaner more quickly. A rested body is a healthy body!

The stress-less solution

Do you want to be more present? Do you want a clearer, brighter mind? Do you want to feel lighter? Do you want to have more energy for your friends, partner and kids? Do you want to stop being so reactive? Of course you do.

Please, please, please try to take a few minutes every day to **just rest**. If that sounds impossible, start with a few minutes a week. Put it in your calendar if that helps, and treat it like family and work commitments because it is ESSENTIAL. Your body works so hard for you all day every day – the least you can do is give it a break. Treat yourself with respect because you deserve it.

How to rest

Here are my favourite ways to rest.

* Write down five things you are grateful for. So simple, yet so effective – try it! When you feel grateful, you automatically feel less stressed.
* Make eight hours of sleep non-negotiable.
* Go into the 'Stress-free Zone' daily (see page 41).

Stress-busters

Combat stress by loading up on vitamins B and C and magnesium, found in wholegrains, fruits and leafy veggies. And eat your oats – they're integral to nourishing a stressed nervous system.

* Cut out the nasty five: alcohol, caffeine, refined salt, soft drink and sugar.
* Enjoy a few cups of chamomile tea a day.
* Meditate daily. If you're new to meditation, it's simply about bringing more awareness into your life, so just sit in silence and connect to your breath.
* Have a bath in aromatherapy oils.

* Read your favourite book.
* Go for a walk in nature.
* Book in for a massage.
* Put your phone on aeroplane mode for an hour or two (baby steps!) during the day. This will give you time to rejuvenate and get things done. I switch off all technology at 9 pm. The blue light and electromagnetic fields mess with melatonin, the hormone that is responsible for inducing sleep.

* Write down any thoughts or tasks before bed.
* Declutter your emails and phone messages. Hit that delete button!
* Keep your emails short and check them only twice a day. I refuse to let emails take over my life. You should too. People will (or will learn to) understand that you can't be on call all the time.
* Schedule in deep breathing exercises. Aim for 10–20 diaphragm breaths every morning.
* Learn to say no. Don't feel obligated to accept a social invitation if you've had a busy or stressful day.
* Enjoy the sunshine for 15–30 minutes a day.
* Go into savasana. Put your legs up against a wall for ten minutes and just breathe.
* Go for an ocean swim. There is nothing better, honestly.
* Tuck yourself up in bed by 10 pm.
* Chat to your best friend.
* Get acupuncture. Bye bye blockages!
* Learn to love restorative exercise. Endorphins are amazing, but we're not designed to push our bodies to the extreme every day. So exercise less, but smarter.
* Give yourself permission to rest. Your body is smart, so listen to it. If you're tired, take a time out.
* Just be. By yourself.

Go into the 'Stress-free Zone' (SFZ) for ten minutes a day

Do you ever take time to be alone? Away from people, phones and emails? You probably don't realise how exhausting it is to be around people all the time, but once you start snatching some alone-time, it will change your life. I recommend 10–30 minutes of solitude a day. Try going for a walk, reading a book, doing meditation, stretching or lying on the grass. It's an incredible way to balance yourself and reconnect with your own body. Have you rested today? Share your Stress-Free Zone with #JSHealthSFZ.

A note on coffee

Let's talk about coffee for a second. You know what I'm going to say, don't you?! I'm sorry, but for those feeling exhausted or anxious, a coffee will not lift you up. Since your body is already running on adrenaline, caffeine will make it worse. If you wake up tired and craving coffee (over food), and then get a second wind of energy late at night, that's a sign of adrenal fatigue. Nourish your adrenals back to life using the stress-busting solutions on pages 40–41. It's fine to enjoy a coffee once a day, but I'd love you to think about how it makes you feel. Jittery? Frantic? Does it cause insomnia? Then cut it out for two weeks and see what happens. You may realise you're calmer, a better sleeper and a nicer person.

Stress-banishing supplements

Trying to curb stress? Consider the following supplements after chatting to your nutritionist or naturopath. For stress, try magnesium to relax muscles and calm the nervous system, B vitamins to adapt to stress and vitamin C to feed the adrenals. When stress has gone too far and you have adrenal fatigue, try herbal formulas containing withania, Siberian ginseng, rhodiola or licorice.

IN YOUR WORDS

I have had a negative guilt-ridden relationship with food my whole adult life. From the minute I finished *The Clean Life* (ebook) I haven't touched gluten, sugar or processed food and I haven't missed any of it at all!

This book is an amazing tool for anyone who has challenges with food and/or their body. Best of all, it makes healthy living so easy, and delicious! *The Clean Life* (ebook) is not about a long list of 'can't haves' or depriving yourself, it's simply easy to understand and [has] easy-to-follow guidelines for building a healthy lifestyle and making positive choices.

Jessica Sepel is unbelievably open and honest about her own health journey which makes her so believable and easy to relate to. She is generous with her knowledge and yummy recipes and her passion for helping people live a clean life shines through [on] every page. I can't wait to buy a hard copy of this beautiful book, I refer to it on a daily basis and want to share it with everyone I know. *– AJ Davis*

Worksheet

Can you identify any stressors in your life? They can be physical, emotional or environmental.

....

....

....

....

....

....

If you're a coffee drinker, record how you feel throughout the day. Then ditch coffee and see if you feel differently.

....

....

....

....

....

....

How will you unwind every day?

....

....

....

When and for how long will you try to go into the Stress-free Zone every day?

....

....

....

PRINCIPLE 6. EMOTIONAL EATING & THE POWER OF SELF-LOVE

Do you want to love your body? Do you want to control your emotions? Do you want to nourish yourself from the inside out?

This principle is all about self-love and exploring the relationship between food and your body. We'll discuss the signs of emotional eating and work out ways to break the cycle. We'll also talk about the art of mindful eating and how it can completely change the way you interact with and think about food. From now on, you're going to eat in tune with your body and you're going to eat with joy. Get ready to end the battle with food.

Let's rewind for a minute

Healing my relationship with food has been my biggest challenge and it was also what inspired me to study health and nutrition. I wanted to gain a better understanding of how the human body works and figure out why I had developed such a negative attitude towards food and my body. I wanted to understand how I became my own biggest burden. Just typing that brings tears to my eyes, because now I feel so incredibly free. I have my moments of self-doubt – I wouldn't be human if I didn't – but when I do, I remind myself we are all in this together. We all want the same things: love and acceptance. And that comes down to loving, respecting and accepting who you are.

Accepting there is no such thing as perfect.
Accepting you are enough.
Accepting you are worthy of getting everything you ever wanted.
Accepting and releasing the need to judge yourself.
Accepting that you cannot blame anyone or anything for your problems or your weight.
Accepting that you – and only you – are in control of your life!

You are entitled to live the best, happiest, healthiest life. But to do so, you need to release the negativity and allow positive thoughts and feelings to flood in.

The more you love yourself, the easier it is to make healthy choices. In my opinion, healthy living is a reflection of how much you love yourself. I invite you to join me in accepting who you are today. To turn those harsh thoughts into acts of self-love. To make healthier choices. To realise you are enough. If you can do that, if you can heal your mind, I promise your health will blossom.

Home exercise

Stand in front of the mirror every morning and state the following affirmation:
'I am enough just as I am. I am beautiful just as I am. I am worthy as I am.' I did this and it slowly healed me. They don't call it brain power for nothing … The mind is an

incredibly powerful organ, so don't underestimate it. The strength of our bodies and sense of wellness are tied to our mental health. Depression, stress and fatigue are mental conditions that, left untreated, can spiral into poor physical health.

The moral of the story? What you tell yourself has a huge impact on your wellbeing, physical and mental resilience. So say those affirmations! Stick them up on your mirror, car and office pinboard. Constantly remind yourself just how gorgeous and worthy you are. It's hard at first but soon it will become a habit.

Emotional eating?

As babies, we eat intuitively: we fuss when we are hungry and stop eating when we are full. Then, as we grow up, many of us lose touch with our true hunger signals. We start eating when we're bored, sad, stressed or happy. We turn to food to deal with our emotions. We forget food is purely there to keep us alive and well. It's here to nourish our bodies – not solve our emotional problems.

As adults, we need to identify those underlying emotional issues that are affecting our relationship with food. That's the first step. The next time you reach for a chocolate bar or a bag of salty chips, ask yourself if you're really hungry or if you're just emotional. Is there something going on in your life that needs attention? Once you've figured out what's causing you to emotionally eat, you can begin to change your habits – and heal your relationship with food. When it comes to dealing with emotions, food is not the answer. Taking care of yourself is the answer.

I used to be a victim of emotional eating. Every morning, the number on the scales would determine my eating patterns. If I liked what I saw, I'd feel empowered, and I'd stick to my diet. If I didn't like it, I'd punish myself through deprivation or the total opposite, by bingeing on the food I'd been missing for so long. I'd berate myself for not having 'more willpower', then the cycle would start over again the next time I 'slipped'. That is no way to live. That's why I'm so passionate about helping people find their way back to eating with love and joy. The self-criticism stops now. Choose self-love instead.

Mythbusters

Repeat after me: 'I don't need to eat everything on my plate.' So many people feel they have to polish off everything on their plates out of fear of offending someone, or because they've been depriving themselves. Food is abundant. It's OK to say no. If you're around 'food pushers', try to get them on your side. Ask your friends and family to support your healthy eating, not sabotage it.

Natural eaters vs dieters

To banish emotional eating for good, you need to let go of the diet mentality and become a natural eater instead. Dieters think about food all the time. They become so preoccupied with food, it starts to take over their quality of life. They have an emotional connection to food. But food is not there to make us feel better – it's there to keep us alive. Natural eaters, on the other hand, don't class food as 'good' or 'bad'. They see it as a source of fuel and nourishment. They enjoy eating, but they know they're eating food to survive. That's it. They know when to stop eating.

If you can shift your mentality and start to see food as abundant and a source of nourishment, a few things will happen. You'll start eating when you're hungry, and stop bingeing and using food to deal with emotions. And as a result, you'll lose weight. Diets don't work because they're a deprivation game. When we deprive ourselves, our bodies get tricked into thinking food is scarce. They then kick into survival mode, slowing down our metabolism and holding on to anything we feed it. You may lose some weight, but you'll pile it straight back on. That's the other problem with diets: they're not sustainable and the stress they cause wreaks havoc on your hormones and mind. Give up the diets. They don't work.

That's what I did. I began to view food as something to keep me alive and well, and I healed myself through counselling, education and meditation. It's all about reconnecting with yourself and your body. The first step towards healing your relationship with food is falling back in love with yourself.

The art of mindful eating

Do you inhale your food? Eat in front of the telly? Scroll through your emails with your fork in the other hand? Beat yourself up over calories and carbs? If so, you're not alone. I was the same. This was the daily battle I had with myself: I ate a meal and classed it as 'good' or 'bad'. I tortured myself with questions like, 'Did I eat too much?', 'How many calories did I just consume?' and 'Why did I eat so quickly? Now I feel sick'. If I ate something 'naughty', I hated myself. I couldn't stop thinking about it for hours, sometimes days. I thought it would make me put on weight instantly. I felt guilty, but above all disappointed that I didn't have the willpower to say no. Scary, right? But true. Then I would binge. Then I would hate myself even more. This never-ending cycle is a sign of 'disordered eating'. It's what caused me to have a very turbulent, sad relationship with my body.

Many of us forget what a powerful impact our thoughts have on our body, at both a spiritual and chemical level. Your thoughts can and will manifest into physical bodily stress – and stress is the number one health concern, in my opinion. And for many – the number one cause of weight gain. To fix my relationship with food, I released my own burden and listened to my body. I'm now a conscious eater. I chew my food. I embrace the flavours and textures. I notice when I am full and I associate food with positive thoughts. I practise gratitude for every bite of food. I know that sounds corny and over the top, but it's true! This attitude shift changed how comfortable I felt in my own body, and eventually, my body shape too. Self-love and respect is the foundation of my health. Wouldn't you like to feel the same?

That's where mindful eating comes in. It's a technique I use to avoid getting caught in the 'diet trap'. Basically, it's about being present and 100 per cent focused on your food when you eat. No distractions. It teaches you to recognise when you're full, allows you to appreciate the plate of goodness in front of you, and removes the guilt factor of eating. A healthier relationship with food will bring you one (huge) step closer to being your healthiest self.

How to be a mindful eater

Use your senses. Look at your food. Taste it. Smell it. Appreciate it. And chew, chew, chew! The plate is not going anywhere. By doing all this, your brain will recognise satiety (fullness) and you'll be less likely to overeat. Remember that food is abundant.

Be grateful. I hate to sound like an airy-fairy health preacher, but the word 'gratitude' can change your life. Try it. Before you eat, take a moment to think about where the food came from, and how lucky you are to have access to it. Food is a gift: it gives your heart, hormones, brain and cells the nutrients they need to function.

Home exercise

In a gratitude journal, write down how lucky you feel to have had access to food today.

Make each meal a pleasurable experience. Sit down to eat, away from computers, phones and TVs. Enjoy the peace and quiet for a few minutes and take three deep breaths before picking up your fork. Eat slowly, chewing and really tasting every morsel before swallowing. This is an amazing way to tune into your own body and rebuild your relationship with food.

Stop the vicious cycle of all or nothing. If you make a 'bad' food choice, let it go! Don't write the rest of the day off. Your body can handle the odd slip-up, but it's when you say 'Oh well, I'll just eat healthy tomorrow' that the problems arise. Your body just doesn't know how to handle an influx of sugary, fatty food.

Practise positive affirmations when you eat. Affirmations are fantastic for releasing negative thoughts and reprogramming your behaviour. They helped me to overcome my anxiety around food. Remember, stress and anxiety impacts our digestion of food. I often tell my clients to 'fake it till you make it', because thinking good thoughts about food doesn't come naturally to most women. But if you keep saying your affirmations, they will become a reality. Try these: 'This plate of food is so good for me', 'My body knows how to use this food' and 'My cells are about to be nourished with so much goodness'.

Let go of the need to eat 'perfectly'. As Aviva Romm M.D. says, 'There is no such thing as a good girl vs. bad girl; no cheater vs. good dieter. There is only choice. And the choice is yours. If you're in the middle of a food battle with yourself, refuse to participate.' If you're being offered food you don't want to eat, feel free to say no. Listen to your body – and then give it what it needs. Let go of everything else. I promise you, no one eats perfectly! Perfect does not exist. Remember, you are good enough.

Stop comparing! Your body and nutritional needs are different from those of your friends, sister and that girl at work. Their eating patterns have nothing to do with yours.

Don't be difficult with food. Try not to let your healthy lifestyle get in the way of your social life. This is one of my biggest challenges. If you're out with family and friends, don't stress about the menu. Just choose the best option available to you. Otherwise, you'll only complicate your relationship with food *and* the people around you!

Ask yourself if you're hungry. If you're reaching for food when you're not hungry, stop and figure out what the underlying issue is. Are you sad? Happy? Stressed? Our emotions often manifest themselves as physical feelings; for example, anxiety can form a knot in our stomachs, which we attempt to 'fix' with food. So just identify the feeling. If you realise you're not actually hungry, do something else that you love: go for a walk, take a bath, have a cuppa, kiss your partner or stalk some health blogs.

Dealing with bingeing

When you get home from your day out at work/school/college, put your bags down and take a cold shower. This calms the frantic pace down and you will find you enter the kitchen with a clarity of mind and make better choices. Food binges occur out of franticness/panic. Don't deprive yourself and treat yourself every week. Get organised and prep what you can. Tune into your body, what is happening and actually ask yourself 'How am I feeling right now?' You will find the answer comes to you, and then you can figure out how to better deal with the emotions. Consider a walk in nature. Call a friend. See a therapist. Go for a massage.

Honour your health

Food should make you feel good. The instant gratification that comes with a greasy/salty/sugary bomb is quickly followed by queasy regret and an energy crash. Ask 'Will this food make me feel well? Will it feed my body the nutrients it needs to function optimally?' If the answer is yes, enjoy it and don't feel guilty about it!

Tune in. Close your eyes and ask what your body is really craving. Chances are it's craving a fresh salad loaded with chicken, fish or avocado, not a chocolate bar. The guilt you will feel after that chocolate bar is far worse for your health. Guilt really harms our relationship with food. If you are craving that chocolate bar, savour it and enjoy it as a treat. Remember to eat it without the guilt and in moderation.

Keep a symptom diary. This is like a food diary, except you write down how you feel before and after each meal. Are you genuinely hungry, or are you eating out of boredom or habit? Tune into and respect your body's hunger and fullness. I eat until I'm about 80 per cent full.

Say goodbye to diets. Fad diets are a thing of the past. They don't work. So throw out the books and magazine articles that say you can lose weight in seven days easily and permanently. All they offer is false hope and they are part of the reason why many women have a messed-up relationship with food. Health is a journey and if you keep up good habits, you *will* lose weight.

Be kind to yourself

Forget about that indulgent meal. *It's what you eat consistently over time that matters. The Healthy Life* is just that – a lifestyle. Think of the 80/20 approach – 80 per cent healthy eating and 20 per cent imperfect eating.

Make peace with food. Pay attention to your body and give yourself permission to eat. If you tell yourself you can't or shouldn't have a certain food, you're pretending you don't have control over your own body. This split-personality thinking, where you 'forbid' certain treats, can lead to intense feelings of deprivation, uncontrollable cravings and, often, bingeing. I used to obsess about every bite that passed my lips and it did more harm than good. Mindful eating is all about that mind–body connection. Remember, our thoughts manifest physically. So eat, drink and be mindful. Release the guilt surrounding food. Say aloud: 'I release and let it go'. Then breathe out. Your body will feel relieved. If you can learn to eat with joy, you'll be well on your way to loving your body.

Be a self-lover to be a mindful eater

It's time to start giving yourself some love! Self-love is the first step to healing your relationship with food so here are my favourite self-love rituals. Pick the ones that resonate with you and start practising them as much as you can. These will do wonders for your wellbeing.

Create a morning routine. For example: open your eyes, stretch, smile, give thanks and drink lemon water. Once you feel refreshed, check your phone and emails. This will set a good tone for your day.

Walk barefoot in nature, even for just a few minutes. Leave your phone behind, connect your feet to the earth and take in the fresh air. Nothing is more rejuvenating!

Write down five things you are grateful for. This really reminds us of what we have and how lucky we are. Gratitude keeps you grounded.

Don't put so much pressure on yourself. While it's important to strive to be your best, there's no need for extra pressure. Start focusing on how much you do, not what you don't do.

Don't worry about what others think. It's so unhealthy. And. It. Does. Not. Matter.

Put 'me-time' in the diary. How delicious does that sound?! Schedule in a walk, reading, yoga, a massage, a TV show or whatever makes you happy – so long as it's away from phones, computers and other people.

Soak in a hot bath with lavender oil and Epsom salts.

Enjoy tea time with a friend or your favourite podcast.

Lie in the sunshine.

Switch off social media. How many times do you check Instagram a day? 10? 20? Social media is taking over our lives. It's preventing us from being present. I'm guilty of overusing it too! Let's all aim for a social media–free day once a week.

Next level self-love

Want to step up your self-love a notch? Here are some ideas to inspire you.

Find your passion. Don't turn your back on your desires. It is so important to wake up and do what you love. In the end, we have one life – you don't want to end up resenting it.

Start meditating. It's a natural stress reliever that also allows you to be more present.

Forgive and forget. If a past situation or grudge is weighing you down, just let it go. Acknowledge it, then release it. That's easier said than done, I know, but you'll feel so much lighter afterwards. I had to do this with an ex-boyfriend and when I forgave him my health and wellbeing blossomed.

Follow your heart and trust your intuition. Your gut feeling is always right.

Reconnect with your inner child. Remember those carefree days when fun and laughter were the only things on the agenda? Try to reclaim them. Dance around, build a sandcastle or do a finger painting. You're never too old to get dirty!

Awaken your spirituality. It doesn't matter what or who you believe in; knowing there's something bigger than us out there keeps us grounded. Aim to connect more deeply with yourself and the world around you.

Visualise your dreams. You can live the life of your dreams – you just have to know you're worthy of it. Every night before bed, I imagine myself living my dream life. I believe I will manifest these thoughts into reality. You can too.

The power of the mind – how I attract good in my life

I've often been told, 'You are so lucky. How did you get this/that/the other?' We are all blessed with certain talents, abilities and circumstances. However, we also have the choice and freedom to be the masters of our destiny. Remember you create your own life. YOU are in control.

But I believe something more powerful is going on in my life. I truly believe all I am receiving and have received is because of my vision and the very simple law of attraction. I am slowly but surely manifesting my dream life into a reality – and it kind of freaks me out sometimes. I put something out there, I vision my dream and it comes alive. It's as simple as that. It does require work and attention, though. Hard work is always required. I am sharing this with you so you, too, can create all that you desire. It's about the power of the mind. Meditate on the life you want to create each day and believe in the power of positive affirmations – try to start the day with positivity.

When I look back on the life I was leading just a few years ago, I see that I was creating my life then too. I wasn't in a healthy frame of mind. Everything was hard. Everything was a challenge. This was my day-to-day mentality and I continued to attract 'hard' and 'challenging' situations.

This is the law of attraction at work. I wasn't living my dream life at all and I was holding onto incredible amounts of stress. **It is my belief that when we hold on emotionally, we hold on physically.** Stress will always stop us from achieving our best state of health.

Now, my living mantra is *let it go.* **LET IT GO.** Now, being in a healthier frame of mind, after lots of self-healing, counselling and education, I have shifted my mentality. I now believe my thoughts will create my reality so I take very seriously what I say and what I think. I am more careful. I know if I state 'I will not get that job' it is likely I will not get it. You can live the life you have always wanted. You just have to DREAM it and BELIEVE you are worth it. Focus on those two words for me. Our body listens to our thoughts and feelings. This is quantum physics. We manifest those thoughts and beliefs physically, without even realising it. When we constantly tell our bodies they are 'fat' or 'ugly' or 'not good enough', we manifest bodily stress.

The power of manifestation

Since I began my healing journey, each day I've spent five to seven minutes in gratitude for my body while visualising the body I desire. I feel incredible gratitude for my body. I literally say to myself, each morning as I open my eyes:

* ✳ 'Thank you for my balanced hormones.'
* ✳ 'Thank you for my comfortable weight.'
* ✳ 'Thank you for my optimal digestion.'
* ✳ 'Thank you for my strong arms and legs.'

My body listens to my thoughts and manifests them.

These affirmations are powerful and my body loves me for them. My body loves me back.

With my business, I simply started writing about my story and the foods I was eating. Everything happened naturally from there – but it didn't 'just happen'. I had a vision. I had a strong dream about the kind of career I wanted to have. I have dreamt of it since I was a little girl (dream big!) and I kept imagining myself living my dream job. Through my self-healing, I began telling myself I was worth it. I was going to have a successful business. But more importantly, one that I would wake up each day and feel excited about. I never let anyone tell me otherwise – and they tried!

I still have moments when I doubt my capabilities and myself. When I doubt it, something knocks me even more and I have to remind myself of my vision. I swap that 'negative' thought to something like 'You are worth it and you can do it'.

On the personal side, until I met my partner, Dean, I literally would visualise my dream partner and living my dream life with him. I could close my eyes each day and imagine it. I was also doing a lot of self-healing work (therapy, yoga, meditation, reading) to build up my self-esteem so I could believe I was good enough to receive my dream partner. This is a huge part of the secret. I also pictured the home I wanted to create with him. I visualised it, felt the feeling of living in it. I believed I would live in it. I literally created a folder that said 'Dream Home Ideas' with the very street I wanted to live on. Just last week, we bought a place on that street. I believe I manifested this dream.

So, dream big. Think positively. And believe you are worth the life of your dreams. You are SO worth it. I encourage you to believe in the power of vision boards. All of the above can be manifested in the form of a vision board. Tell me – what is on your vision board? What are you manifesting for yourself?

Home exercise

Create your own vision board and pin up your affirmations as well as healthy/inspirational photos.

See a counsellor. I can't rave on about therapy enough. Therapy helped me to identify my emotional pain and see things from a different perspective. It taught me to 'observe' rather than 'react' and to simply let go. By talking about your fears, problems and dreams out loud, you release them into the universe and can start to take action.

Trust that the universe is on your side.

How to improve your mood – naturally

Forget chocolate, coffee and clubbing – here's how to lift your spirits the all-natural way.

6 WAYS TO BOOST YOUR SELF-ESTEEM

1. Do something for someone else.
2. Look in the mirror and state one thing you love about yourself.
3. Do your favourite form of exercise.
4. Write in a gratitude journal.
5. Indulge in a day of pampering.
6. Validate someone you love – tell them how much they mean to you.

NUTRITION

- Cut out caffeine (coffee, soft drink, energy drinks) – especially if you're stressed or feeling low.
- Eliminate processed and packaged foods.
- Avoid artificial sweeteners. Aspartame is linked to mood disorders. Try stevia instead.
- Add a portion of protein, good fats and complex carbs to your plate. These macronutrients keep your blood sugar stable. When your blood sugar drops, so does your mood.
- Increase your intake of mood-boosting omega-3s (found in oily fish, walnuts, flaxseed, chia seeds and dark leafy greens).
- Reduce alcohol intake. Notice how drinking makes people giddy/sad/violent? All mood disorders.
- Cleanse your gut and liver. Serotonin, the 'feel-good' hormone, is made in the gut, so give your body a break and reduce that toxic load with a seasonal detox.
- Drink more water! Dehydration can cause fatigue and agitation.
- Eat foods high in tryptophan. These include nuts, seafood, turkey, poultry and eggs.
- Eat good quality complex carbohydrates. These include sweet potato, quinoa, legumes and brown rice.

LIFESTYLE

- Exercise – ever heard of endorphins?
- Pencil in some downtime. Dedicate a few minutes a day to REST.
- Sleep for 8 hours. Sleep = repair. We're happiest when we're well rested.
- Try acupuncture.
- Forgive. It's amazing how much it will benefit you.
- Laugh more! Yes, there is scientific evidence to back this up.
- Schedule in some YOU time and don't feel guilty about it.

SUPPLEMENTS

- Vitamin D. Low vitamin D levels are directly linked to depression, so make sure you get 15 minutes of sunshine a day or invest in a good quality supplement (at least 1000 IU/day).
- Fish oil: 2–3 g a day is great.
- B vitamins. Especially B6 or a good quality B complex is advised.
- Pop a probiotic – remember serotonin is made in the gut.
- Herbs can be useful too. See a good naturopath or herbalist for advice.
- Zinc and magnesium can also boost your mood.

MY FAVOURITE MANTRAS

'I listen to my body and give it exactly what it needs.'

'Eat in tune with your body. Eat with joy.'

'Isn't it about time you felt great?'

*'Deprivation only leads to a more complicated relationship
with food and your body. Give yourself permission.'*

*'Forgive yourself for your past. You are not your past. If you didn't eat
perfectly today, that's alright because perfect doesn't exist. Now let it go.'*

*'I trust that my body knows how to break these foods down.
'My body will heal itself naturally.
'My body works in my favour.
'Food nourishes my cells to keep me alive and well.'*

*'One step at a time. Small dietary changes
make a huge difference to the body.'*

'I love and care for my body and it cares for me.'

'I love and approve of myself. I am beautiful, just as I am.'

'The guilt we feel around food adds huge amounts of stress to the body. Let go of the guilt and watch your body heal.'

'I promise to forgive myself for any choice or attitudes that I had in the past, and look to a brighter, happier, healthier future.'

'Slow down. Breathe. Take it all in.'

'Small changes go a long way. Make one simple change a week.'

'I am grateful for my body and all it does for me.'

'I move my body because I love it, not because I hate it.'

'I allow myself to feel good being me.'

'I accept the beauty of my body shape.'

'A rested body is a healthy one.'

'I view food as nourishment, not the enemy.'

Worksheet

Fill out a symptom diary for a week. Did you notice any patterns about the way you felt before and after eating? Does eating affect your self-love?

....

....

....

Next time you have a meal, commit yourself to eating mindfully. Write down your experience. What did the food look like? Smell like? Taste like? How long did it take you to eat? How did you feel afterwards?

....

....

....

Is there anything negatively influencing your eating (e.g. stress, work colleagues)? What five activities (e.g. bath, walk in nature) will you use to curb emotional eating?

....

....

....

What self-love activity have you done for yourself today or this week? Commit to doing something nice for yourself every day.

....

....

....

Home exercise

Write down five things you'd like to do more of. Commit to doing at least two out of the five this week. I can tell you this made a huge difference not only in my outlook of the week ahead, but also in my overall attitude. When I focused on doing things I truly wanted to do and made a commitment to making some of them happen, I felt an excitement and freedom I hadn't felt in a long time. It didn't feel like another item on the to-do list; it felt like honouring myself.

PRINCIPLE 7. MOVEMENT

Move your body – but not too much

Exercise is so important for cardiovascular health – and even more fantastic for the mind. So say yes to your endorphin hit, but don't take it to the extreme. **The key is to be active.** This does not mean compulsively exercising twice a day to 'burn off' your eating sins. It's a seductive and prevailing idea, but it's dangerous to your overall wellbeing. We're just not designed to push our bodies to the limit, day after day. There's no need.

If you overdo it at the gym, you'll exhaust your adrenals – those all-important hormones that we talked about earlier in the book. Over-training depletes the body, leading to hormonal imbalance, high cortisol levels (which cause fat to cling on to the tummy, no thanks!), fatigue, insomnia and even musculoskeletal breakdown. When you're exhausted, an intense workout can feel good – but only temporarily. Within hours, you'll be awash with aches and fatigue. This kind of distress causes the body to go into crisis mode: it cannibalises muscle, stores fat, induces fatigue, impairs cognitive function (like creativity) and promotes injuries and anxiety. Why? Because your body is smarter than you are. It does everything to make you slow down. The longer you ignore its requests, the louder its demands will become.

Your body needs time to move, rest *and* recover. So when it comes to working out, I recommend exercising less – but smarter.

That's what I did and I feel more energetic than ever before. I don't slog it out at the gym day in, day out. I don't exercise until I can't breathe. Instead, I try to live a really active lifestyle. In a typical week, I do interval sessions, yoga , Pilates and weight training. While the resistance sessions are short, I work hard: enough to burn energy, maintain heart health and keep my metabolism firing, but not too much that I feel depleted and achy. Intense workouts are great, but not all the time. As for the gentler forms of exercise like yoga, I believe they keep me grounded. I find them restorative and allow me to tune into myself. I also include one to two rest days every week and relieve all guilt about it. My body loves rest days.

Benefits of yoga

To exercise your body and mind, you can't go past yoga. I disliked it at first, but now I truly believe it's one of the best ways to move. The benefits are incredible:

* better posture and flexibility
* improved digestive function
* mental clarity and focus
* stable blood pressure
* tension release
* improved strength and endurance
* reduced stress and anxiety
* anti-ageing
* feelings of calm and wellbeing.

Haven't you noticed yogis are always happy?

MY WEEK IN WORKOUTS

Monday – 45 minutes weight training and HIIT (high-intensity interval training)

Tuesday – Rest day or 1 hour brisk walk/yoga

Wednesday – 30-minute jog outdoors

Thursday – 45 minutes weight training or Pilates class + 30-minute brisk walk

Friday – Rest day or yoga

Saturday – 1-hour walk with friends or family + (sometimes) Pilates class

Sunday – Rest day or 'light' walk

Now it's your turn. From now on, I want you to move your body daily. Pick 2–3 forms of exercise you enjoy, and schedule them into your week. I don't care what you choose, so long as it puts a smile on your face. That way, you're more likely to stick to it. Along with a couple of workouts that get your heart rate up, pencil in some yoga or Pilates – your body will love you for it.

Change your mentality, change your body

Just like with anything else, what you tell yourself about exercise is so important. To reap the most benefits, you need to start exercising because you love it – not because you hate it. Stop putting pressure on yourself. Instead of exercising 'to lose weight', do it because it's a mood booster, mind clearer and fantastic for your heart. The weight loss will come naturally. This is why I advocate low-impact activities with a mental aspect like yoga. By forcing you to become aware of your body, they allow you to tune in to what it needs. They're a nice break from clock-watching during cardio, or blasting music to block out the pain. That is not the point of exercise. If you listen to your body, it will reward you by making you look and feel better than ever.

Diet and exercise

If you're worried that cutting back on your workout regime will lead to weight gain, remember the saying: you can't outrun a bad diet. In other words, 90 per cent of your health is about what you put into your mouth.

Does intense exercise suit you?

I used to exercise twice a day and my weight just crept up. Now, while some of us thrive on intense exercise – it boosts our mood and energy, and maintains our weight – for others it's disastrous. It comes down to the nervous system: if it's balanced, you can handle the intensity of spinning; if it's out of whack, step away from the bike and move your body in more restorative ways.

I go on and on about exhaustion and stress being the number one causes of weight gain. It's crazy how many stressed-out people go to boot camp at 8 pm after a twelve-hour work day, when their body is screaming at them to slow down and REST. In the long term, this can result in 'sympathetic dominance', which is when the nervous system is constantly active. It means your body is always in 'fight or flight' mode. This is a major reason why many people find it hard to lose weight. When you're forever trying to run away from the 'tiger' (i.e. financial, family or relationship stress), your body will protect itself by sending blood to the legs and arms (because you need those to 'escape'!), shutting off your digestion, releasing glucose (for energy) and shooting out cortisol. This all leads to – you guessed it – hormonal imbalance. And that will make it hard for you to achieve the body you want.

I advise most people with taxing jobs to enjoy gentle exercise after work and on the weekend. Yoga, Pilates, brisk walking and meditation are all fabulous. When I ask people to cut back on their extreme exercise regime, they're often resistant. But after they swap a few tough workouts for restorative ones, they're amazed at the results. When the body is rested, it's better able to burn fat. If you're slaving away at the gym and nothing is happening weight-wise, ask yourself whether that exercise is really serving you.

PRINCIPLE 8. BEAUTY FROM THE INSIDE OUT

I believe when we heal our relationship with our bodies, our health thrives. And when we're healthy, so is our appearance. In a basic evolutionary way, the signs of beauty – lean muscle, bright eyes, lustrous hair – are a reflection of inner health. When it comes to beauty, what's on the inside counts. If you simply focus on external beauty – by caring more about your foundation than your fatty acid intake – you'll be left with a 'skin deep' beauty that's unsustainable, unsatisfying and ultimately unconvincing.

Do you want clear skin? Sparkly eyes? Strong nails? Thick, healthy hair? Then concentrate on what you're putting into your body. By increasing your intake of enzymes, minerals, antioxidants and nutrient-rich foods, you will get that radiant glow from within we all know and love.

WHAT IS AN ANTIOXIDANT?

Antioxidants neutralise the effects of 'free radicals', substances that damage the body's cells. By doing so, they fight the signs of ageing and boost immunity. Think of them as your body's beauty protectors.

Worksheet

Based on your schedule and energy/stress levels, write down a new exercise regime. Try it for one week, recording how you feel before and after each session.

After one week, what have you learnt about exercising less, but smarter?

....
....
....
....
....
....
....
....

Choose three stretches or yoga poses to do each morning.

....
....
....
....
....
....

Home exercise
Create a mood board of fun, fit photos to inspire you to move your body.

I eat fish three times a week for beauty on the inside and out.

Swap your soft drink for vitamin water. These delicious vitamin waters give you a glowing complexion.

Experiment with and get excited about veggies. Eating colourful vegetables will give you good health and glowing skin.

I enter the Stress-free Zone for 10 minutes every day and it has changed my life. It balances my day and clears my head.

The beauty hotlist

These minerals and nutrients fuel your body and feed your skin in the best possible ways. Load up on them for gorgeous, glowing skin and hair.

NUTRIENT/ MINERAL	BENEFIT	SOURCES
Zinc	Helps to rebuild collagen, smooths skin, and heals scars and wounds	Pumpkin seeds, seafood (especially shellfish and oysters), meat, liver, legumes, mushrooms and eggs
Magnesium	Detoxifies the skin, slows down the ageing process and combats breakouts	Dark leafy greens (like spinach), nuts, seeds, fish and brown rice
Silica	Strengthens skin tissue, hair and nails	Oats, leeks, green beans, strawberries, cucumbers and mangoes
Potassium	Maintains our body's fluid levels, reducing puffiness	Bananas, beetroot, sweet potatoes, lentils and avocados
Selenium	Fights disease and ageing by reducing cell damage and inflammation	Brazil nuts, sunflower seeds, fish, shellfish, mushrooms and eggs
Vitamin E	Protects, repairs and nourishes your skin from the inside out	Nuts, seeds, spinach, kale, sweet potatoes, egg yolk and dairy products
Vitamin C	Essential for the production of collagen. It also builds tissue, keeps skin elastic and prevents sagging	Lemons, oranges, capsicums, broccoli, cauliflower, papaya, tomatoes and strawberries
Vitamin A	Thickens and stimulates the skin, reducing wrinkles and increasing blood flow. It also helps to form new skin cells	Sweet potatoes, egg yolk, liver, meat and fish. Betacarotene converts into vitamin A, so eat plenty of carrots, sweet potatoes and dark leafy greens (Sensing a pattern here?)
Essential fatty acids	High quality omega-3s, -6s and -9s reduce inflammation, promote cell growth and control the oils and fats in our body	Nuts and seeds (especially walnuts and chia), avocados, coconuts and coconut oil, olives and olive oil, oily fish and tahini

Best and worst beauty foods

Our skin cells are renewed every six to eight weeks. That's why it's so vital to replenish our cells with the nutrients they need. It also means it's never too late to start looking after your skin. If you want a glowing complexion, the key is to cut out the crap – that is, sugar, alcohol and processed foods – and eat your way through a rainbow of fresh wholefoods. Avoid foods that can increase inflammation in the body and affect the way you feel and look. In the case of beauty, you really are what you eat. The key is to rid the body of inflammation by eating the anti-inflammatory foods in the table below.

BEST – EAT THESE FOODS	WORST – AVOID THESE
• Low-GI foods: berries, wholegrains, beans, legumes, eggs, lean animal protein, fish, nuts and seeds • High-fibre foods: fruit, vegetables, legumes, oats, flaxseed and psyllium husk • Good fats: avocados, nuts, seeds and oily fish • Seafood: loaded with zinc, omega-3 fatty acids and selenium • Fruit and veggies: full of vitamins, especially A and C • Nuts: high in zinc, selenium, vitamin E, niacin and omega-3 • Lean meat: great source of protein, niacin, selenium, vitamin E and zinc	• Refined sugar: inflammatory • Processed dairy: inflammatory • Alcohol: full of sugar and creates toxic build-up • Transfats: 'bad' fats found in fries, cakes, pizzas, etc. • Processed foods: toxic to the body • Gluten and wheat In short, if it comes out of a packet, don't eat it!

The beauty solutions

Follow these tips to get skin, hair and nails that scream health!

Eat nutritious foods. Feed your skin by making sure every plate is brimming with enzymes and minerals. Sip a green juice daily for bonus points. And try my Skin Glow Balls on page 272.

Join the raw-volution. Aim to start each meal with a bowl of raw greens (like rocket) to increase your enzyme load and fire up digestion. Sprouts are also amazing.

Clean the gut and liver. We absorb all of our nutrients in the gut, which is why gut health is key to making us look and feel beautiful. When our bodies are clogged with toxins, they can't perform at their best. The metabolism slows down, throwing off digestive and liver function and accelerating the ageing process. See page 28 for detox tips.

Ask a nutritionist or naturopath about doing a gut and liver cleanse. They will work with you to ensure your body eliminates toxins through the liver and kidneys so that impurities don't flood through the skin.

MY FAVOURITE BEAUTY BITES & TIPS

Veggies Especially greens: the darker, the better

Herbs and spices Basil, parsley, mint, ginger, turmeric

Fruit Avocados, bananas, berries, pomegranate, lemons

Nuts and seeds Particularly almonds and pumpkin seeds

Coconut oil

Aloe vera juice Drink every morning for its anti-inflammatory properties, and soothing and healing effects on the skin and gut. It also stimulates the growth of new cells and allows the skin to heal quickly.

Salmon

Protein Its amino acids work to build and repair skin. Enjoy animal protein as well as plant sources like chlorella and spirulina. Both are fantastic for inner health.

Drink water 1.5–2 L a day (including herbal teas). Staying hydrated is the easiest and most effective beauty tip, in my opinion.

Cut out sugar Sugar causes hormonal havoc and breaks down collagen, leading to wrinkles. It really is a sweet poison.

Avoid dairy Dairy is mucus-forming, acidic and contains an insulin-like growth factor. It's said to stimulate growth of oestrogen too – and excess oestrogen causes acne in some women. If you struggle with skin issues, take two weeks off dairy and see if it clears up. If you can't live without dairy, swap to organic sources and limit yourself to two portions a day.

Feed your skin with good fats Essential fatty acids are crucial for healthy, glowing skin. They also balance hormones and reduce inflammation in the body. Say hello to virgin organic coconut oil, cold-pressed extra-virgin olive oil, avocado, walnuts, cold-pressed flaxseed oil, chia seeds and oily fish, or invest in a fish oil supplement that contains EPA and DHA.

Add antioxidants to your diet Eat an array of these foods daily: blueberries, pomegranate, beetroot, acai berries, goji berries, spinach, raspberries, nuts, seeds, green tea and 70 per cent cocoa dark chocolate.

Zinc it up Zinc is my favourite mineral. It's known for rebuilding collagen, which prevents the signs of ageing and skin damage (like wrinkles and stretch marks). It also assists with scar repair and hormonal balancing.

Learn to love vitamin C Vitamin C is fabulous for our skin and very high in antioxidants. It also nourishes the adrenal glands, helping with the stress response. For doubly amazing results, use vitamin C serum on your skin.

Sleep It's called beauty sleep for a reason, so try to catch 8 hours of shut-eye a night.

Rest, rest, rest If you're stressed, it will show on your skin in the form of inflammation or breakouts. Combat this by scheduling in daily downtime such as a power nap, yoga, Epsom salt bath or popping your legs up against a wall. Those who rest well, age well!

How to reduce cellulite

Bumpy, dimpled skin – most women contend with cellulite at some point in their lives. Cellulite is simply normal fat beneath the skin and it appears the way it does because it's pushing against connective tissue. While cellulite is not a sign that you're unhealthy or overweight, it's a condition most would prefer to get rid of. **The good news is, you CAN reduce cellulite with your diet.**

Ditch the salt. Just recently I noticed a few little bumps on my thighs, something I have not had in a long time. Hmm. I decided to cut out salt for a week (using herbs and spices instead) and the bumps have significantly reduced. Salt dehydrates the cells in the body, which can form the appearance of cellulite.

Eat alkaline. Enjoy your fresh fruit and veggies. Alkaline foods help combat acidity and toxic build-up in the body that often accumulates and can form cellulite. Greens at every meal is my golden rule.

Ditch the sugar. Keep your blood-sugar levels stable. Eat regularly and ensure your meals and snacks are protein-rich. Avoid all processed sugar and reduce fruit to two portions/day. Berries and citrus fruits are fab!

Get your blood flowing. Use a dry body brush each day. Exercise daily. Do a coffee scrub. Treat yourself to a massage regularly.

Drink a green juice daily. Or use a green wholefood powder. This will help you increase your antioxidant profile, which helps to reduce damage to skin cells.

Drink plenty of water. Obviously! Water helps to flush the toxins out of the body. Add some lemon juice for that extra metabolism boost.

Detox. Toxic build-up can increase cellulite. Keep your liver healthy and cut out the toxins – alcohol, refined sugar, refined carbs, transfats (processed foods) and take-out foods.

Sweat it out. Exercise and have saunas.

Swap coffee for green tea. One coffee a day max.

Keep alcohol to the weekends. Red wine is the best option, in my opinion.

Reduce stress. Stress is responsible for most of our body woes. Breathe deeply. Practise yoga. Rest every day.

Cellulite? Start dry body brushing. It's incredible for promoting circulation and lymphatic drainage, which in turn gets rid of cellulite and plumps up the skin. I do it a few mornings a week. How to use a dry body brush. Pick a soft, naturally bristled brush. Starting at your feet, brush in small, upward movements towards your heart. Use light pressure.

Skin-loving supplements

Under the guidance of a practitioner, consider the following supplements:

* a good quality multivitamin: the best ones include vitamins A, E and C, selenium and B vitamins
* vitamin C: 2 g a day
* zinc: 10–30 mg a day
* high quality fish oil (with EPA/DHA) or primrose oil: 2–3 g

DIY pampering

You don't need to splurge on fancy face masks. Most products contain natural extracts, so just go straight to the source. Chances are you already have all the ingredients you need in the fridge. Your skin absorbs up to 80 per cent of what you put on it, so please, please, please go for natural, organic and chemical-free skincare brands. These are stocked at most health-food stores, as well as online. **No time?** For a quick fix, simply apply mashed strawberries to your skin. They're super high in vitamin C. To treat your skin to a deliciously cleansing mask, mix together:

Avocado and banana face mask

To get the glow factor, mix together:

1 avocado (great source of omega-3, vitamin E and antioxidants)

1 tbsp Manuka honey (antimicrobial)

juice of ½ lemon (rich source of vitamin C)

1 banana, mashed (full of betacarotene and potassium)

Apply to your skin and allow to absorb for 20 minutes before rinsing off.

Oat and lemon face mask

2 tbsp oats

2 tbsp natural yoghurt

juice of ½ lemon

1 tbsp apple cider vinegar

splash of water

Combine in a bowl and leave the on skin for 15 minutes before rinsing off.

MY SKINCARE REGIME

I use Burt's Bees products to nourish and take care of my skin. Why? Because they're 99 per cent natural, eco-friendly and leave my skin hydrated, soft and supple.

- ✴ Burt's Bees Intense Hydration Cream Cleanser
- ✴ Burt's Bees Intense Hydration Day Lotion
- ✴ Burt's Bees Intense Hydration Eye Cream (at night)
- ✴ Burt's Bees Peach and Willowbark Deep Pore Scrub (a couple of times a week)

Other brilliant buys:

- ✴ Rosewater spray – hello, hydration!
- ✴ Vitamin C serum
- ✴ Vitamin A, E and C-based creams
- ✴ Rio Rosa Mosqueta Rosehip oil (at night)
- ✴ Coconut oil: a great body moisturiser and scalp treatment
- ✴ WotNot Natural Sunscreen SPF 30+

Make-up

When you're eating right and living a happy, healthy life, your skin will thank you by looking amazing. You won't need make-up, but wearing it is half the fun. I like to wear a little make-up – but I **go down the natural route most of the time**. Here's what I use:

* tinted moisturiser with SPF or a mineral powder
* shimmer on cheeks and forehead
* gold eyeshadow to accentuate my green eyes
* mascara: my daily essential!
* blush or bronzer for that sun-kissed look.

Luscious locks

Want beautiful, shiny hair? As always, there's a natural solution (or eight).

Load up on good fats. Walnuts, flaxseed, fish and avocado will give your hair that healthy shine.

Up your vitamin C intake. This nifty vitamin boosts collagen production, which keeps hair thick and strong. Rich sources include citrus fruits, capsicums, strawberries and leafy green vegetables.

Pop a B vitamin. B complex vitamins increase scalp circulation and rejuvenate the hair follicles, leaving you with lovely thick locks.

Enjoy iron-rich foods. Found in lamb, beef, oysters, legumes, beans, spinach, dark leafy greens, nuts and seeds, iron is key to hair growth.

Invest in a zinc and silica supplement. These minerals promote hair growth, so ask a practitioner for a supplement. To up the ante, include cucumber, zucchini, mango, beans, celery, asparagus, oysters, Brazil nuts and eggs in your diet.

Nourish with vitamin E. This vitamin boosts the body's ability to produce keratin, meaning it plays a huge role in preventing hair breakage. You can get vitamin E in supplement form, or by eating almonds, pine nuts, spinach and olives.

Give yourself a massage. Do you love a hairdresser's scalp massage as much as I do? There's no reason why you can't do it yourself. Grab some rosemary or coconut oil and knead your head gently for five to ten minutes. This will stimulate circulation.

Check your thyroid. If you've got a sluggish thyroid, you may experience hair thinning or breakage. Combat this by enjoying foods high in iodine, such as nori, kombu and wakame. See page 35 to learn how to keep your thyroid healthy.

Got a breakout? Don't stress – simply pour a little apple cider vinegar onto cotton wool and dab on the spot. It should disappear in no time!

Worksheet

What are your biggest skincare concerns?

....
....
....
....

Using the info in this chapter, how will you try to combat them the natural way?

....
....
....

What three food swaps will you make for healthier skin and hair?

....
....
....
....
....
....

It's time to compliment yourself! What are your best features and assets and why? Don't be shy!

....
....
....
....

PRINCIPLE 9. SLEEP

Sleep. **We all love it, but too many of us don't get enough.** A few more experience agonising, erratic sleep patterns like insomnia. A good night's sleep is a huge part of the health equation. It allows your body to rest and repair. That's why, if my friends, family and clients are feeling out of sorts, the first thing I ask is, 'How many hours of sleep do you get a night?' Everyone who knows me knows I have a non-negotiable commitment to getting eight hours of shut-eye every single night. No exceptions. I owe my health, energy, stable weight and motivation to sleep – honestly! While we all know how fantastic we feel after a really great sleep, many people don't realise just how important sleep is.

Why sleep rocks

Getting your forty winks comes with a ton of benefits. These are the major ones.

Repairs the body. While you sleep, your body is busy producing extra protein molecules. These molecules build new cells and repair the damaged ones, in turn strengthening your body's ability to fight infection. So if you seem to catch every cold that comes around, sleeping more will help.

Reduces stress. A good night's sleep lowers your blood pressure and cortisol (the stress hormone) levels in the body. High blood pressure and cortisol can lead to a laundry list of health complications, none of them good. Sleeping is the best way to chill out.

Helps with weight control. Do you ever feel ravenous after a night out? Or when you're jetlagged? Sleep regulates the hormones that control your appetite, so when you don't get enough sleep, that balance is interrupted. Your body releases the nasty 'ghrelin' hormone, which stimulates hunger. Cue tummy growling. Lack of sleep also slows down the metabolism, which leads to weight gain over time.

Enhances mood. We all know how true this is! Sleep affects the way we feel and interact with others. When we don't get enough, we end up feeling irritable and moody. When we sleep for eight hours straight, we feel fresh and ready to take on the world.

Take sleep seriously

Studies have shown that limited sleep can lead to long-term mood disorders such as depression and anxiety, not to mention chronic fatigue. So make sure you treat sleep like you would a doctor's appointment: it's non-negotiable.

Enhances your beauty. There's nothing worse than being told 'you look tired'. Sleep affects your appearance, so snooze more and for longer. Doing so will reduce puffiness and dark circles and leave you with flawless, radiant skin because your skin cells will have the *time* to repair overnight.

The sleep solutions

If you can sleep better, you'll look and feel better. It's that simple. Your body loves rest as much as you do. Here's how to get a great night's sleep, every night.

Restore sleeping patterns – and stick to them. Go to bed and wake up at the same time every day. If you can tuck yourself in early, say 9 or 10 pm, your body will love you for it.

Turn off technology and bright lights from 9 pm. As you're unwinding and getting ready for bed, switch off computers, TVs, mobile phones and lights. They mess with the pineal gland, the part of your brain that produces melatonin (the sleep hormone). Candles are so much prettier anyway.

Switch off the smartphone. Phones are the worst of all technologies when it comes to interrupting sleep. They're brightly lit, small (forcing us to squint) and full of distractions. Try to put your phone on aeroplane mode after dinner … I know it's hard, but think of it as a character-building exercise.

Keep your room quiet, dark and cool. Your bedroom should be a peaceful haven with no distractions. Shut the blinds or hang curtains and make sure it's nice and cool inside.

Avoid exercising right before bedtime. Exercising floods your body with adrenaline and cortisol, which are the last things you want when you're trying to sleep.

Close the kitchen early. Aim to finish dinner by 7.30–8 pm and avoid any heavy meals or late-night snacking. Give your body a chance to digest the food before bed.

Don't work in your bedroom. If possible, keep your work and sleep spaces separate. This changed my quality of sleep dramatically.

Jot down your thoughts. Do you have thoughts running through your mind so fast, they literally keep you awake at night? Keep a notebook next to your bed and write down any problems or tasks before you go to bed. This will allow you to let them go, relieving stress and worry and opening you up to a good night's sleep.

Cut the coffee. Avoid stimulants like caffeine, smoking and soft drink before bed. As a general rule, stop drinking caffeine – black/green tea and coffee, even cacao – after 3 pm.

Avoid spicy foods at night. For some people, curries, garlic and chilli are too stimulating.

Soak up the sunshine. Get outside and enjoy 15–30 minutes of sunshine a day. This will give you a vitamin D hit and boost melatonin production.

Do yoga and meditation. Both are powerful at improving sleep and lowering stress levels. It may take time to get used to the breathing and centring, but I promise you'll be grateful when you do.

Breathe slowly and deeply. Most of us walk around sucking in shallow breaths, so indulge in 20 deep breaths before bed. Watch your belly rise and fall, rise and fall, rise and fall …

Use lavender oil. Dab some lavender oil on your temples before bedtime, or add a couple of drops onto your pillow. It's known for a calming effect on the mind and body.

Have an Epsom salt bath. I can't even explain how amazing this is! Epsom salts are made up of magnesium, which works to relax and soothe your muscles. Soak in a bath for 20 minutes, then roll straight into bed. You'll sleep like a kitten in a cosy corner.

Enjoy tryptophan-rich foods. Tryptophan is the precursor to melatonin, the hormone that puts us to sleep and it's found in protein. Try to include nuts, seafood, turkey, poultry or eggs on the dinner menu.

Put your legs up on a wall. I love this. It forces you to relax. If you forget and hop into bed, just pop your legs up on the headboard!

Sip on a hot drink before bed. This is an incredibly soothing ritual that will set your body and mind up for sleep. Try chamomile tea, or whip up my Ayurveda Hot Chocolate (see page 301).

Reduce sugar and alcohol. As you've probably picked up, these two stimulants do you absolutely no favours! They spike your blood sugar and you're more likely to wake up in the middle of the night after consuming them.

Sleep supplements

Boost your slumber with magnesium, homeopathic melatonin or valerian. Ask your herbalist or naturopath for guidance.

IN YOUR WORDS

When I found your website, what really drew me in, is that you have a combination of many things I was looking for. I realised I CAN enjoy food, I CAN control myself, I CAN think better about myself. I CAN understand my body and its needs.

I can't say I am able to do this completely yet, but I know for sure I am getting there. For that, I really wanted to thank you. I don't tell this to people around me, mainly due to shame of myself, but I was really desperate. I really honestly hated myself. I said before that I can't love myself, I take that back. I may not be where I want to be yet, but I know for sure that this time I am on the right track. It's a huge relief knowing that I don't have to put my body under stressful situations (little amounts of food, and ever-lasting hours of exercise). For all those things, thank you Jess!! *– Deyanira*

Worksheet

How many hours of sleep do you get a night?

....

What do you think is affecting your sleep?

....

....

....

....

....

What three to five things will you incorporate into your life to get
a better night's sleep?

....

....

....

....

....

PRINCIPLE 10. WEIGHT LOSS

It's time to end the battle with your body. To nourish it instead of starving it. To let go of whatever is holding you back from being your happiest, healthiest self. To start feeling great about yourself. If you can do that, you will find your optimal weight.

Weight-ing on the mind

Weight has become the biggest concern for women around the world. From what I have seen, learnt and experienced myself, women identify themselves by their weight. It determines who we are and what we can control – and this has led to an incredibly complex relationship with food and our bodies.

Many of us see eating as a form of control over our lives. We use food to 'escape' or make us feel better. We eat when we're happy or sad, rather than when we're truly hungry. By doing all this, we've lost the connection with our own body. We've stopped listening to what it needs – and that is holding us back from losing weight successfully and healthily. For a lot of women, food serves as a temporary relief from something or someone. But it's not food we are hungry for. It's other things. Uncovering exactly what it is we're trying to fix/control/eat our way out of is the first step to achieving a healthy weight that we are happy with.

My story about weight

As I mentioned at the start of the book, I struggled with my body image for most of my teenage years and early twenties. Like many girls, I tortured myself to the point where food was the enemy and my body was a burden. My relationship with my body was turbulent: I was a carb-restricting, fad-dieting, anxiety-ridden, scale-fearing, self-loathing and self-doubting mess. My days were either 'good' or 'bad' and they revolved around food. I weighed myself incessantly. If I liked the number on the scales, I'd congratulate myself. If the number had crept up, I would bury myself in self-loathing. I would feel like a failure. So I'd end up bingeing and then, wallowing in guilt – which I now know was *worse* for my health than the junk food itself. It was a never-ending cycle. Then something clicked. I realised hating my body was affecting everything in my life, so I committed myself to understanding what nutrition was all about. I freed myself from deprivation. I literally woke up one day and said, 'I've had enough. I would rather be heavier than diet like this.' I was frustrated that food had such power over me. My obsession with dieting and food clouded my ability to listen to what my body really needed.

When I began to learn how the body actually works, my mentality shifted. I viewed food as a source of nourishment, not the enemy. I ditched dieting and fed myself REAL foods. I didn't feel the urge to eat as much. I ate in a way that healed my body.

The result? My palate changed, my appetite shifted and over time, those excess kilos – the ones that were just *not meant to be on my body* – fell away. Just like that.

When you feed your body with goodness and love, it is so, so good to you in return. It's the most empowering, amazing feeling.

Get rid of the guilt

The mind is a powerful thing. When I gave myself permission to eat any food that tickled my tastebuds, I actually binged less. I found I didn't want those 'naughty' foods so much. It wasn't long before I realised I only craved them because I was rebelling. Self-sabotaging, even. So let go of the guilt and allow yourself to eat anything. You'll end up choosing wisely and the weight will fall off.

Seize control

I ate nourishing wholefoods – and did so with joy. I followed my ten principles – I healed my gut, loved my liver and balanced my hormones and blood sugars. I had three meals a day with two snacks in between. This kept my metabolism firing and blood sugars stable. I got 15–30 minutes of sunshine daily. (It's best to expose your tummy to the sun. Low vitamin D has been linked to weight problems and the vitamin is essential for good thyroid function.) I learnt to appreciate my body. I started saying affirmations and the positive thoughts triggered healing and a sense of self-respect.

We can't reach our optimal weight until our hormones are balanced. This goes beyond having a good diet; it requires more sleep, less stress and internal happiness. The body burns fat better when you feed it wholefoods and repopulate it with healthy flora. We're overfed, yet starved of nutrients. We're eating the wrong foods and that's causing us to be nutritionally unsatisfied. But we're not solely to blame – it's the way food is marketed.

Once we find happiness, motivation and balance in all aspects of our lives, healthy eating becomes second nature and weight falls off with ease. If we fuel our body with goodness – from both food and supplements – it will restore natural vitality. Since no two people are the same, no two diets should be the same either. One size does not fit all.

Thoughts ➤➤ Reality

The mind–body connection is real. So when we think positive thoughts about our body, it's able to transform more easily.

Calorie-counting chaos

Compulsively counting calories and eating to an 'average' calculated by a computer or someone who has NEVER met you is absurd. Our bodies are not calorie-counting machines. We're all different biochemically and physiologically, with varying metabolisms: your body will break down food differently from mine or your mum's depending on bodily functions such as digestion or how well your liver is working. It's not as simple as calories in and calories out. I used to track my calories and carb intake, but doing so only added extra stress and weight to my body. The trick to weight loss is to listen to your body, not an app. Think about it this way: if there was one diet that worked for everyone, wouldn't we all be on it by now? Health is a lifestyle. It's long term, not a fad. The most effective changes are the ones you can sustain for the rest of your life.

MYTH	TRUTH
1. Artificial sweeteners (like those in Equal, Splenda, sugar-free gum and energy drinks) help you lose weight.	Wrong! Fake sugars are both toxic and addictive, and among the worst things for your health. They are chemicals that suppress your satiety (so you don't know when you're full or satisfied) and spike your insulin, leading to mood disorders, hormonal imbalance and weight gain.
2. Work out for hours and you'll get the body of your dreams!	False! Over-exercising can make you hungrier. It can also result in high cortisol and adrenal exhaustion, which causes hormonal havoc. A tired, exhausted and stressed body clings on to fat. The trick is to exercise less, but smarter.
3. Fat will make you fat.	No, it won't! Low-fat and fat-free foods are loaded with SUGAR and bulking agents. The body stores extra sugar as fat. Good fats are essential to support cell growth, balance hormones, protect the organs and help the body absorb nutrients. They also give you an energy boost and keep you fuller for longer.
4. If you eat less calories than you burn, you'll lose weight.	False! The body regulates our metabolism, and it's far more complex than calories in, calories out. Focus on eating high quality wholefoods for a clean, lean body. Do that, and your metabolism will rev up automatically.
5. Don't snack.	Wrong! To keep your blood sugars stable, you must eat every 3–4 hours. When you don't eat for a long period of time, your body thinks it's being starved and goes into survival mode – and holds on to fat.

Treat yourself

Why is it that when we eat a deliciously decadent food – something that makes us smile and feel good – we bury ourselves in guilt and self-loathing? I decided to put a big end to this a couple of years ago. As a nutritionist, my problem is not eating badly all the time, but feeling like I *have* to eat well all the time. I can become TOO strict with my diet. It's surprisingly easy because I am exposed to healthy options.

We need to trust our bodies more. Will one indulgent meal cause a skin breakout? A significant weight gain? Destroy our good habits? No. We need to enjoy the foods we love. Release the idea that we have to eat perfectly all the time. This is why I have implemented 'Treat Yourself Tuesday'. I choose one day a week to enjoy something indulgent – a true treat. When you put an end to the deprivation mentality, something amazing happens. You will find yourself not wanting it so badly. You will find yourself being able to control how much you eat. You will find yourself savouring rather than shaming. Share your Treat Yourself Tuesday indulgence with #JSHealthTreatYourself.

Don't deprive yourself – you'll only be frustrated and more likely to overeat later. Deprivation only needs to a complicated relationship with food. And often a food binge. If you splurge, move on – don't let the guilt ruin it.

Top weight-loss tips

The 7-Day Slim-down Meal Plan (see page 120–121) goes into much more detail about how to eat your way to weight loss, but these guidelines will get you started.

Drink lemon water upon rising. This is an amazing way to alkalise your body and awaken the digestive system. Try my Meta-boost Drink (see page 301) to jolt your digestion and metabolism into top gear.

Limit caffeine. Enjoy ONE coffee a day (before lunch) and that's it. If you suffer from anxiety, poor sleep or hormonal complications like PMS, eliminate caffeine completely for a week or two and feel the difference. Swap to green tea – it's a fab fat burner.

Start your day with a good, protein-rich brekkie. Forget cereal or toast – these are blood-sugar disasters that wreak havoc on the waistline. Go for an egg-based breakfast or protein smoothie.

Eat protein with every meal. Protein is thermogenic, meaning it requires a lot of energy to break down, which in turn boosts your metabolism. It also stabilises blood sugars, reducing cravings and keeping you fuller for longer.

Practise portion control. Just because food is abundant, doesn't mean we have to eat all of it. Sit down to a balanced plate of food: protein, carbohydrates, vegetables and good fats. Give yourself a chance to rest and digest afterwards. Cut down the size of your dinner especially.

Go gluten-free. Gluten is highly inflammatory and hard to digest, so opt for brown rice, quinoa, legumes, pumpkin and beans instead.

Cut back on starchy foods. Particularly bread, pasta, cereals and crackers. Cut out carbs after 3 pm. This works for me but not for everyone.

Stop having artificial sweeteners and diet soft drinks. They create a toxic build-up in the body and mess with hormones, especially insulin.

Learn to love your veggies. Eat them with every single meal – aim for five serves a day if you can. Green, red, yellow and orange veggies are packed with fibre to keep you full and loaded with B vitamins for purifying your system. A clean body is a lean body!

Eat through the rainbow. Variety is the spice of life. I know it's easy to get stuck in a food rut, but try to mix it up. When we limit ourselves to the same foods all the time, we miss out on vital nutrients.

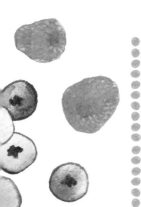

FAT-BURNING FOODS

We'll cover this more in Nutitrion 101, but for now, pop these metabolism-boosting foods on your shopping list.

- Broccoli
- Berries
- Seaweed
- Spirulina
- Lemon

- Turmeric
- Green tea
- Grapefruit
- Lean protein and fish

Heal your gut. If you are not digesting and absorbing your food, weight loss can be a struggle. See page 14 for tips.

Keen to quit sugar? Read *I Quit Sugar* by Sarah Wilson and *Sweet Poison* by David Gillespie. Sugar is one of the biggest barriers to weight loss. It's addictive and throws the entire body out of whack, so try to cut out the white stuff.

Take care of your liver. Your liver is a fat-burning organ. If your liver is clean, you will be able to burn fat better. See page 28.

If it comes from a box, don't eat it. Packaged foods are processed and almost always contain ingredients that counteract weight loss, such as high fructose corn syrup and transfats. Think of packaged food as dead food – yuk.

Increase fibre intake. Fibre aids weight loss and keeps you fuller for longer. Add high-fibre foods to your daily diet, such as psyllium husk, konjac noodles, chia seeds, flaxseed, fruit and veggies.

Save alcohol for special occasions only. It's a sugar-laden toxin your liver doesn't need.

Drink more H_2O. Water revs up the metabolism, keeps you full and reduces cravings.

Stop inhaling your food. *Those who chew more, eat less.* Chewing not only signals to your brain that you're eating, but it also puts less strain on digestion.

Don't eat fat-free products. Good fat will boost metabolism and keeps you fuller for longer.

Consider cutting back on dairy. I recommend no more than two serves of dairy per day. I've found organic natural yoghurt and whey protein the best sources. They are easier to digest than milk and contain beneficial bacteria for the gut.

Supplements that support weight loss

To function properly and reach its optimal weight, your body needs the right amount of nutrients. That's where supplements come in. These ones are great for aiding weight loss:

- ✳ Multivitamin High in B vitamins, which fire up the metabolism and correct any nutritional deficiencies that are important for fat-burning
- ✳ Fish oil Loaded with omega-3, which burns fat and balances hormones
- ✳ Chromium Fabulous for balancing blood sugars
- ✳ PGX/Glucomannan powder Made from konjac root, this high-fibre supplement helps to reduce appetite and cravings, and keep blood sugars stable.

Live a healthy lifestyle

Get more sleep. Aim for at least eight hours every night. Research shows that sleep regulates our appetite hormones, therefore assisting in weight loss.

Go into the Stress-free Zone every day. Find a stress reliever that suits you, and do it daily. It could be meditation, deep breathing, yoga, tai chi, barefoot walking, drinking tea or reading. Taking the time to chill out will keep your adrenal glands healthy and your hormones balanced.

Stop eating two to three hours before bedtime. Give your body the chance to digest dinner.

Exercise! It triggers the fat-burning hormones and speeds up metabolism. Plus, who doesn't love endorphins?! Interval training (also known as HIIT) and weight training are fantastic for weight loss. Just don't overdo it.

Ready to get your heart rate up? Try this HIIT routine

Jog for a minute at a moderate pace. Run as fast as you can for 30 seconds to a minute. Repeat eight times. I do this 2–3 times a week.

Do yoga. It may be slow and gentle, but it's an amazing form of exercise. Yoga tones the body, balances hormones, aids digestion and burns energy.

Practise mindful eating. When you fully engage in the eating experience, your body breaks down food better. So chew, taste and appreciate your food.

Get organised on a Sunday. Hit the markets or health-food store, stock your fridge and prepare some meals for the week. This will keep your healthy eating on track.

Let it go

Emotional baggage = physical baggage. I believe that when you're holding on to negative emotions (like sadness or stress), you hold on to extra weight. If you think that may be the case for you, try to uncover what's getting you down. Seek professional help if you have to. And then learn to let it go.

Stop weighing yourself

While you're at it, get rid of the scales for three to six months. Weighing yourself obsessively only puts your mind and body under enormous amounts of stress. If you can release that stress, you'll give yourself the best chance to find that optimal weight.

It's all in the mind

Our thoughts become our reality. Believe you CAN lose weight and you WILL. Instead of thinking, 'weight loss is hard', tell yourself 'it is easy and effortless'. Say these positive affirmations every day and watch the magic happen.

How to handle a bad body moment

I truly believe negative self-talk is more harmful to our health than any bad food choice. It's a silent stress but luckily, it can be reversed through the power of positive thinking. We all doubt ourselves from time to time – it's how we move past it that matters. Here's what I do.

* I focus on a part of my body I DO like. I look in the mirror and say, 'Oh, my legs are looking fab today – I'm so lucky to have them!'
* I remind myself that those negative thoughts are from my inner mean girl – and she doesn't deserve my time or energy.
* I think about all of my good and incredibly healthy practices. I thank myself for taking care of my body most of the time.
* I remind myself that my body is unique and I stop comparing.
* I tell myself I am enough.

Affirmations to aid weight loss

Pick the ones that resonate with you the most and say them daily! Stick your affirmations to your bathroom mirror for maximum effect.

* I love myself for who I am.
* I accept the beauty of my body shape.
* I let go of negative habits and thoughts about food.
* I make decisions that serve me best.
* I let go of any guilt I hold around food choices.
* I accept myself for who I am.
* I am grateful for the body I own and all it does for me.

MY DAILY ROUTINE

This routine has helped me keep the weight off for a few years now.

Morning: Wake up, breathe deeply, sip on lemon water with a pinch of cayenne pepper, exercise, dry body brush, enjoy a protein-rich brekkie (find my favourites in the recipe section),and see clients in clinic.

Afternoon: Enjoy a protein-rich lunch, see more clients or pump out a blog post, savour a low-GI snack, and go for a barefoot walk or into the Stress-free Zone.

Evening: Eat a light, healthy dinner, enjoy affectionate family time, switch off technology by 8 pm, sip on herbal tea and get ready for an eight-hour sleep.

Worksheet

Write down how you feel about your body right now. Then write down how you want to feel about your body. What affirmations will get you there?

....
....
....
....
....
....

What parts of your body do you love?

....
....
....
....
....
....

What nutrition and lifestyle changes will you make to reach your optimal weight?

....
....
....

Do you have emotional baggage? Are you holding any grudges? Write these down and then let them go.

....
....
....
....

Nutrition 101

MY PHILOSOPHY ON FOOD

We all have to eat – but what, how and when we eat affects our health and happiness. I don't subscribe to any dietary labels; instead, I believe in fuelling and nourishing my body with real wholefoods. That means clean unprocessed foods that are as close to their natural state as possible. No additives, no preservatives and no artificial ingredients. The body recognises and knows how to break these 'clean' foods down, whereas processed foods are foreign. Choose nutrient-rich food that serves as medicine for the body and soul.

My diet looks like this most of the time:

* no refined sugar or gluten
* gluten-free grains
* good fats
* high quality animal protein, sustainably caught fish, beans and pulses
* a little organic dairy
* small amounts of low-fructose fruits such as berries
* loads of colourful and green veggies.

I believe in eating sustainably – for both ourselves and the world! Health and nutrition is a lifestyle.

THE JSHEALTH RULEBOOK

- Stop fad dieting.
- Enjoy clean, unprocessed foods.
- Eat through the rainbow.
- Drink water all day long.
- Eat slowly and mindfully.
- Chew, chew, chew.
- Buy local and organic produce where possible.
- Stop depriving yourself.
- Listen to your body and its hunger signals.
- Be kind to yourself.
- If you can't pronounce it, don't eat it.
- Move your body daily.
- Breathe deeply.
- Go into the Stress-free Zone every day.

TOP TIP

Wheat vs gluten – what's the difference? Gluten refers to the protein composite in food processed from wheat and other grains. While wheat is the most common source of gluten, gluten can be found in other grains such as barley, rye and spelt.

ALL ABOUT NUTRIENTS

Good health comes down to finding the right balance of macronutrients in your body. Everyone has a unique optimal balance, and tuning in to your body's needs will help you find yours. Many of us focus on the protein, carbs and fats we consume – all of which are very important for our energy – but we rarely stop to think about the nutrient density of food. Nutrients not only sustain and support us, but they also help us flourish.

Before you eat, ask yourself, 'Will this food nourish me? Will it feed my cells the nutrients they need to function properly?' Wholefoods are the answer. They are loaded with nutrients and enzymes, both of which are necessary for every chemical process in the body. Too many 'diet plans' home in on strict macronutrient ratios – low carb (Atkins), high protein (Dukan) and high fat (Ketogenic diet) – when food quality is what matters. If you eat natural foods and eat according to your body's needs, you will inevitably find a macronutrient balance that suits you. These are the macronutrients your body needs to perform at its peak. (The nutrition plan on page 93 will guide you on the specific foods to enjoy and those to avoid.)

CARBOHYDRATES

Contrary to popular belief, carbs are not the devil. They are actually the body's chief source of energy. They're also the easiest macronutrient to absorb, since they convert quickly into glucose for energy. However, to sustain energy, it's better for our bodies to absorb glucose slowly. That's why it's important to go for 'complex' rather than 'simple' carbs.

COMPLEX CARBS (BEST SOURCES)	SIMPLE CARBS (LESSER SOURCES)
• Wholegrains: rye, spelt and sourdough • Gluten-free grains: quinoa, brown rice and buckwheat • Starchy vegetables: sweet potato, beetroot and pumpkin • Oats • Low-GI fruits: berries, citrus fruits and stone fruits e.g. peaches • Beans and legumes	• White bread • White rice • Cereals • Pastries • Potatoes • Chips • Candy bars • Refined sugar

GLUTEN

Gluten is a two-part protein found in grains, namely wheat, rye and barley. It's called a 'sticky' protein because it holds together the nutrient stores of the plant it's in (which explains why it's often used to bind together processed foods). Main gluten sources are bread, cereal, cakes, biscuits and crackers. Sources of hidden gluten are gravies, soups, sausages, bottled sauces and some marinades. Grains have no defence mechanism against being eaten and so defend themselves with poison: anti-nutrients that punch holes in the intestinal lining and cause irritation and inflammation. This stops the absorption of nutrients and affects the immune system.

If you do not know if you're sensitive to gluten, cut it from your diet for at least three weeks, and then reintroduce it. If you feel better off gluten (or worse when you bring it back), then it's likely causing problems.

SUGAR

If you want to feel, look and perform better, the single best thing you can do is cut down on refined sugar. It encourages weight gain, and fat cells manufacture oestrogen, leading to hormonal imbalance. Sugar is inflammatory and spikes your insulin levels, which can result in depression, obesity and/or sugar addiction. It irritates the gut and feeds bad bacteria, wreaking havoc on the digestive system. By leaching important nutrients from the body, it also messes with your hormones, mood, weight balance and digestion. And it causes wrinkles.

Artificial sweeteners are even WORSE. Avoid chemicals such as saccharin (Sweet'n Low), aspartame (Equal) and sucralose (Splenda). They cause a toxic build-up in the body and trigger your sugar cravings. High fructose corn syrup is another ingredient to steer clear of.

Want to learn more? Watch the documentary That Sugar Film. *Ensure you avoid packaged foods because many that are marketed as healthy are not. Got a sweet tooth? Go to page 100 to find out about sugar substitutes.*

TIP-TOP CARBS: FRUIT AND VEG

If you only take one thing away from this book, make it this: **eat more greens!** The darker, the better.

To nourish your body with the highest quality food, try to buy organic and locally grown produce. If you don't have access to organic fruits and veggies, at least buy the most seasonal, freshest ones you can.

Why switch to organic? Eating organically will decrease your exposure to pesticides, and increase your nutrient intake. Fruit with thick skins (like bananas) tend to be safer than those with thin ones (like grapes).

If you can't afford to buy organic all the time, use this guide to help allocate your pennies.

'DIRTY DOZEN' (THE MOST SPRAYED)	CLEANEST OF THE BUNCH
• Apples	• Asparagus
• Celery	• Sweetcorn
• Strawberries	• Peas
• Peaches	• Avocado
• Spinach	• Papaya
• Nectarines	• Broccoli
• Grapes	• Cauliflower
• Capsicums	• Bananas
• Potatoes	• Mangoes
• Lettuce	• Onions
• Blueberries	• Kiwifruit
• Kale	• Pineapples

TOP TIP

Missed the farmers' markets? To wash off residual pesticides and herbicides from conventional produce, place your fruits and veggies in water with a couple of tablespoons of apple cider vinegar. Let them soak for at least 10 minutes before rinsing.

IN YOUR WORDS

I have lived with endometriosis for over four years. It stopped me from going about my everyday life, unable to work, see friends and just enjoy my days.

I had heard about Jess through a friend and decided to give it [the nutrition plan] a go instead of opting for surgery. Going to Jess was the best decision I have ever made. Jess changed the way I ate as well as my quality of life. I went from having unbearable pain to eventually no pain at all. Thanks to Jess I can now go about everyday [life] happily and healthy. *– Tyler-Rose Bedil*

FAT

After years of 'fat' talk, modern nutritional science is finally realising that fat isn't the problem. Research shows that only transfats are bad.

Good fats are absolutely vital for good health and wellbeing. They make hormones, protect organs and reduce inflammation. If you eat the right healthy fats, your brain, skin, hormones AND waistline will thank you for it.

Seriously!

CHEWING THE FAT ... ON FAT
There are a few different kinds of fat – and they all affect the body in their own way.

SATURATED FATS	These mainly come from animal sources. Too much saturated fat can increase your risk of cardiovascular disease, but sticking to virgin organic coconut oil and unprocessed organic meat will do wonders for your satiety (fullness). **Verdict: saturated fats are part of a well-balanced diet**
TRANSFATS	While they occur naturally in some foods, most transfats are made during food processing. By partially hydrogenating unsaturated fats, food manufacturers can create synthetic fats that are easier to cook with and less likely to spoil. As such, transfats are found in most packaged foods and foods such as doughnuts and burgers. **Verdict: even small amounts of transfats can put you at higher risk of cardiovascular disease**
UNSATURATED FATS	Monounsaturated: eating foods rich in monounsaturated fats (mufas) improves blood cholesterol levels, which can decrease the risk of heart disease. Mufas also regulate insulin levels and control blood sugars, so add avocado and drizzle that cold-pressed extra-virgin olive oil on your salad! **Verdict: healthy fat** Polyunsaturated (including omega-3s and omega-6s) (pufas): these fats are found mostly in plant-based foods and oils. Like mufas, eating pufas improves cholesterol levels, decreasing the risk of heart disease and type 2 diabetes. **Verdict: super healthy**

OMEGA – WHAT NOW?

Omega-3s and -6s are known as 'essential fatty acids'. Our bodies can't produce these on their own, so we must get them from food. Most people don't get enough omega-3s, which leads to things like dry skin, fatigue, depression, hormonal imbalance, poor immunity and stiff joints. On the flipside, when we do eat fatty acids, we're rewarded with satiety, hormonal equilibrium (read: no more PMS!), healthy brain function, better mood, lower blood pressure, improved stress response, heart health and weight loss. Up your intake of omega-3s by eating oily fish, flaxseed, egg yolks, walnuts and dark leafy green veggies.

WILL FAT MAKE ME FAT?

You won't get fat from eating fat. That is a myth. Eating a moderate amount of good fat will keep you fuller for longer. You will only store fat if you overeat or fill your body with artificial, processed food like refined sugar. So if you're trying to lose weight, cut out the bad fats, but keep the good ones. Stick to one small serving of fat per meal – see the 7-Day Slim-down Meal Plan for more details.

WHAT'S THE DEAL WITH CHOLESTEROL?

Cholesterol is a fat-like substance in the body, mostly produced in the liver. It actually produces sex hormones and bile, making it very important for health. However, too much cholesterol can lead to a build-up of fat in the arteries.

To manage cholesterol, we need to stay away from sugar and transfats, and some saturated fats. However, there is still an ongoing debate about how saturated fats can affect cholesterol levels. While there is so much conflicting research on the link between saturated fats and heart disease, transfats can definitely be dangerous in the long term. The problem is, transfats are in most refined foods, including vegetable oil, margarine, cookies, crackers and baked goods. These baddies are guilty of causing weight gain and clogged arteries. On the other hand, good fats (like omega-3s) have the opposite effect – they reduce high cholesterol. So enjoy oily fish and walnuts, and ask a practitioner about taking a high dosage fish or krill oil supplement. To sweep out excess cholesterol in the body, increase your fibre intake – sprinkle ground flaxseed, oat bran and psyllium husk into smoothies and porridge. See page 91 for the best fibre sources. This will also help take care of your liver (see page 28).

PROTEIN

Protein is crucial for the healthy growth and development of the muscles, blood, skin, hair, nails and organs. I see so many clients who don't eat enough protein. When I ask them to increase their daily intake, they notice a huge difference in energy and satiety. It also speeds up the metabolism and produces healthy hormones. It helps us to build lean body mass, which burns fat most effectively. Most of the neurotransmitters in the brain are composed of amino acids, the building blocks of protein.

Although there are plenty of vegetarian protein sources (like beans, legumes and nuts), the body absorbs animal protein much better. Try to buy organic meat; it may be more expensive, but it's far more nutrient dense. If you're a vegetarian, I urge you to learn about protein combining – see page 96 for more details.

Every meal and snack should include a palm-sized portion of some form of protein. For example, 100–150 g lean chicken breast contains 20 g of protein. If you're training a lot, you'll need to up your protein even more.

FIBRE

Fibre is in charge of keeping the digestive system moving. Many people are just not getting enough fibre – and it's usually those who are wanting to lose weight. Fibre actually enhances long-term weight loss. It is also fabulous for:

* stabilising blood sugars
* keeping the bowels regular and healthy
* lowering cholesterol
* decreasing the risk of colon cancer
* cleansing the body from excess hormones.

Aim to get 30–40 g of fibre a day through wholegrains (e.g. oats), dark leafy greens, fruit, nuts, flaxseed, chia seeds and psyllium husk. If you eat these foods, your bowels should start working more regularly. If not, follow the steps on page 17 to repair gut health.

IN YOUR WORDS

I just wanted to thank you SO MUCH. After reading *The Clean Life* I feel so much better about myself. I feel so happy to have read your story. The feelings you went through are EXACTLY the same as mine. I have a passion for health and the body but up until now I could never implement it in my own life! Since reading your book I feel I have whole new look on life. Yesterday I ate a chocolate bar and I did not even feel guilty one bit. I really wanted one and thought to myself I can't deprive my body of everything it wants or feels like, so I ate it. I enjoyed it. And went on with my day. This is AMAZING – usually I would feel so guilty and try to compensate with a workout or lose control and eat crap for the rest of the day. I feel ready to love myself, love my body and only then will I look better on the outside. *– Sophie L*

WATER

H_2O is by far the best drink to keep your body hydrated and healthy. Aim for 1.5–2 litres a day, and start with two glasses first thing in the morning. Not only does this replenish fluids after sleep, but it also fires up the metabolism. Then, sip all day long, but try to avoid drinking at mealtimes. Water dilutes the digestive enzymes, which can affect nutrient absorption. Natural spring water is best, but the chemicals released from plastic bottles can be toxic. Invest in a stainless steel bottle as well as a good water filter to remove harmful bacteria, chlorine and fluoride from tap water.

MICRONUTRIENTS

The body also needs **micronutrients**, which are made up of the following.

Vitamins and minerals

Vitamins and minerals pack a powerful punch. The body only needs a small amount of them, but they're essential for growth, muscle response, digestion, healthy hormones and the absorption of nutrients. For women, it's important to get enough iron for energy, and iodine for breast health. For men, zinc is necessary for healthy sperm. And where do you get these vitamins and minerals? Wholefoods!

Phytochemicals

Phytochemicals are plant-based foods rich in vitamins, minerals and antioxidants that protect our bodies from damage. This confirms why eating a diet high in plant foods is one of the keys to good health. The best sources of phytochemicals include beans, fruit and vegetables, so eat through the rainbow.

Antioxidants

Antioxidants is a buzzword, and for good reason. They're compounds found in foods that counter 'free radicals', thus preventing (or at least delaying) the process of cell damage. In other words, they fight ageing. There are a few types of antioxidants, such as betacarotene and vitamin C, most of which are found in orange and green veggies.

WHAT ABOUT SUPPLEMENTS?

While we *can* get our nutrients from food, many people struggle to find the time to buy fresh produce and prepare home-cooked, wholefood meals. What's more, much conventional produce is grown in mineral-depleted soils. I understand this is the reality of our fast-paced lifestyles, but we're not getting enough nutrient-rich foods as a result. That's where supplements come in. They can help to ensure we're getting the proper nutrition we need every day. When the body lacks essential vitamins and minerals, it unbalances, causing low energy, stress, weight gain and crazy hormones. Take supplements above and beyond a healthy diet (under a practitioner's guidance).

CLEAN IN-AND-OUT NUTRITION PLAN

There's no way of escaping this: a large percentage of health comes down to what you put in your mouth. So if you want a lean, healthy, energetic body, you need to clean up your diet and get your eating patterns on track.

Enter *The Healthy Life* plan. Here are the foods you should be eating and avoiding, and why. You're going to learn **how to eat well**, in a way you can sustain for the rest of your life. The recipe section has tons of meal ideas, all geared towards helping you achieve optimal health and weight loss.

THE 'YES' FOODS

Carbohydrates

Carbs are essential for energy, but the kind of carbs you choose will determine just how energetic you are. While some wholegrains are fine, if you're cleansing or have digestive problems, cut out gluten for a trial period. I bet you'll feel much better.

HEALTHY WHOLEGRAINS	GLUTEN-FREE GRAINS	OTHER GLUTEN-FREE ALTERNATIVES
• Rye, sourdough or spelt bread (1 slice) • Mountain bread wraps (1–2) • Pumpernickel/Ezekiel bread (1 thin slice) • Rolled oats (⬚ cup uncooked) • Oat bran (¼ cup uncooked) • Ryvita (2)	• Quinoa (½ cup uncooked) • Brown or wild rice (½ cup uncooked) • Millet (½ cup uncooked) • Amaranth (½ cup uncooked) • Buckwheat (½ cup uncooked) • Gluten-free noodles: buckwheat, kelp, konjac, soba and black bean (1 cup cooked) • Corn thins (3–4) • Brown rice cakes (2)	• Chia seeds • Flaxseed/buckwheat crackers • Gluten-free oats • Mung bean/black bean pasta • Sweet potato vermicelli

Vegetables

Choose seasonal, local and organic produce where possible. Have at least three cups of veggies a day and unlimited greens. Opt to steam, stir-fry, grill or pressure cook your veggies, or eat them raw – just don't microwave them.

VEGGIES WITH LOW CARB CONTENT (LOAD UP ON THESE WITH EACH MEAL)	STARCHY VEGGIES (LIMIT TO ½ CUP PER MEAL)
• Asparagus • Eggplant • Brassica veggies: Brussels sprouts, broccoli, cauliflower, cabbage, kale. These need to be cooked well as they contain goitrogens, which can mess with the thyroid. • Cabbage • Celery • Zucchini • Cucumber • Fennel • Capsicum • Dark leafy greens: silverbeet, bok choy, Swiss chard • All lettuces • Mushrooms • Onions, garlic, leek • Radish • Rocket • Tomato • Green beans • Seaweed	• Carrots • Sweet potato • Pumpkin • Yams • Beetroot • Parsnip • Peas • Corn

Fruit

Aim to buy fresh, seasonal and organic fruit where possible. Since fruit is still a starch, limit yourself to two serves a day, and enjoy them in the morning on an empty stomach. The correct serving sizes are listed in brackets in the table opposite; typically, 1 serve = 1 medium-sized piece of fruit or half a cup of berries.

TOP TIP

Gluten-free flours to bake with include buckwheat flour, coconut flour, almond meal and quinoa flour. I'll let you in on a secret: these are even yummier than white flour!

MY FAVOURITE FRUITS (THAT ARE LOW-GI!)	FRUITS THAT I EAT OCCASIONALLY	AVOID
• Granny Smith apples (1) • Berries: strawberries, blueberries, raspberries (½ cup) • Goji berries (¼ cup) • Figs • Citrus fruits: lemons, grapefruit, oranges (1) • Papaya (1 medium-sized) • Kiwifruit (2–3) • Passionfruit (2–3) • Stone fruit: nectarines, plums, peaches (1)	• Dates (2) • Small banana (1) • Small mango (1) • Grapes (1 small bunch) • Cherries (6–8) – but low GI • Watermelon (1–2 wedges) • Lychees (6–8)	• Dried fruits: high in sugar and sulphur preservatives • Stewed fruits, unless homemade

Beans and legumes

These are both a starch and a protein source and high in fibre. If you suffer from digestive issues, don't consume too many beans and legumes – they can cause stomach upsets when eaten in large amounts. One portion = ½ cup. Choose from:

* black beans
* kidney beans
* mung beans
* white beans
* lima and butter beans
* chickpeas
* lentils
* split peas.

PROTEIN

Protein feeds every cell in your body, so aim for one palm-sized portion at every meal. When buying fish and seafood, use the *Australia's Sustainable Seafood Guide www.sustainableseafood.org.au* to find out what types are caught in a way that's beneficial to the earth and your health. And grass-fed meat is not just a hippy trend – grass-fed animals have higher levels of omega-3s, B vitamins, vitamin E, and much less transfats. This means they're great for your cholesterol and heart health. For an easy protein hit, throw chickpeas and seeds over salads.

And while we can get most of our protein needs from food, I'm a big believer in increasing protein consumption to stabilise blood sugars and help with muscle recovery and weight control. That's why I include protein powder in my diet. Having protein within the first 60 minutes of waking up is essential for optimal health, so I make a protein smoothie most mornings. In terms of protein powder, opt for a whey, rice or pea protein. If you suffer from digestive issues or lactose intolerance, choose pea or rice protein. Many powders on the market are full of junk, so ensure you choose one that is free from artificial sweeteners, colours and preservatives, is gluten-free, naturally sweetened (with stevia), low carb (below 3 g), high in protein (around 20 g per serve) and non-GMO. See my JSHealth natural vegan mix opposite.

ANIMAL	VEGETARIAN	WHEY
• Organic free-range eggs (1–2) **Seafood and fish** • Wild Alaskan salmon, Atlantic salmon, ling, mackerel, barramundi, sardines, trout, snapper (150–200 g). Smaller white fish are better to avoid mercury. • Tinned or bottled tuna (90–150 g), maximum 2 per week to limit mercury levels. • Prawns (6–8) • Lobster (1 cup) • Oysters/mussels (6) **Meat and poultry** • Free-range and organic poultry and game: chicken, turkey, duck, ostrich, kangaroo (100–150 g) • Grass-fed lean red meat: lamb, veal, beef, pork (150 g) *Avoid* sausages, deli and smoked meats.	• Beans and legumes: lentils, chickpeas etc. (½ cup, cooked) • Tofu and tempeh (100 g) • Hummus/tahini (2–3 tbsp) • Dairy products: organic natural yoghurt, goat's/sheep's milk yoghurt, goat's cheese (100–200 g) • Nuts and seeds (¼ cup) While eggs and dairy products are complete proteins, nuts, grains, seeds and beans are not. If you're vegetarian, you should be 'protein combining' in order to provide your body with the amino acids it needs to function. This involves combining legumes + grains (e.g. lentils + quinoa) or beans + legumes (e.g. kidney beans + chickpeas).	• Whey/rice/pea protein powder (30 g)

JSHealth natural vegan mix

Contains about 20 g of protein. This is amazing in smoothies or on porrige.

1 tbsp chia seeds

2 tbsp ground flaxseed

¼ cup walnuts

¼ cup pumpkin seeds

1 tsp spirulina

Dairy and dairy substitutes

Dairy is the subject of rich debate in the health world and it's important for its calcium levels. But milk is pasteurised and homogenised, making it a highly processed food. Plus, casein – the protein in milk – is a potent growth promoter. However, dairy can be oestrogenic and cause an array of hormonal issues for women. Overall, the decision to eat or not eat dairy is up to you. But always opt for organic sources. If you absorb it well, enjoy two portions a day. If you bloat or get a sore stomach afterwards, there are plenty of alternatives.

CHEESE	YOGHURT	OTHER	DAIRY SUBSTITUTES
Stick to the white kind: • Goat's cheese/ fetta (2–3 tbsp) • Cottage cheese (2–3 tbsp) • Ricotta (2–3 tbsp) • Other white cheeses (2–3 slices)	• Natural/Greek-style yoghurt with little to no sugar (100–200 g) • Goat's/sheep's yoghurt (100–200 g) • Coyo (100 g) Sweeten your yoghurt with stevia, ground cinnamon or a little raw honey.	• Organic or A2 cow's milk (1 cup/ day) • Organic butter (1 tsp)	If you cannot tolerate dairy, try 1 cup a day of the following alternatives: • Almond Milk (see page 306) • rice milk • hemp milk • coconut milk or coyo

Whey is a liquid by-product created in the cheese-making process. It's very high in protein.

HOW TO FIND A HEALTHY YOGHURT

Some supermarket brands contain more hidden sugar than a chocolate bar, so look for the following words on yoghurt labels:

- organic
- natural (i.e. not flavoured)
- low/full fat (depending on your taste preference)
- less than 5 g sugar per 100 g serve
- no added fruit, sugars or sweeteners
- no more than 3–4 ingredients.

The best of the bunch in Australia include Barambah Organics, five:am, Coyo, Meredith Dairy sheep yoghurt, Jalna Greek-style yoghurt.

Soy

We need to be careful about soy. Most soy products, like soymilk and tofu, are GMO, which can depress thyroid function, mess with hormones, and slow down digestion. There is mixed evidence on this so I stick to a low-soy diet, personally. However, fermented soy products contain beneficial bacteria for the gut, and the fermentation process destroys the anti-nutrients (phylates) that bind to essential nutrients needed by the body. On *The Healthy Life* plan, you're allowed to enjoy miso, natto, tempeh and tamari (wheat and gluten-free soy sauce). If you have an underactive thyroid, cut out ALL soy products, even fermented ones.

Good fats

Here's my list of good fats you can enjoy on *The Healthy Life* program:

- ¼ avocado
- 1 tbsp cold-pressed extra-virgin olive oil or virgin organic coconut oil
- ¼ cup mixed nuts and seeds
- 1 tbsp nut butter

Did you know? You can get calcium from sources other than dairy such as dark leafy greens and sesame seeds.

Raw nuts and seeds

Nuts and seeds are high in essential vitamins and minerals, and contain the kind of essential fatty acids that are vital for good health. Choose unroasted and unsalted varieties. It's best to soak all nuts and seeds or buy 'activated' ones. Soaking breaks down phytic acid and enzyme inhibitors, the substances that make nuts and seeds so difficult to digest for some. To 'activate' nuts, seeds, legumes and grains – and neutralise those inhibitors – put them in a bowl/jar. Cover with water, then add the juice of ½ lemon and 1 tsp salt. Leave to soak for between 7 and 12 hours, then drain and place in the fridge. If you don't like the soft texture, you can put them in the oven (or dehydrator) at the lowest possible temperature for 24–48 hours. I love to sprinkle ground cinnamon and grated nutmeg onto mine.

I've found that in the health world, gluten-, sugar- and dairy-free people are going nuts for nuts! Nut milk, nut butter and raw cakes are all easy swaps but we need to be careful not to overdo it. Allow one-quarter cup of nuts and seeds up to twice a day. If you're trying to lose weight, stop at one-quarter cup. Choose from:

* almonds
* cashews
* walnuts
* pecans
* macadamias
* hazelnuts
* Brazil nuts
* sesame seeds
* sunflower seeds.

Condiments

Jazz up your meals using these condiments. Allow 1–2 tablespoons per serve per person from the following:

* vinegars – Bragg apple cider vinegar, white wine vinegar, balsamic vinegar
* cold-pressed extra-virgin olive oil/cold-pressed flaxseed oil (for dressings)
* Dijon or wholegrain mustard
* tamari
* tahini/hummus
* lemon/lime juice
* homemade guacamole
* homemade pesto (see my Homemade Walnut Pesto on page 252)
* homemade tomato sauce or tomato paste.

Cooking oils

Enjoy in moderation – 2 tablespoons a day, even though they are good fats from the following:

Cook over high heat
* virgin organic coconut oil
* macadamia oil
* ghee

Cook over medium heat
* sesame oil
* cold-pressed extra-virgin olive oil

Fresh/dried herbs and spices

Not only do herbs and spices add flavour to your meals, but they're also incredibly nutritious. If you're buying spice mixes at the supermarket, check that they don't contain added salt or sugar.

Table salt is heavily refined and, as such, stripped of minerals. I prefer rock, Celtic and Himalayan salt, as they contain traces of important minerals.

HERBS AND SPICES	RECOMMENDED SALTS (NO MORE THAN 1 TSP/DAY)
• Garlic • Turmeric • Cayenne pepper • Mint • Coriander • Parsley • Basil • Sumac • Chives • Oregano • Zaatar • Cumin • Cinnamon, ground • Ginger • Rosemary • Sage • Thyme • Chilli flakes	• Himalayan salt • Celtic sea salt (to season) • Vogel's Herbamare herb and vegetable salt

TOP TIP

To reduce your sodium intake, cut back on packaged foods (like cereals and breads), bottled sauces (soy, oyster and tomato), and frozen meals. I love using spice mixes from health-food stores to jazz up my meals. My favourite brands are Mrs Dash and Bragg.

Natural sweeteners

Got a sweet tooth? Never fear – there are some natural sweeteners that will tingle your tastebuds. Only enjoy the following in small amounts (1 tsp a day):

* raw honey
* pure maple syrup
* blackstrap molasses
* rice malt syrup.

For natural sweeteners that won't spike your blood sugar, stop sugar cravings and aid weight loss, choose from the following spices and flavourings:

* stevia (my preference)
* ground cinnamon
* vanilla bean/powder
* grated nutmeg.

Stevia is sweeter than processed sugar, yet does not contain any of the nasties. Of the natural alternatives, it's the best option as it's low in kilojoules and doesn't spike blood sugar.

Superfoods

Boost your smoothies, oats, yoghurt and salads with these extras – they're called superfoods for a reason! But all wholefoods are superfoods in my opinion, especially greens. One serve of the following is 1 tablespoon:

* cacao powder
* cacao nibs
* bee pollen
* maca powder
* mesquite powder
* spirulina
* chia seeds
* flaxseed
* goji berries
* acai berry powder
* maqui berry powder.

Beverages

Hydration is the cornerstone of great health, so drink up.

* filtered water (1.5–2 L a day)
* herbal teas (enjoy throughout the day)
* freshly squeezed veggie juices
* caffeinated drinks such as coffee/tea (one a day, max).

The limited list

I avoid or limit the following foods:

* high-sugar fruits: grapes, watermelon, dates, dried fruits
* all tinned food: fresh is best!
* corn (unless it's organic)
* stock cubes (unless organic) or pre-made stocks; best to make your own
* Marmite or Vegemite
* factory-farmed eggs
* farmed meats: chicken, turkey, pork, beef, veal, sausages, smoked/deli meats, tinned meats
* factory-farmed fish (max twice a week): tuna, farmed salmon, shark, swordfish
* soy products: tofu, soymilk, soybeans
* dairy products: cow's milk, powdered milk, cheese, cream cheese, butter
* pre-packaged foods: even the 'low fat'/diet ones
* high fructose corn syrup
* agave and maple syrup: small amounts only
* refined sugar: white and brown sugar, lollies, chocolate, ice-cream, energy bars, jellies, jams
* wheat products: bread, pasta, noodles, cookies, cakes, pies, cereals, waffles, pita bread, bran, couscous
* commercial condiments are packed with sugar and preservatives: packaged salad dressings, tomato/BBQ sauce, relish, chutney
* deep-fried and microwaved foods
* gluten-free diet products made with cornstarch, rice starch or potato starch; these are incredibly processed and high in sodium
* alcohol: a glass of red wine is healthy.

Hidden nasties

Watch out for these synthetic additives and ingredients in processed foods:

* refined salt
* MSG
* sweeteners: artificial sweeteners, sucrose, sucralose, malt, glucose or high fructose corn syrup
* vegetable oils: canola, sunflower, safflower, soybean
* milk solids, milk powder or processed milk
* soy
* corn: corn starch, maize, cornflour
* potato starch
* yeast
* egg powder
* white flour.

Booze

First, clean eating and alcohol don't mix. The body processes alcohol first, meaning that carbs and fats get stored as fat rather than being used as fuel. If you're going to have a drink, choose spirits such as dry gin or vodka with sodawater with fresh lime or lemon, or red wine, as it's high in antioxidants and lower in sugar. Organic versions have fewer preservatives. Alcohol is a neurotoxin and should be drunk in moderation. It's equally important to socialise and enjoy the pleasures of life, so do have that glass of wine on the weekend. Make sure you have a healthy meal first. Drinking should be a rare treat, not something you rely on to have fun or deal with other problems.

The never, ever list

Don't have these foods – even if you're starving!

* artificial sweeteners such as Equal, Splenda
* foods fried in unhealthy oils, especially canola, sunflower, margarine, safflower, soybean and peanut oil
* soft drinks, including Diet Coke.

IN YOUR WORDS

Your blog and Instagram are so inspiring. Keep being amazing! – *Jenni*

I just wanted to say another thank you for inspiring me every day. I have been really stressed with school and studying for the MCAT; and you are always a light in my day through all of your positivity! Thank you for constantly inspiring me! – *Cal*

Thank you for reminding me that it is OK to indulge, to feel human, to prefer Pilates over slaving away at the gym. You have reignited my passion for health and my belief in myself, my mantras and that my dream life is the one I am living right now – it is in my hands. I am a miracle. – *Natalie*

The golden rule? If you don't understand it, don't buy it.

THE JSHEALTH EATING GUIDE

When it comes to eating, I follow a simple formula. Every main meal contains a complex carbohydrate, a quality protein, a good fat and lots of greens. These macronutrients send messages to the brain, maintaining our energy and controlling appetite.

My plate is usually made up of one-quarter protein, one-quarter grains or starchy veggies and half greens. I eat a LOT of greens! As for snacks, they always contain some kind of protein to keep my blood sugars stable and cravings at bay. I also drink 1.5–2 litres of water daily, and I'd like you to do the same. Yes, you'll be sipping all day long! Carry a water bottle everywhere, and drink 2–3 gulps every chance you get.

You get to eat a lot on my eating guide. The aim is to eat five small meals a day – three 'main' meals and two snacks – to keep your metabolism firing and cravings at bay. You may find that four meals suits you better, and that's fine. Once you're back in tune with your body, you'll know how often and how much you need to eat.

All I ask is that you make healthy eating a priority. Don't use work or the kids as an excuse to eat junk food. Don't skip meals – you'll only sabotage yourself later on by overeating or bingeing. If you can't foresee nutritious food coming your way – like on a road trip – you have to make it yourself. If you're going to do this, health has to become a lifestyle. Use the JSHealth meal-by-meal guide on page 105 as best you can. Please make snacking a habit. When you don't feed your body often, it releases excess cortisol. Long-term, this can slow down your metabolism, lower immunity and promote belly fat. Cortisol plonks visceral fat directly onto your abdomen, covering those beautiful muscles you work so hard for. If you want a lean body, you have to fuel it properly and reduce stress.

THE FOOD GROUPS

Forget that food pyramid you were given at school – a healthy diet should include the three main food groups in each meal. And no, carbohydrates should not dominate your plate!

Examples of foods that should be on your plate:

FATS	COMPLEX CARBOHYDRATES	PROTEIN (ANIMAL & VEGETABLE)
• Raw and unsalted nuts and seeds • Oily fish, e.g. salmon • Extra-virgin olive oil • Virgin organic coconut oil	• Wholegrains/gluten-free grains • All beans and legumes • All vegetables • Low-GI fruits	• Fish • Chicken • Red meat • Dairy • Lentils and beans

Along with variation, the key is to combine these three macronutrients correctly. The food charts in this chapter will help you do that. They contain lists of my favourite nutrient sources, as well as portion sizes.

Raw foods

For optimal health, 50 per cent of your plate should be raw. This isn't as hard as it sounds: simply load up on salad leaves and raw veggies. For the best results, sit down to each meal, and eat it calmly and mindfully. Keep a food diary. Tracking your eating will help you identify patterns as well as how certain foods make you feel.

IN YOUR WORDS

Jess came along at the exact right time in my life. After a year of chemotherapy I had no idea how to understand or look after my body. Jess has such a realistic approach to health and wellness and serves up endless inspiration that has empowered me to transform my life for the better. She has the biggest heart and is a truly beautiful human inside and out. *– Jess Watt*

The meal-by-meal guide

If you fuel your body with real food, it will reward you by functioning beautifully. Now, one of the hardest parts of embarking on a healthy eating plan is figuring out what to eat – but luckily, you won't have to. Just follow the instructions in the following tables, then head to pages 128–129 for tons of recipes and meal ideas. These guidelines are for those wanting to achieve optimal health and weight loss.

Pre-breakfast

Start your day with a nourishing routine. You deserve it. Here's mine:

1. Wake up to warm lemon water with a pinch of cayenne pepper or fresh ginger, or try my Meta-boost Drink (see page 301).
2. 10–20 deep belly breaths.
3. Write down 3–5 things to be grateful for. Be aware of the blessings in your life and you'll attract more good vibes.
4. Visualise your dream body and life. Say, 'With the power of my thoughts, I can create the body I desire.'

   One positive thought in the morning can change your whole day.

Breakfast

Eating a wholesome breakfast is a huge part of the health equation. It kickstarts your digestion and metabolism, and feeds your body with the vitamins and minerals it needs to perform. Please don't skip it! If you do, you will set yourself up for a day on the blood-sugar rollercoaster, and trigger the release of stress hormones like cortisol. Try to eat within 1 hour of waking, and always include **protein** and **fat**. Studies show that those who eat breakfast lose weight faster. So tuck in!

Choose one from each column.

CARBS	PROTEIN	FAT
• 1–2 cups non-starchy veg • Greens are unlimited; eat as much as you want! • 1 fruit • ½ cup veg protein (e.g. lentils and beans) • ½ cup starchy veg (e.g. pumpkin) • 1 gluten-free grain	• 200 g Greek-style yoghurt • 1–2 boiled/poached eggs • 3 egg whites • 2 tbsp LSA mix • 3 tbsp ricotta • 2–3 slices smoked salmon • ¼ cup raw nuts/seeds • 1 scoop protein powder	• ¼ avocado • 1 tbsp cold-pressed extra-virgin olive oil/ virgin organic coconut oil (when cooking) • 1 tbsp flaxseed/chia seeds • ¼ cup raw nuts • 1 tbsp nut butter • 2 tbsp hummus/tahini

TOP TIP

While you're munching . . .

Go outside and get a vitamin D hit. Fifteen to twenty minutes of sunshine a day keeps thyroid problems, depression and weight gain at bay.

Snack

Mid-morning is a great time to have your green juice, coffee and a small snack. Snacks must contain a **protein** component. If you look at my Instagram feed, you'll see that I always have a nutritious snack between main meals – and it's not just because I think eating is one of life's greatest pleasures!

Choose one from each column.

CARBS	PROTEIN	FAT
• 1–2 cups non-starchy veg • Greens are unlimited; eat as much as you want! • 1 low-GI fruit • 2 rice cakes	• 200 g Greek-style yoghurt • 1 boiled/poached egg • ¼ cup raw nuts/seeds • 1 scoop natural protein powder • 3 tbsp cottage cheese • 1 tbsp nut butter/ hummus	• Found naturally in starch and protein; try carrots with hummus or 10 raw nuts/seeds with a handful of blueberries

TOP TIP

Avoid boxed cereals. Breakfast cereals are marketed as convenient 'health foods'. The reality is, they contain high amounts of sugar and sodium, and are essentially blood-sugar disasters waiting to happen. Make your own muesli instead. For Bircher Muesli see page 146.

Lunch

When lunchtime rolls around, think of combining **dark leafy greens** with one to two servings of **protein**, one unit of good **fat** and one unit of **starch** – your choice of starchy veggies, gluten-free grains or legumes. Most people feel fuller when they add a portion of fat to their lunch. It does wonders for energy levels and banishes sugar cravings in the afternoon. Lunch will ensure your body slowly releases energy for the rest of the day so you don't experience the dreaded afternoon slump.

Choose one from each column.

CARBS	PROTEIN	FAT
• 1–2 cups non-starchy veg • 1–2 cups greens • Greens are unlimited; eat as much as you want! • 1 low-GI fruit • ½ cup veg protein (e.g. lentils and beans) • ½ cup starchy veg (e.g. pumpkin) • 1 gluten-free grain	• 150 g chicken breast • 150–200 g fish • 150–200 g lean beef/ lamb • 1–2 eggs • ½ cup veg protein (e.g. lentils and beans)	• ¼ avocado • ¼ cup seeds • 1 tbsp cold-pressed extra-virgin olive oil/ cold-pressed flaxseed oil/tahini • 1 tbsp nut butter

Make extra food for dinner so you have plenty of leftovers for lunch the next day. This is truly the easiest way to stay on track during the working week.

CRAZY FOR RED MEAT?

If meat is a big part of your diet, consider Meatless Mondays. Try to eat only plant-based meals on that day, or at least enjoy a vegetarian dinner.

Snack

In the mid-afternoon, reach for a **protein-rich** snack to keep your blood sugars stable until dinner (and to prevent you from falling victim to the vending machine). If you're on a weight loss journey, steer clear of starches after 3 pm. However, if you exercise in the afternoon, you'll need to combine protein with a starch to reduce cortisol levels. Choose one from each column.

Avoid coffee and fruit in the afternoon – they won't do your stress or blood sugar levels any favours.

CARBS	PROTEIN	FAT
• 1–2 cups non-starchy veg • Greens are unlimited; eat as much as you want!	• 200 g Greek-style yoghurt • 1–2 boiled/poached eggs • ¼ cup raw nuts/seeds • 1 scoop natural protein powder • 3 tbsp cottage cheese • 1–2 tbsp nut butter/ hummus	• Found naturally in protein here. Try a boiled egg, a handful of nuts, a protein shake, homemade frozen yoghurt or carrot sticks with hummus

Dinner

Dinner should be your smallest meal of the day. As your body is winding down and preparing for sleep, it's your job to feed it one last hit of nutrition before it 'fasts' overnight. So think **protein** with **non-starchy veggies**, including lots of **greens**. A small portion of **starchy carbs**, like sweet potato, quinoa or brown rice, is OK as well (unless you're trying to lose weight).

Choose one from each column.

CARBS	PROTEIN	FAT
• 1–2 cups non-starchy veg • Greens are unlimited; eat as much as you want! • 2 cups veg protein (e.g. lentils and beans) • ¼ cup starchy veggies (e.g. sweet potato)	• 150 g chicken breast • 150 g fish • 150–200 g lean beef/ lamb • 1–2 eggs • 1 serving natural protein powder • ½ cup veg protein (e.g. lentils and beans)	• ¼ avocado • 1–2 tbsp cold-pressed extra-virgin olive oil/ cold-pressed flaxseed oil/virgin organic coconut oil (for cooking/dressings) • ¼ cup nuts/seeds

Post-dinner plan

Do you have a sweet tooth? I believe in moderation, so I encourage you to treat yourself *once or twice a week* after dinner. If you really savour healthy desserts, bliss balls or raw chocolate mousse will be more than enough. Check out the sweet treats section on page 124 for some not-so-naughty ideas.

Then, in the lead-up to bed:

* sip on a cup of herbal tea with a dash of stevia or ground cinnamon
* soak in an Epsom salt or lavender oil bath
* switch off technology
* read a chapter of your book – or get intimate with your partner!
* take 10–20 deep belly breaths
* get 8 hours sleep for rest, repair and weight control.

PORTION SIZES

Food provides us with the nutrients we need to function, but most of us eat too much. **Respecting our body's hunger and satiety signals** is the best way to combat overeating. These tips and tricks will help get you there.

1. Serve dinner on a smaller plate.
2. Eat slowly and chew each mouthful 20 times.
3. Enjoy the tastes and textures of food.
4. Put your knife and fork down after each mouthful.
5. Drink 2 glasses of water 20 minutes BEFORE meals, not during.
6. Have a protein-rich snack in between meals – this will help you control your appetite.
7. Dish out protein and carb portions the size of your palm.
8. If you're stressed or anxious, forgo food for a walk, tea, bath or sex!
9. Set one smazll health goal per week. If you're overwhelmed, you're likely to turn to food as comfort and overeat.
10. Practise self-love and remind yourself your body is a temple. Why would you want to fill it until you're terribly uncomfortable?
11. Remember that food is abundant. You're lucky to know your next meal is coming soon.

THE 80/20 APPROACH

Believe it or not, indulging is good for you – so long as it's not all the time! This approach will heal your relationship with food, and bring a sense of balance and satisfaction to your life. Personally, I eat super cleanly 80 per cent of the time, and indulge WITHOUT GUILT for the other 20 per cent. And I no longer have intense cravings.

Why? Deprivation ➤ obsession ➤ bingeing ➤ guilt

It's all about moderation. Once a week I savour:

- ✳ a scoop of good quality gelato
- ✳ 2 glasses of red wine or champagne
- ✳ frozen yoghurt
- ✳ 2–4 pieces of chocolate
- ✳ a piece of apple crumble.

French women have it down pat: they enjoy indulgent foods, but eat them in moderation and with mindfulness. The scales won't tip after an indulgent meal or two. But they *will* if you indulge daily.

SWAP THIS FOR THAT

Sugar or sweetener ➡ Stevia

Milk chocolate ➡ 70–85 per cent cocoa dark chocolate or homemade raw chocolate

Vegetable or sunflower oil ➡ Virgin organic coconut oil, olive oil

Margarine ➡ Organic butter

Soft drinks ➡ Water with fresh lemon/lime

Processed bread ➡ Lettuce cups or gluten-free bread

Wheat pasta ➡ Zucchini, mung bean, konjac or brown rice pasta

Potato chips ➡ Kale Chips (see page 270) or natural popcorn

Cow's and soymilk ➡ Almond or rice milk

Factory-farmed eggs ➡ Free-range organic eggs

Factory-farmed meat ➡ Grass-fed organic meat

Table salt ➡ Himalayan or Celtic sea salt

Fries ➡ Cinnamon Sweet Potato Fries (see page 243)

Chai latte ➡ Chai tea with extra ground cinnamon

Hot chocolate ➡ Ayurveda Hot Chocolate (see page 301) or hot cacao

Fudge ➡ 2 fresh dates filled with almond butter

Store-bought banana bread ➡ My Gluten-free Banana Bread (see page 152)

Plastic water bottles ➡ Aluminium, BPA-free water bottles

Natural deodorant ➡ Aluminium-free deodorant

THE GUIDE TO EATING OUT

Try to limit restaurant meals to twice a week, max.

Health-wise, eating out can be tricky. But you shouldn't give up your social life just because you're trying to be healthy! Just do the best you can with what you've got. Trust yourself to make good choices.

Take-out options: the good and the bad

	GOOD	BAD
CONTINENTAL	Lean protein (grilled, steamed or barbecued) Green veggies or salad Optional: Small serve of brown rice, quinoa or sweet potato on the side Ask for salad dressings on the side	Fried foods and creamy dressings
CHINESE	Lean protein stir-fry Colourful veggies (steamed or stir-fried) Soup with rice noodles and protein Ask for food to be cooked in less oil	Dumplings Spring rolls Fried meats
THAI	Lean protein Asian veggies (e.g. bok choy and Chinese broccoli) Steamed fish with ginger Stir-fries made with lime, lemongrass, ginger, basil, chilli or garlic (sauce on the side) Tom yum soup Thai beef salad	Spring rolls Chicken wings Moneybags Pad Thai Satay sauce
INDIAN	Chicken tikka/tandoori chicken (oven-baked or grilled) Veggies Brown, jasmine or basmati rice Roti	Creamy curries Fried foods Gravies

VIETNAMESE	Vermicelli salad with beef/chicken Soup with rice noodles and protein Rice paper rolls Vietnamese-style salad	Fried foods Creamy sauces Dumplings
JAPANESE	Miso soup Edamame Sashimi (white fish is best) 1 x fish/chicken sushi roll with brown rice Chicken/beef with Asian veggies (ask for less sauce or a sauce on the side as they are high in sugar)	Tempura dishes Mayo and heavy sauces Teriyaki sauce
ITALIAN	Grilled chicken/veal/steak Steamed or grilled veggies Italian garden salad Choose thin, gluten-free pizza bases topped with loads of veggies, and ask for no cheese	Creamy pasta dishes Processed meat toppings Thick bases with lots of cheese

TIPS AND TRICKS

- Enjoy a protein-rich snack before going out. This will curb your hunger and prevent you from overeating.
- Go fresh. The first thing I look at on a menu is the salad selection. If there are limited options, check out the sides – you'll usually find a garden salad or steamed veggies to enjoy before or with your main meal.
- Avoid table salt and cheeses. Goat's cheese is fine.
- Opt for grilling and steaming. Say no to fried foods! I often ask for the chef to use less oil – not because I fear fat, but because I'm concerned about the type of oils they choose.
- Choose grilled fish, chicken or lean meat for your main. If you're a vegetarian, skip the pasta and rice-based mains and choose veggie stir-fries, minestrone soup or a variety of sides and salads.
- Order extra veggies instead of rice/potatoes. Our bodies just don't need the extra fuel.
- Ask for dressings and sauces on the side. Cold-pressed extra-virgin olive oil, balsamic and lemon-based dressings are best.

Vegetarian tips

Here are some key nutrition points for vegetarians to consider for adequate vitamin and mineral intake. Vegans can take note of these tips too but avoid eggs, dairy and fish options.

* Increase B12 vitamin intake: eggs, lentils and beans, nutritional yeast and greens.
* Increase zinc intake: eggs, seeds (pumpkin and sunflower), nuts and seafood. Sprinkle seeds on salads.
* Increase iron: spinach (drizzle with lemon juice), lentils, eggs, tahini, nuts, blackstrap molasses and silverbeet.
* More protein: seeds, nuts, eggs, legumes, quinoa, broccoli, dairy, avocado, rice/pea protein powder and supplement with chlorella/spirulina.
* Six small meals throughout the day to stabilise blood sugar.
* I always suggest using supplements above and beyond a healthy diet for vegetarians and vegans. Consider iron and a good multivitamin/B complex.
* Incorporate smoothies and juices into your diet for extra protein and vitamins.
* Avoid the refined starches (just because you are more limited does not mean your diet should be based on these): white bread, white rice, bagels, cereals and pasta.
* Combination eating for amino acid profile (protein): for example, legumes with grains, legumes with nuts and seeds, nuts with tofu, and legumes with dairy.

Some extra meal ideas (lunch or dinner) for vegetarians/vegans

* Mung bean/black bean pesto pasta with fresh rocket and pumpkin seeds. Top with some goat's cheese if you wish.
* A brown rice bowl with steamed broccoli, avocado, tempeh and sesame seeds. Drizzle with olive oil and tamari.
* Quinoa/brown rice sushi. Add some sliced egg/tempeh into the rolls. Use tamari/tahini as the dipping sauce.
* Goat's cheese, lentil and beetroot salad.
* Big green salad with quinoa, grilled zucchini, sprinkles of pumpkin seeds and beetroot.
* Mixed bean salad with roasted sweet potato and avocado.
* Lentil and vegetable soup.
* Brown rice cakes topped with grilled salmon, avocado and fresh spinach leaves. Drizzle with lemon and olive oil.
* Open omelette with roasted tomato, mushrooms and onion. Top with a little goat's cheese/parmesan.
* Quinoa/brown rice stuffed peppers/capsicums. Add veggies, herbs and gluten-free grain of choice to your peppers. Roast in the oven with olive oil and rock salt.
* Grilled salmon salad with fresh spinach, avocado and beetroot. Add a dollop of hummus/tahini.

- Tempeh stir-fry with veggies of choice, e.g. broccoli, green beans, onion, mushrooms, kale, etc. Add those greens!
- Zucchini pasta with pesto, hemp seeds and sliced avocado.
- Kelp noodle salad with steamed/grilled vegetables and tempeh.
- Cauliflower pizza with your favourite vegetable toppings and some goat's cheese/salmon.
- Baked eggs with tomato, kale, mushrooms and ricotta. Add a dollop of pesto.
- Vegetarian felafel with a green salad
- Peanut tempeh stir-fry with green vegetables of choice. Combine natural peanut butter, tamari, fresh ginger and sesame oil to make a sauce and add. Top with crushed peanuts

Still at school?

Are you a high-school or uni student who's struggling to make healthy choices? It can be difficult to stay healthy under peer pressure, but with a little preparation and willpower, you can become the 'fit friend' everyone wants to be.

Here's how to do it.

- Take healthy leftovers for lunch.
- Make a batch of bliss balls to snack on.
- Pop wholesome snacks into your bag. Raw nuts, dates, berries and veggies with hummus are all great, easy-to-carry options.
- Sip on herbal teas whenever you can.
- Pep up your water with fresh lemon and mint.
- Inspire people! Share healthy recipes and Instagram accounts with your friends and family.
- Keep a food diary.
- Plan your meals for the week.
- Don't compare your diet/body with your friends'. You're unique!

PREP FOR SUCCESS!

- Set aside a day to stock up your fridge and pantry.
- Make and freeze hearty soups.
- Cut up veggies for the week.
- Make and freeze a loaf of Signature Gluten-free Loaf (recipe on page 141).
- Roll up some bliss balls or homemade granola bars for snacks on the go.
- Make an extra serving of dinner for lunch the next day.

FOOD DIARY

Writing down what and when you eat (and how you feel afterwards) is one of the best ways to connect with your own body and identify true hunger signals. Use this food diary to track your eating patterns, as well as your progression towards optimal health – and the body of your dreams!

	MONDAY	TUESDAY	WEDNESDAY
BREAKFAST			
MID-MORNING SNACK			
LUNCH			
MID-AFTERNOON SNACK			
DINNER			
SUPPER			
EXERCISE			
SYMPTOMS			

THURSDAY	FRIDAY	SATURDAY	SUNDAY

Progress Sheet

HEALTH CONCERN/GOAL: ....
....

	MEASUREMENTS	ENERGY	SLEEP	EMOTIONAL STATE	CURRENT SUPPLEMENTS / MEDICATIONS	DIGESTION / BOWEL MOVEMENTS
WEEK 1						
WEEK 2						
WEEK 3						
WEEK 4						
WEEK 5						
WEEK 6						
WEEK 7						
WEEK 8						

Self-love Planner

Fill this out every morning if you can. I print out lots of copies and stick them to my fridge so I don't forget.

What is today's affirmation? ....
....

What am I grateful for today and why? ....
....

What do I hope to achieve today? ....
....

What is one eating habit I am going to change or attempt to create this week? (e.g. cut back on caffeine, enjoy a snack between meals)
....

How am I feeling today? ....
....

How am I going to manage any negative thoughts or feelings? ....
....

What will I do today to look after ME? (e.g. meditation, reading, bath)
....

How will I move my body today? ....
....

What is on today's to-do list?

Priorities ....

Things that can wait: ....

7-Day Slim-down Meal Plan

FOR OPTIMAL WEIGHT LOSS

Almond and Herb-crusted Snapper (see page 178)

LIQUIDS: 2 L water (add a squeeze of lemon or chlorop - optional) + unlimited herbal teas
Pre-breakfast:
Meta-boost Drink (see page 301) or warm lemon water with a pinch of cayenne pepper or ginger

BREAKFAST

MID-MORNING SNACK

This is a great time to have your 1 coffee for the day. Go for piccolo, long black, or add a dash of organic milk/almond milk and sweeten with stevia, if you wish. Green tea is even better!

LUNCH

MID-AFTERNOON SNACK

Top tip: Cut carbs out from this point on for optimum weight loss results.

DINNER

SUPPER

OTHER

	MONDAY	TUESDAY	WEDNESDAY
BREAKFAST	Green egg bowl: 1–2 boiled eggs, ¼ avocado, sautéed spinach, mushrooms, onion, kale, silverbeet or green of choice. Optional: add 1 slice Signature Gluten-free Loaf (see page 141) or find at health-food store or 2 brown rice cakes	JSHealth Protein Smoothie (see page 134)	Egg white omelette with sautéed mushrooms, spinach and tomato + ¼ avocado. Optional: add 1 slice Signature Gluten-free Loaf (see page 141) or find at health-food store or 2 brown rice cakes
MID-MORNING SNACK	Chopped carrots, cucumber, celery and/or fennel with 1–2 tbsp hummus or tahini Tip: Keep these in the fridge for when you get hungry.	1 sliced green apple with a sprinkle of ground cinnamon and lime juice + a small handful of almonds	Chopped carrots, cucumber, celery and/or fennel with 1–2 tbsp hummus or tahini
LUNCH	150 g grilled chicken breast, large green salad, 1 cup mushrooms, ½ steamed broccoli, 1 raw carrot, 1 Roma tomato. Drizzle with My Super Clean Dressing (see page 215)	150 g grilled salmon, asparagus and spinach salad. Add ¼ avocado and any leftover roasted veggies like cauliflower.	Chopped salad with cucumber, celery, fennel, onion, tomato and herbs in your food processor. Top with 150 g sliced chicken breast or grilled fish. Drizzle with Slim Down Dressing (see page 215).
MID-AFTERNOON SNACK	Slim-Down Smoothie (see page 134)	Veggie nori rolls: fill nori sheets with chopped veggies and 1–2 tbsp tahini or hummus then roll up	Slim-Down Smoothie (see page 134)
DINNER	150 g Asian-style Snapper (see page 182), stir-fried greens (bok choy, kale, spinach, broccoli, etc.) in tamari, garlic and fresh ginger	150 g Lemon and Herb Chicken (see page 186) on Broccoli Mash (see page 229) + side green salad	Broccoli Soup (see page 235) + 150 g Grass Fed Eye Fillet with Sautéed Garlic and Thyme Mushrooms (see page 198). Marinade in healthy marinade of choice (see page 259) + serve with green salad
SUPPER	Chamomile tea	Rooibos chai tea with ground cinnamon, nut milk and stevia. Top tip: This delish drink kicks those late-night sweet cravings.	Chamomile tea

OTHER
1 green juice (or 1 serving of green superfood powder) daily
Preferably no more than 1–2 portions of dairy/day

3-Step Overnight
Pudding (see page 158)

Broccoli Mash
(see page 229)

Sweet Berry Omelette
(see page 145)

THURSDAY	FRIDAY	SATURDAY	SUNDAY
Brekkie salad: 1–2 boiled or poached eggs, 1 cup rocket and/or spinach leaves, ¼ sliced avocado, 1 sliced tomato + handful of sprouts/fermented veggies. Drizzle with lemon juice, add a pinch of Himalayan salt and black pepper.	3-Step Overnight Pudding of choice (see page 158)	Sweet Berry Omelette (see page 145): 2 beaten eggs, handful of fresh/frozen blueberries, 1 tbsp psyllium husk, 1 tsp ground cinnamon, 2 tbsp nut milk, stevia. Add a serving of protein powder for a protein boost.	JSHealth Protein Pancakes (see page 143)
1 sliced green apple with a sprinkle of ground cinnamon and lime juice + a small handful of almonds	2 JSHealth Sugar-free Protein Balls (see page 269)	Grapefruit with a sprinkle of stevia powder and ground cinnamon	2 JSHealth Sugar-free Protein Balls (see page 269)
Chopped up carrots, cucumber, celery and/or fennel with 1–2 tbsp hummus or tahini	150 g grilled chicken breast + sautéed broccoli, green beans, mushrooms and onion + ½ cup cooked quinoa or brown rice	Chopped salad with cucumber, celery, fennel, onion, tomato and herbs in your food processor. Top with 150 g sliced chicken breast or grilled fish. Drizzle with Slim Down Dressing (see page 215).	Superfood salad with 1–2 boiled eggs, ¼ avocado, steamed broccoli, carrot and spinach leaves. Drizzle with My Super Clean Dressing (see page 215) or tahini and lemon juice.
¼ cup walnuts + a sprinkle of ground cinnamon	Slim-Down Smoothie (see page 134)	Veggie nori rolls: fill nori sheets with chopped veggies and 1–2 tablespoons tahini or hummus then roll up. Or 2 JSHealth Sugar-free Protein Balls (see page 269)	Slim-Down Smoothie (see page 134)
150 g fish, beef, or tempeh stir-fry (see page 210) and sautéed broccoli, spinach, silverbeet, kale and/or bok choy in garlic, olive oil and tamari	Japanese-style Salmon (see page 175) and sautéed asparagus, mushrooms and broccoli. Season with mixed spices of choice.	Chicken or fish Lettuce Cups (see page 209)	Zucchini and Mint Soup (see page 235) + Herb and Almond-crusted Snapper (see page 178) + Cauliflower Rice (see page 201) + steamed green beans (add olive oil, lemon juice and rock salt)
Peppermint tea	Rooibos chai tea with ground cinnamon, nut milk and stevia. Top tip: I love using almond milk for its creamy texture.	Chamomile tea	Rooibos chai tea with ground cinnamon, nut milk and stevia.

Vegan tip: Swap meat, fish or egg option for tempeh. Swap non-vegan breakfast choice with a vegan breakfast option in the recipe section.

THE HEALTHY KITCHEN

Go organic and free-range where possible.

Veggies

Artichokes
Asparagus
Beetroot
Broccoli
Broccolini
Brussels sprouts
Cabbage
Capsicum
Carrot
Cauliflower
Celery
Chives
Cucumber
Eggplant

Endive
Fennel
Garlic
Green beans
Kale
Leeks
Lettuce (cos, butter, iceberg)
Mushrooms (all kinds)
Okra
Onion
Parsnip
Pumpkin
Radicchio

Radish
Rocket
Seaweed (dried/fresh)
Silverbeet
Snow peas
Spinach
Spring onions
Sprouts
Squash
Sweet potato
Tomatoes
Watercress
Zucchini

Fruit

Apples (green)
Avocados
Bananas*
Berries (fresh and frozen)
Cherries
Cranberries, dried
Dates*
Figs
Grapefruit

Grapes*
Kiwifruit
Lemon
Lime
Mangoes*
Nectarines
Oranges
Papaya
Peaches

Pears*
Pineapple*
Plums
Pomegranate
Rhubarb*

Note: Only eat occasionally due to their high sugar content. Also limit dried fruit.

Fresh Herbs & Spices

Allspice	Cumin, ground	Pepper: Black peppercorns
Basil	Curry powder	Rosemary
Bay leaves	Dill	Sage
Cayenne pepper	Garlic	Salt: Himalayan, Celtic or Herbamare salt
Chilli	Ginger	
Chives	Mint	Sumac
Cinnamon, ground	Oregano	Thyme
Coriander	Paprika	Turmeric
Coriander, ground	Parsley	Zaatar spice

Protein

Beef	Good quality whey, rice or pea protein powder	Turkey
Chicken		
Eggs	Kangaroo	
Fresh fish – white fish is best (snapper, ling, cod, flathead) or Wild Alaskan salmon	Lamb	
	Tinned or bottled tuna, wild salmon, mackerel or sardines	

Nuts & Seeds

Ensure these are raw or activated. Refrigerate so they don't go rancid.

Almonds	Cashews	Pumpkin seeds
Black or white sesame seeds	Flaxseed	Sunflower seeds
	Hazelnuts	Walnuts
Brazil nuts	Pecans	

Dairy

Cottage cheese – low fat or full fat

Goat's or sheep's milk yoghurt

Kefir

Organic butter

Ricotta – low fat or full fat

White cheese such as mozzarella

Yoghurt, natural or Greek-style (no added sugar and preferably organic)

Dairy Alternatives

Almond milk (sugar-free)

Coconut milk, coconut cream and coconut yoghurt (coyo)

Rice milk

Flour & Baking (all gluten-free)

Almond meal

Baking powder (aluminium-free, gluten-free)

Baking soda (aluminium-free, gluten-free)

Buckwheat flour

Coconut flour

Hazelnut meal

Quinoa flour

Grains & Pasta (all gluten-free)

Amaranth

Black bean pasta

Brown rice and brown rice pasta

Buckwheat

Corn thins

Gluten-free Oats

Konjac noodles

Millet

Mung bean pasta

Plain brown rice cakes

Quinoa

Vermicelli rice noodles

Wild rice

Oils

Cold-pressed extra virgin olive oil (for salads or low–medium heat cooking)

Cold-pressed flaxseed oil (keep refrigerated; great in salad dressings or smoothies)

Virgin organic coconut oil (for high-heat cooking)

Vinegars

Apple cider vinegar

Balsamic vinegar

Red wine vinegar

White wine vinegar

Condiments & Spreads

Dijon mustard, wholegrain without added sugar

Miso paste

Nut butters (ABC, almond, cashew, peanut)

Raw sauerkraut or kimchi

Tahini and hummus

Tamari sauce (a wheat-free soy sauce alternative)

Sweeteners

Pure maple syrup (small amounts only)

Raw honey or Manuka honey (small amounts only)

Rice malt syrup (small amounts only)

Stevia (powder or natural, vanilla and coconut-flavoured stevia liquid)

Unlimited: Vanilla bean powder, ground cinnamon, allspice and grated nutmeg – these are spices that sweeten my food

SUPERFOODS

These are bonus foods, not essentials.

Acai berry (powder/ frozen)

Bee pollen

Cacao nibs

Cacao powder

Chia seeds

Desiccated coconut, coconut chips, shredded coconut

Ground flaxseed

LSA (ground linseed, sunflower and almond meal)

Maca powder

Maqui berry powder

Psyllium husk

Protein powder (whey, rice and pea)

Spirulina

BEVERAGES

Caffeinated drinks: coffee, English breakfast tea, chai, green tea. Drink before lunchtime and try to limit yourself to 1 coffee a day.

Coconut water

Non-caffeinated herbal tea: chamomile, ginger, dandelion, liquorice, rooibos chai, nettle and peppermint

Roasted dandelion root 'coffee'

Spring and alkaline water

MY PERSONAL PRODUCE LIST

Living The Healthy Life *comes down to good preparation – and regular shopping trips! I make sure my fridge and pantry are always stocked with these goodies.*

PANTRY

Almond butter

Almond meal and coconut flour for baking

Apple cider vinegar

Bottled tomatoes

Clean and natural whey protein powder

Cold-pressed extra-virgin olive oil and virgin organic coconut oil

Gluten-free pasta: konjac,

soba or black bean noodles

Grains: quinoa, organic gluten-free rolled oats

Herbal teas: chamomile and rooibos chai are my favourites

Natural, gluten-free and sugar-free muesli

Raw nuts and seeds

Spices: ground cinnamon, grated nutmeg, cumin, paprika, turmeric, fennel seeds, chilli flakes, garlic and ginger

Superfoods: cacao, bee pollen, maca powder, goji berries, chia seeds, psyllium husk

Sweeteners: Raw honey, maple syrup and stevia

FRIDGE

Activated or raw nuts and seeds (store in an airtight jar)

Almond milk (a sugar-free brand or I make my own)

Berries

Carrots

Cold-pressed flaxseed oil (for salad dressings and smoothies)

Fermented veggies

JSHealth Signature Gluten-free loaf (see page 141)

Green apples

Greens: kale, spinach, rocket, cos lettuce, avocados, silverbeet, zucchini, broccoli and sprouts

Herbs from my garden: mint, parsley, coriander, rosemary and basil

Lemons

LSA (ground linseed, sunflower and almond meal)

Organic Dijon mustard

Organic Greek-style yoghurt (no added sugar)

The ingredients for *The Healthy Life* salads (see page 214)

Unhulled tahini

ESSENTIAL KITCHEN TOOLS

Here are my must-have kitchen tools that I can't live without. I recommend researching products to find brands that suit your needs.

Alligator chopper – quick and easy way to chop onions and julienne vegetables

A set of sharp knives

A set of pots and saucepans – small, medium and large

A set of non-stick frying pans – small and large

A non-stick wok – large

A variety of spoons – for measuring and mixing

Baking dish

A high-powered blender – I use Vitamix and Hamilton Beach

Bread tin

Wooden chopping boards

Electric beaters

Food processor – I use Kenwood

Garlic crusher

Grater

Grill pan

Juicer – I'm obsessed with my Breville

Kettle – for all that herbal tea

Masher

Measuring cups

Mixing bowls – small, medium and large

Mortar and pestle

Peeler – good for minimising pesticides on fruit and vegetables

Salad spinner

Scales

Spatula

Steamer – the best way to prepare your veggies and keep in the nutrients

Stick blender – to purée vegetables

Tongs

Vegetable spiraliser

Healthy Recipes

My aim for this section is to prove that healthy eating can be beyond delicious, and to inspire you to get into the kitchen! Most of my diet is gluten-free, sugar-free and dairy-free, as are most of these recipes.

The ones that have gluten and dairy can be easily made with alternatives.

Share your creations with us on #thecleanlife and #jshealth.

A quick note when reading recipes:

V *Vegetarian recipes*

F *Freezer-friendly recipes*

All recipes pictured are the first recipe on the opposite page.

Breakfast

They're not lying when they say breakfast is the most important meal of the day – and it's the one I look forward to the most! A healthy breakfast is what sets up my day. In this chapter you will see just how creative you can get with healthy ingredients. Whether sweet or savoury, there are literally endless ways to create delicious breakfast meals that will keep you full until lunchtime. All my breakfasts are vegetarian and can easily be altered for vegan alternatives. From on-the-go breakfast, to relaxing weekend spreads, this chapter lays out my favourite morning starts that will make you never skip breakfast again!

3-Step Smoothie

A delicious AND healthy start to the day. Smoothies are packed with vitamins, minerals and healthy fats to get your brain and your metabolism revving. And you'll need a good blender. The key to a good blender is power, so look for anything with 350 watts or more. The best ones are multi-taskers that can be used to make anything from smoothies to soups, and are well worth the investment. Vitamix, Breville, Oster, Hamilton Beach and Cuisinart are all fantastic brands. I sometimes make my smoothies thick enough to eat from a bowl like a dessert smoothie!

ONE

Add 1 cup water, coconut water or your choice of milk to your blender. For the milk, try my Almond Milk (see page 306), coconut milk or rice milk. Then add 1 cup ice cubes.

TWO

Now for the creative part: pick and mix! Add a serving of protein, fibre, good fats, superfoods and/or flavourings or sweeteners from the table below.

GOOD FATS	FIBRE	PROTEIN	SUPERFOODS	FLAVOURINGS OR SWEETENERS
• ¼ avocado • ¼ cup coconut flakes • 1 tbsp ground flaxseed • 1 tbsp nut butter • 2 tbsp nuts or seeds • 1 tbsp tahini	• ½ green apple • ½ banana, fresh or frozen • ½ cup berries, fresh or frozen • 2 dates – chopped and pitted • 2 tbsp oats • ½ pear • 1 tbsp psyllium husk	• 1 egg, raw • 2 tbsp LSA (ground linseed, sunflower and almond meal) – vegan friendly • 3 tbsp natural yoghurt • 1 serving (approximately 2 tbsp or 30 g) whey, pea or rice protein powder – pea and rice protein powders are vegan friendly	• 1 tbsp acai powder or ½ block of frozen acai • 1 tbsp bee pollen • 1 tbsp raw cacao powder • 1 tbsp chia seeds • 1 tbsp goji berries • 1 tbsp maca powder • 1–2 tsp maqui berry powder • handful fresh spinach, kale, parsley or mint	• ½–1 tsp ground cinnamon • a squeeze of lemon or lime • 1 tsp maple syrup or raw honey • ½ tsp grated nutmeg • a pinch of sea salt • 1 tsp stevia powder or 3 drops of stevia liquid • ½ tsp vanilla powder

THREE

Blend in a high-powered blender until the smoothie is your desired consistency!

My Favourite Smoothie Combinations

JSHealth Protein Smoothie

1 serve protein powder (or protein of choice)

1 cup Almond Milk (see page 306), filtered water or coconut water

1 tsp chia seeds

½ cup frozen berries

½ frozen banana (optional)

½ cup baby spinach leaves

1 tsp vanilla powder

½ tsp ground cinnamon

½ cup ice cubes

1 tsp stevia powder

Cinnamon Tahini Smoothie

2 tbsp vanilla protein powder or LSA

½ frozen banana

1 tbsp chia seeds

1 tbsp tahini

½ tsp ground cinnamon

2–3 drops vanilla stevia or 1 tsp stevia powder

1 cup Almond Milk (see page 306)

1 cup ice cubes

a small handful of walnuts (for topping)

Heal Your Gut Smoothie

1 serving vanilla or pea protein powder

½ cup frozen berries

1 tsp glutamine powder

1 tbsp psyllium husk

1 tbsp slippery elm powder

1 tsp ground cinnamon

1 tsp Manuka honey, stevia powder or 2–3 drops vanilla stevia liquid

1 cup ice cubes

1 cup coconut milk or Almond Milk (see page 306)

Slim-down Smoothie

1 serve vanilla protein powder

1 cup unsweetened Almond Milk (see page 306) or water

1 cup ice cubes

1 tsp cinnamon

2–3 drops vanilla stevia or 1 tsp stevia powder

Carrot Cake Smoothie

1 small carrot, grated

2 tbsp pecans

2 fresh dates, pitted

1 tsp ground cinnamon

a pinch of grated nutmeg

2 tbsp almond meal

a pinch of Celtic sea salt

1 tsp stevia powder or maple syrup

1 cup coconut milk

1 cup ice

Antioxidant Smoothie

1 serve protein powder

1 cup Almond Milk (see page 306), coconut water or any dairy milk

a good handful of spinach

½–1 frozen banana

½ cup frozen raspberries

½ cup frozen blueberries

1 tbsp chia seeds

1 tsp maqui berry powder or acai powder

1 tbsp psyllium husk

1 tsp ground cinnamon

1 cup ice cubes

mint leaves and chopped almonds (to serve)

Glorious Green Smoothie

2 stalks kale (remove the stems and just use the leaves)

1 cup coconut water or filtered water

a handful of fresh mint leaves

1 cup baby spinach leaves

½ green apple

juice of ½ lemon

2 tbsp chia seeds

1 tsp stevia powder

a handful of ice cubes

½ banana

chia seeds, sunflower seeds and chopped walnuts (to serve)

1 tsp turmeric (optional)

Cinnamon, Banana & Walnut Smoothie

2 tbsp protein powder or LSA

2 tbsp raw walnuts

½ frozen banana

1 tbsp natural yoghurt (optional)

1 tsp stevia powder or maple syrup

1 tsp ground cinnamon

½ tsp grated nutmeg

1 tsp vanilla powder

a squeeze of lemon

1 cup milk or Almond Milk (see page 306)

1 cup ice cubes

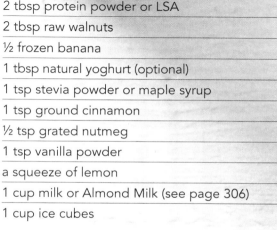

Blueberry, Orange and Ricotta Hotcakes

Sunday morning: rain, tea, PJs and slippers. That's when you'll find me whipping up this recipe.

2 eggs or 3 egg whites

1 banana, mashed

¼ cup ricotta + 2 tbsp extra (to serve)

1 tsp vanilla extract

2 tbsp honey + extra (to serve)

¼ cup milk of choice

½ cup almond meal

2 tbsp psyllium husk

1 tsp baking powder

½ tsp ground cinnamon

2 tbsp desiccated coconut

½ cup blueberries + extra (to serve)

½ tsp virgin organic coconut oil

orange segments (to serve)

1. Whisk the eggs, banana, ricotta, vanilla extract, honey and milk together.

2. In a separate large bowl, combine the almond meal, psyllium husk, baking powder, cinnamon and desiccated coconut.

3. Slowly pour the wet ingredients into the dry ingredients, stirring until combined. Gently stir through the blueberries.

4. Melt the coconut oil in a large non-stick frying pan over a medium–high heat. Pour ⅓ cup of the mixture into the pan. When bubbles start to form (after around 4 minutes), turn the hotcake over. Cook for a further 3 minutes on the other side or until golden brown. Place on a serving plate and repeat with the rest of the mixture.

5. Serve with orange segments, blueberries, ricotta and a drizzle of honey.

SERVES 2 (MAKES 4)
PREP TIME: 25 MINUTES, INCLUDING COOKING

Jess's Health Bowl

This breakfast smorgasbord is full of antioxidants, protein and healthy fats to jump-start your day. Mix and match your toppings – the combinations are endless! It's my quick go-to breakfast on a busy day.

CINNAMON PROTEIN YOGHURT

200 g natural yoghurt or a dairy-free yoghurt such as coyo

2 tbsp LSA

1 tsp stevia powder

1 tsp ground cinnamon

1 tsp vanilla powder (optional)

¼ cup raw almonds, activated

½ cup berries of your choice

½ banana, sliced

2 tbsp pumpkin seeds

mint springs (to garnish)

1. To make the Cinnamon Protein Yoghurt, mix the yoghurt, 1 tbsp LSA, stevia powder, cinnamon and vanilla powder, if using, in a bowl that can be put in the freezer. (You can freeze the yoghurt for 30 minutes and enjoy as frozen yoghurt. I recommend making a big batch and storing it in the freezer.)
2. For the health bowl, spoon frozen yoghurt in the centre of the serving bowl and add all the remaining ingredients including 1 tbsp LSA. Garnish with mint before serving.

SERVES 1
PREP TIME: 10 MINUTES

Chocolate Peanut Butter Smoothie Bowl

Is there any combination more delicious than chocolate and peanut butter? This smoothie combines both flavours for a protein-packed treat.

1 frozen banana

1½ tbsp natural peanut butter

1 tsp ground cinnamon

1 tbsp raw cacao powder

1 tbsp LSA

1 tsp rice malt syrup or stevia powder

1 cup ice cubes

½ cup milk of choice

1 serving chocolate protein powder (optional)

1. Process all the ingredients in a blender until thick and smooth. Pour into a bowl and add your favourite toppings to serve. Suggestions include crushed nuts, cacao nibs and a sprinkle of raw cacao powder.

SERVES 1
PREP TIME: 10 MINUTES

Signature Gluten-free Loaf

I make this loaf every week and keep it in the fridge. It goes with everything and is completely unprocessed, unlike most breads you buy. It is gluten-free and very high in fibre. I love to slice up a loaf with eggs for breakfast most mornings.

DRY

2 cups almond meal

½ cup LSA or ground flaxseed

½ cup chia seeds

¼ cup crushed almonds

¼ cup psyllium husk

1½ tsp baking powder

1 tsp Himalayan pink rock salt

1 tbsp slivered almonds (to decorate)

WET

3 eggs

2 tbsp virgin organic coconut oil

⅓ cup milk or Almond Milk (see page 306)

olive oil (to serve)

1. Preheat the oven to 180°C (160°C fan-forced).
2. In a large mixing bowl, combine all the dry ingredients except the slivered almonds.
3. Whisk all the wet ingredients together in a measuring cup.
4. Slowly add the wet mixture to the dry, stirring until everything is well combined. If the batter is too wet, add extra almond meal; if it is too dry, add more almond milk.
5. Lightly oil a standard loaf tin (approximately 21 cm x 11 cm) with coconut oil spray, then coat liberally with extra almond meal to prevent it from sticking. Spoon the batter into the tin, sprinkle the top with the almonds and place in the preheated oven.
6. Bake for 35–45 minutes. To check if it's cooked, insert a skewer into the middle of the loaf. If the skewer comes out dry, it's done. If the top is starting to brown, cover with foil and continue baking until the loaf feels more solid than normal bread.
7. When cooked, remove the loaf from the oven and cool in the tin. Remove the loaf and slice. Serve with olive oil.
8. Keep covered in the fridge for up to one week. It also freezes well.

MAKES 1 LOAF

PREP TIME: 1 HOUR, INCLUDING COOKING

MORE VARIATIONS

This recipe is a basic gluten-free loaf. You can alter it to make it sweet or savoury.

Zucchini Loaf Grate 2 zucchini into a colander, add a pinch of salt and let it sit for 10 minutes. Squeeze dry, then add to the batter before baking.

Carrot and Walnut Loaf Fold 2 grated carrots, ¼ cup roughly chopped walnuts, 2 tbsp stevia powder or maple syrup, 1 tsp ground cinnamon, ½ tsp vanilla powder and ½ tsp grated nutmeg into the batter.

Date and Coconut Loaf Fold ¼ cup shredded coconut, 4 chopped fresh dates, 1 tbsp maple syrup or stevia powder and 1 tsp ground cinnamon into the batter.

4-Step Pancakes

ONE

In a mixing bowl, whisk 2 eggs or 3 egg whites. For vegan-friendly pancakes mix 1 tbsp ground flaxseed with 3 tbsp water. Allow it to sit for 20–30 minutes until the mixture thickens.

TWO

Now it's time to mix the batter! From the table below, combine and stir a serving of binder, fruit, fibre, liquid and sweetener or flavourings with the whisked eggs and ½ tsp baking powder.

BINDER	FRUIT	FIBRE	MILK	SWEETENER OR FLAVOURINGS
• 1 cup almond meal • 1 cup buckwheat flour • ¼ cup coconut flour • ½ cup rolled gluten-free oats • 1 serving (approximately 30 g) protein powder	• ½ green apple, grated • ½ banana, mashed • ½ cup berries • 2 tbsp dried cranberries • 2 tbsp goji berries • ½ pear, grated	• 1 tbsp chia seeds • 1 tbsp ground flaxseed • 1 tbsp LSA • 1 tbsp rolled oats or oat bran • 1 tbsp psyllium husk	• ¼ cup milk of your choice. Try plain, coconut, rice milk or Almond Milk (see page 306).	• ½ tsp ground cinnamon • a handful of shredded coconut • a squeeze of lemon or lime • 1 tsp maple syrup, raw honey or rice malt syrup • a pinch of grated nutmeg or ground ginger • 1 tsp stevia powder or 3 drops stevia liquid • ½ tsp vanilla powder

THREE

Melt the coconut oil in a large non-stick frying pan over a medium heat. Ladle in one-third of the mixture and cook each side for 2–3 minutes, or until lightly golden. Repeat with the rest of the mixture.

FOUR

Serve with your choice of toppings and be creative! I recommend:

- ½ banana, sliced
- a handful of fresh berries: raspberries, cranberries or blueberries
- a handful of cacao nibs
- a shake of ground cinnamon
- a handful of shredded coconut
- 2 fresh figs, sliced
- 2 tbsp goji berries

- 2 tbsp Greek-style yoghurt
- orange slices
- 2 tbsp ricotta or cottage cheese
- 1 tbsp tahini mixed with a drizzle of raw honey or maple syrup

SERVES 1

MAKES 3 PANCAKES

Carrot Cake Pancakes

2 eggs or 3 egg whites

2 tbsp Almond Milk (see page 306)

1 cup almond meal or ¼ cup coconut flour

1 tbsp oat bran

1 small carrot, grated

5–10 walnuts, crushed

1 tbsp maple syrup

¼ tsp baking powder

½ tsp ground cinnamon

¼ tsp grated nutmeg

1 tsp vanilla powder

1 tbsp ricotta or cottage cheese (optional)

1 tbsp shredded carrot (for the topping)

1 tbsp Greek-style yoghurt (for the filling)

JSHealth Protein Pancakes

3 egg whites or 2 eggs

1 cup almond meal (or binder of choice)

1 tbsp LSA

¼ banana, mashed

a small handful of shredded coconut

½ cup berries

1 tbsp psyllium husk

1 tsp vanilla extract

1 tsp ground cinnamon

1 tsp stevia powder or 3–4 drops stevia liquid

2–3 tbsp Almond Milk (see page 306)

Peanut Butter & Banana Pancakes

This creamy, peanut-buttery breakfast tastes like dessert! To finish, make a sauce by mixing together the peanut butter, a little water and stevia until runny.

1 cup almond meal

3 egg whites or 2 eggs

1 tsp ground cinnamon

½ tsp vanilla powder

1½ bananas, mashed

1 tbsp desiccated coconut

½ tsp baking powder

3–4 drops vanilla stevia

⅓ cup Almond Milk (see page 306)

a pinch of sea salt

1 tbsp virgin organic coconut oil

TO FINISH

1 tbsp peanut butter

a pinch of stevia powder

1 banana, sliced, fried or fresh

1 tsp shredded coconut

1 tsp maple syrup

raw cacao nibs

Sweet Berry Omelette

This sweet twist on a savoury breakfast classic is inspired by The Holistic Ingredient. Berries add an antioxidant boost to this protein-rich dish. If you like, add 1 tbsp raw cacao powder to the mixture and whisk together for a chocolate omelette.

3 egg whites or 2 eggs

1 tbsp almond meal

1 tsp stevia powder

½ cup mixed berries, fresh or frozen

2 tbsp natural yoghurt

1 tbsp shredded coconut

1 tsp virgin organic coconut oil

1–2 heaped tbsp sunflower and pumpkin seeds

a pinch of ground cinnamon (to serve)

1. Whisk the eggs, almond meal, stevia powder, a few berries (leave some for later), 1 tbsp of the yoghurt and a little of the shredded coconut in a bowl.
2. Melt the coconut oil in a medium-sized non-stick frying pan over a medium heat.
3. Pour the mixture into the pan and allow to cook. Wait for either bubbles to form on the surface or the edges to start to brown. Once the edges begin to brown, flip the omelette and cook for another 1–2 minutes.
4. Turn the heat off and let the omelette sit for a couple of minutes.
5. Transfer the omelette to a plate and fill with the remaining yoghurt, the seeds, and the remaining berries and coconut. Sprinkle with cinnamon, fold over and serve.

SERVES 1
PREP TIME: 15 MINUTES, INCLUDING COOKING

Tahini and Vanilla Smoothie Bowl

Give your smoothie a fun twist by adding tahini – sesame is a fantastic source of calcium, potassium and magnesium.

1 frozen banana

1 tbsp tahini

2 tbsp LSA

1 tsp maple syrup

1 tsp ground cinnamon

1 cup ice

½ cup milk of choice

1 tsp vanilla powder

1. Process all the ingredients in a blender until thick and smooth. Pour into a bowl and add your favourite toppings to serve. Suggestions include berries, crushed nuts and a sprinkle of ground cinnamon.

SERVES 1
PREP TIME: 10 MINUTES

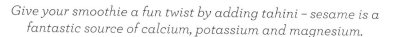

Bircher Muesli

My darling partner, Dean, adores Bircher ... and so do I. We make a big batch on Sunday evenings and it lasts in the fridge for several days. If you struggle with breakfast decisions in the morning, this is the recipe for you. Plus, it's super easy to transport to class or the office – double win on a busy morning!

1 cup rolled oats (gluten-free option: quinoa flakes)

1 cup water or milk for soaking (I do half and half)

1 tbsp shredded coconut

¼ cup mixed sunflower and pumpkin seeds

½ cup slivered almonds

¼ cup goji berries or dried cranberries

1 green apple, grated

a handful of strawberries or berries of choice

2 tbsp Greek-style yoghurt

½ tsp ground cinnamon

1 tbsp raw honey, maple syrup or stevia powder (optional, to serve)

extra berries, fresh mint and a pinch of ground cinnamon (to serve)

1. Soak the oats in water or milk overnight. Make sure the oats are completely covered.

2. The next day, mix all the ingredients together in a bowl. The texture must be thick but smooth.

3. To serve, drizzle with honey, top with fresh mint, a sprinkle of cinnamon, extra berries or even my 4-Step Granola (see page 164).

SERVES 2
PREP TIME: 10 MINUTES + SOAKING OVERNIGHT

Berry and Banana Breakfast Nice-cream

1 frozen banana

1 cup frozen mixed berries

a handful of cashews

1 tbsp almond butter

½ tsp ground cinnamon

¼ tsp vanilla extract or powder

a pinch of Himalayan salt

1 tsp stevia powder or raw honey

2–3 tbsp unsweetened Almond Milk (see page 306)

2 tbsp natural or coconut yoghurt (optional)

1. Combine all the ingredients in a blender or food processor and blend until smooth. Freeze for an hour before serving with natural or coconut yoghurt, if desired. If you don't have time to freeze the nice-cream, try adding an extra frozen banana and cashews for texture.

SERVES 1
PREP TIME: 10 MINUTES

Green Egg Wrap

Sneak a big dose of greens into your morning meal – it adds beautiful colour AND good health.

½ head broccoli, steamed

½ cup baby spinach leaves

2 eggs or 3 egg whites, beaten

2 tbsp LSA or psyllium husk

½ tsp baking powder

juice of ½ lemon

1 tbsp milk of choice

Himalayan salt and ground pepper

½ tsp virgin organic coconut oil

tomatoes, rocket and avocado (to serve)

1. In a food processor, combine the broccoli and spinach and blitz until smooth.
2. Combine the broccoli mixture and the remaining ingredients (besides the coconut oil) in a bowl and stir well.
3. Melt the coconut oil in a medium-sized non-stick frying pan over a medium heat.
4. Pour the mixture into the pan and allow to cook. Wait for either bubbles to form on the surface or until the edges start to brown. Once the edges begin to brown, flip the omelette and cook for another minute or two.
5. Turn off the heat and let the omelette sit for a couple of minutes before you transfer it to a plate.
6. Top with Homemade Walnut Pesto (see page 252), tomatoes, rocket, avocado and a drizzle of lemon. Fold the omelette over and enjoy.

SERVES 1
PREP TIME: 15 MINUTES, INCLUDING COOKING

3-Step Porridge

Warm, creamy and so comforting. There's nothing like a bowl of porridge with delicious toppings to start a chilly morning.

ONE

Soak your chosen grains in water, Almond Milk (see page 306), rice milk or coconut milk overnight. Try ⅓ cup amaranth, ⅓ cup hulled buckwheat, ⅓ cup rolled oats or ⅓ cup quinoa grains or flakes.

TWO

Add 1 cup water, milk or Almond Milk to ⅓ cup of grains and bring to the boil. Once boiling, reduce the heat, cover and simmer until the grains are soft (approximately 10 minutes).

THREE

Mix your choice of fruit, nuts, spice or sweeteners into the porridge and serve. Try:

- a handful of almond flakes, pecans, walnuts or pistachios
- ½ apple or pear, grated or sliced
- ½ banana, sliced
- ½ cup berries of choice
- a handful of cacao nibs
- 1 tbsp raw cacao powder
- 1 tsp ground cinnamon, grated nutmeg or ground ginger
- 2 tbsp coconut cream or milk
- 2 chopped dates – for a creamy sticky date pudding
- 1 tbsp ground flaxseed
- 2 tbsp LSA
- mango, sliced
- 2 tbsp natural yoghurt
- 1 tbsp nut butter – try almond butter for a creamy texture
- orange segments
- peach, sliced
- 3 drops stevia liquid or 1–2 tsp stevia, maple syrup, raw honey or rice malt syrup
- 1–2 tbsp tahini

SERVES 1

Carrot Cake Porridge

⅓ cup rolled oats

½ carrot, grated

3 walnuts, crushed

1 tbsp natural yoghurt

a pinch of Himalayan salt

1 tsp ground cinnamon

½ tsp grated nutmeg

1 tsp vanilla powder

1 tsp honey or stevia powder

½ cup water and ½ cup Almond Milk (see page 306)

1 tbsp vanilla protein powder (optional)

Sticky Date Porridge

1 tsp vanilla extract or powder

2 egg whites

⅓ cup rolled oats

2 tbsp chopped pecans

2 fresh dates, pitted

½ tsp ground cinnamon

a pinch of Himalayan salt

½ cup water and ½ cup Almond Milk (see page 306)

1 tsp stevia powder or maple syrup (optional)

1 tsp mesquite powder (optional)

Peanut Butter & Banana Porridge

⅓ cup rolled oats

1 tsp ground flaxseed or chia seeds

¼ banana, mashed

1 tbsp natural crunchy peanut butter

1 tsp stevia powder, raw honey or maple syrup

1 tsp ground cinnamon

½ tsp vanilla powder

a pinch of grated nutmeg

½ cup Almond Milk (see page 306) and ½ cup water

Chocolate & Berry Porridge

⅓ cup rolled oats

2 tbsp chia seeds or ground flaxseed

1 tbsp raw cacao powder

½ cup mixed berries or ½ banana, mashed

1 tbsp stevia powder or raw honey

1 tsp ground cinnamon + extra to dust

a pinch of grated nutmeg

½ cup milk of choice and ½ cup water

1 tbsp virgin organic coconut oil (optional)

Paleo Carrot Porridge

Tasty grain-free breakfast choice for my paleo friends!

1 large carrot, grated

1–2 tbsp ground flaxseed

a handful of raw walnuts, crushed

1 tsp ground cinnamon

a pinch of grated nutmeg

1 tbsp stevia powder or raw honey (enough to sweeten it up)

2 tbsp vanilla protein powder (optional)

Top with 2 tbsp Greek-style yoghurt, coconut yoghurt or tahini, and sprinkle with extra ground cinnamon.

Gluten-free Banana Bread

Ahh …. warm banana bread topped with fresh ricotta, cinnamon and a drizzle of raw honey alongside a cup of chai. This combination makes me so happy. My recipe is gluten-free, sugar-free and packed with nutritious ingredients. See? You never need to feel deprived when you embrace a healthy lifestyle. There is always a healthy version of your favourite treats.

DRY

2 cups almond meal

½ cup LSA or ground flaxseed

¼ cup roughly chopped walnuts

¼ cup psyllium husk

1½ tsp baking soda

2 tsp ground cinnamon

1 tsp vanilla powder

2 tbsp stevia powder, raw honey or maple syrup

4 fresh dates, pitted and chopped (optional)

2 tbsp raw cacao powder (optional, for a chocolatey banana loaf)

WET

3 eggs

2 tsp virgin organic coconut oil, melted

1 tsp vanilla extract

3 ripe bananas, mashed + extra ½ banana to decorate

¼ cup milk or Almond Milk (see page 306)

Greek-style yoghurt, ground cinnamon and maple syrup (to serve)

1. Preheat the oven to 180°C (160°C fan-forced).
2. Combine all the dry ingredients in a large mixing bowl.
3. In a measuring cup, whisk all the wet ingredients together.
4. Add the wet mixture to the dry, mixing as you go until everything is well combined. If the batter is too wet, add extra almond meal; if it's too dry, add more almond milk.
5. Lightly oil a standard loaf tin (approximately 21 cm x 11 cm) with some coconut oil spray, then coat liberally with some extra almond meal to prevent the loaf from sticking. Spoon the batter into the tin. Top with the extra ½ banana, sliced lengthways.
6. Bake for 45–50 minutes. To check if it's cooked, insert a skewer into the middle of the loaf. If the skewer comes out dry, it's done. If the top is starting to brown, cover with foil and continue baking.
7. When cooked, remove the loaf from the oven and cool in the tin. Remove the loaf and slice. Serve with yoghurt, ground cinnamon and a drizzle of maple syrup or nut butter if desired.
8. Keep covered in the fridge for up to one week. The loaf also freezes well.

MAKES 1 LOAF
PREP TIME: 1 HOUR 5 MINUTES, INCLUDING COOKING

THE LOWDOWN ON GLUTEN-FREE BREAD

When choosing a gluten-free loaf at the supermarket, be aware that most brands are very processed, high in sodium and don't taste very nice. I recommend either making your own bread, or visiting a health-food store and choosing a sprouted loaf.

Green Smoothie Bowl

Sneak in a couple of servings of veggies any time with this nutrient-rich smoothie.

1 cup baby spinach leaves

¼ avocado

3 Brazil nuts

1 frozen banana

juice of ½ lemon

a handful of mint leaves

1 tbsp spirulina powder (optional)

2 tbsp LSA

1 tsp stevia powder

½ tsp ground cinnamon

½ cup ice cubes

½ cup coconut water

chopped Brazil nuts, cashew butter, sesame seeds and psyllium husk (to serve)

1 tsp turmeric (optional)

1. Process all the ingredients in a blender until thick and smooth. Pour into a bowl and top with Brazil nuts, cashew butter, sesame seeds and a sprinkle of psyllium husk.

SERVES 1
PREP TIME: 10 MINUTES

Turmeric Omelette

Perfect for a quick breakfast, lunch OR dinner – with the added health and anti-inflammatory benefits and a spicy kick of turmeric.

2 eggs

1 tbsp psyllium husk or ground flaxseed

½ tsp ground turmeric

½ tsp paprika

Himalayan salt and ground pepper

1 tsp virgin organic coconut oil

1. In a mixing bowl, combine all the ingredients (except the coconut oil) and beat well.
2. Melt the coconut oil in a medium-sized non-stick frying pan over a medium heat.
3. Pour the mixture into the pan and allow to cook. Wait for either bubbles to form on the surface or until the edges start to brown. Once the edges begin to brown, flip the omelette and cook for another 1–2 minutes.
4. Turn the heat off and let the omelette sit for a couple of minutes.
5. Place the omelette on a plate and add your favourite extras. I like fresh spinach, ¼ avocado and leftover roasted carrots. Fold over.

SERVES 1
PREP TIME: 10 MINUTES, INCLUDING COOKING

Zucchini and Avocado Fritters with Lemon Coconut Yoghurt

The perfect brunch, this is one to make for the family and friends on a cosy Sunday morning.

FRITTERS

2 zucchini, coarsely grated

Himalayan salt and ground pepper

2 eggs, lightly beaten

1 cup baby spinach leaves, shredded

¼ cup basil leaves, finely chopped

½ cup almond meal

½ tsp ground cumin

½ tsp ground coriander

1 tbsp psyllium husk

1 tbsp virgin organic coconut oil

LEMON COCONUT YOGHURT

¼ cup coyo

juice and zest of ½ lemon

Himalayan salt and ground pepper

paprika

sliced avocado and baby rocket leaves (to serve)

1. To make the fritters, place the grated zucchini in a colander with some salt. Sit for 10 minutes to release the moisture. Squeeze dry with your hands.
2. In a mixing bowl, combine the zucchini and all the remaining fritter ingredients except the coconut oil and mix well.
3. Melt the coconut oil in a large non-stick frying pan over a medium heat, then add large spoonfuls of the zucchini mixture in batches. Use a spatula to gently press the mixture to flatten.
4. After 3 minutes, turn the fritters and cook the other side for 2 minutes or until golden brown. Repeat until the batter is used up.
5. To make the lemon coconut yoghurt, combine the coyo, and lemon juice and zest in a small bowl. Season and sprinkle with paprika.
6. Serve the fritters with avocado, rocket and a dollop of lemon coconut yoghurt.

SERVES 2 (MAKES 6 FRITTERS)
PREP TIME: 30 MINUTES, INCLUDING COOKING

3-Step Overnight Pudding or 'Bircher Muesli'

A morning saviour! Get out the door fast and fuelled with a breakfast you make the night before. Try soaking your Bircher in a Mason jar so they're super simple to take on the go. For my family's favourite Sunday morning Bircher Muesli see page 146.

ONE

Soak your chosen base overnight in ½ cup water, Almond Milk (see page 306), coconut milk or rice milk:

- 3 tbsp chia seeds – for a chia pudding
- ⅓ cup hulled buckwheat
- 3 tbsp ground flaxseed
- ⅓ cup rolled oats
- ⅓ cup quinoa flakes
- or a mixure of all of the above.

TWO

The morning after soaking your base, mix or top with your choice of fruit, seeds, nuts or superfoods:

- 1 tsp acai powder
- ½ green apple or pear, grated
- ½ banana, mashed or sliced
- ½ cup berries of your choice
- 1 tbsp raw cacao powder
- a small handful of shredded coconut
- 2 dates, pitted and chopped
- 2 figs, fresh
- 2–3 tbsp goji berries
- grapefruit segments
- 3 tbsp natural yoghurt
- a handful of raw mixed nuts, such as walnuts, hazelnuts or slivered almonds
- 1 tbsp nut butter
- peach or mango, sliced
- 2 tbsp protein powder

THREE

Then mix or top with your favourite flavours for a sweet or spicy kick:

- ½ tsp ground cinnamon
- shake of grated nutmeg or ground ginger

- a squeeze of lemon
- 1 tsp stevia powder
- ¼ tsp vanilla powder

SERVES 1

Chocolate Pudding

⅓ cup organic rolled oats

¼ banana, mashed (optional)

1 tsp stevia powder or maple syrup

½ cup Almond Milk (see page 306)

1 tbsp raw cacao powder

2 tbsp chia seeds

½ tsp ground cinnamon

1 tbsp natural or coconut yoghurt

1 tbsp nut butter (optional)

Sticky Date Pudding

⅓ cup rolled oats

2 tbsp pecans, chopped

1 tsp stevia powder or maple syrup

½ tsp vanilla powder

½ cup milk of choice

½ tsp ground cinnamon

1 tbsp chia seeds

2 fresh dates, pitted and chopped

Vanilla & Berry Pudding

⅓ cup rolled oats

1 tbsp chia seeds

1 tbsp psyllium husk

½ cup mixed berries

¼ banana, sliced

½ tsp ground cinnamon

1 tsp stevia powder

1 tbsp natural yoghurt

2 tbsp mixed nuts and seeds

½ tsp vanilla powder

a squeeze of lemon juice

½ cup milk of choice

Antioxidant Hit Pudding

1 tbsp maple syrup or stevia powder

1 tbsp acai or maqui berry powder

½ cup milk of choice

2 tbsp natural yoghurt

½ green apple, grated

⅓ cup rolled oats

2 tbsp chia seeds + extra to sprinkle

a squeeze of lime juice

a handful of mixed nuts (to serve)

a handful of blueberries (to serve)

Mint and Raspberry Smoothie Bowl

Packed with antioxidants and vitamins thanks to the magical acai berry.

1 x 100 g packet frozen unsweetened acai

½ frozen banana

½ cup frozen raspberries or blueberries

1 tbsp cashew butter

½ cup milk of choice

1 tsp raw honey

1 serving vanilla protein powder (optional)

¼ cup mint leaves + extra (to serve)

fresh raspberries, shredded coconut, mixed seeds and mint leaves (to serve)

1. Process all the ingredients in a blender until thick and smooth. Pour into a bowl and top with fresh raspberries, coconut, seeds and mint leaves.

SERVES 1
PREP TIME: 5 MINUTES

Egg Nourishment Bowl

About Life, a local health café, inspired me with this bowl of nourishment and it keeps me full for hours.

⅓ cup quinoa

½ bunch kale, leaves cut into bite-sized pieces, stems discarded

a handful of cherry tomatoes

2 eggs, whisked

2 heaped tbsp Homemade Walnut Pesto (see page 252)

1 tbsp cold-pressed extra-virgin olive oil

1 tbsp linseeds

1 tbsp slivered almonds, or nuts of your choice (optional)

½ avocado, sliced

Himalayan salt and ground pepper

1. Bring the quinoa to the boil in a saucepan as per packet instructions. Put the lid on, reduce the heat, and simmer for 10–15 minutes.
2. Steam the kale and tomatoes for 3 minutes, then take off the heat.
3. Once the quinoa is cooked, add the eggs to the quinoa and continue to cook over a low heat, stirring frequently. This will take 3–4 minutes.
4. Once the eggs have set, mix in the pesto. Then fold in the kale and cherry tomatoes and turn off the heat.
5. Transfer to a bowl. Lightly drizzle with the olive oil and top with the linseeds, almonds, if using, and avocado. Season and serve.

SERVES 1
PREP TIME: 20 MINUTES, INCLUDING COOKING

Breakfast Protein Balls

These are for the busy bees who struggle to get breakfast in. Please, please don't skip breakfast. Give these a try. They're rich in protein, good fats, slow-releasing carbs, and they will give you all the energy you need to start your day. Make a batch on the weekend to last you the week.

1 cup organic rolled oats

½ cup LSA or ground flaxseed

¼ cup chia seeds

¼ cup raw nuts of your choice

½ cup dried cranberries or goji berries (or a mixture of both)

2–3 fresh dates, pitted and chopped

½ cup almond butter

2 tbsp virgin organic coconut oil, melted

1 tsp ground cinnamon

1 tbsp raw honey or stevia powder

¼ cup desiccated coconut (optional) + extra to sprinkle

⅓ cup filtered water

1. In a high-powered blender or food processor, combine all the ingredients except the water and blend until the mixture is smooth.
2. Slowly add the water to bring the mixture together and until the desired consistency is achieved. Make sure it's not too wet – you may not need all the water.
3. Roll into balls, sprinkle with extra coconut, if desired, and refrigerate. These can be kept in the fridge for 7 days.
4. Enjoy 2–3 balls for brekkie.

MAKES 12 BALLS
PREP TIME: 15 MINUTES

4-Step Granola

Who doesn't love delicious, crunchy granola with creamy Greek-style yoghurt?
These healthy ideas are sugar-free, gluten-free and free from any salt and preservatives
– and guaranteed to turn you into a granola addict like me!
This recipe makes four cups. It can be stored it in an airtight container for a week.

ONE

Preheat the oven to 180°C (160°C fan-forced).

TWO

Now for my favourite part! Pick and mix 2 cups of raw base ingredients, 1 cup of protein or good fats, 1 serving of fruit, 1 serving of extra flavour and 2 tbsp of sweetener from the table below:

RAW BASE INGREDIENT (2 CUPS)	PROTEIN OR GOOD FAT (1 CUP)	FRUIT (1 SERVE)	EXTRA FLAVOUR (1 SERVE)	SWEETENER (2 TBSP)
• hulled buckwheat or buckinis • coconut flakes – great for a paleo-style Bircher • oats • quinoa flakes • a mixture of all of the above to make 2 cups	• mixed raw nuts, try almonds, walnuts, pecans and/or hazelnuts • mixed seeds, try sunflower seeds, pumpkin seeds, chia seeds and/or flaxseed • a mixture of all of the above to make 1 cup	• 1 banana, mashed – this can caramelise the granola • ⅓ cup cranberries, dried • ½ cup fresh dates, pitted and chopped • ⅓ cup goji berries • 3 tbsp orange zest • ⅓ cup mulberries • ⅓ cup sultanas, raisins, currants, apricots, dried figs or pitted dates	• 2 tbsp raw cacao powder – for chocolatey granola • 1 tsp ground cinnamon • ½ tsp grated nutmeg or ground ginger • pinch of Celtic sea salt • ½ tsp vanilla powder	• raw honey • maple syrup • rice malt syrup • stevia powder or 3–4 drops stevia liquid – for a sugar-free version

THREE

Combine ⅓ cup melted virgin organic coconut oil with the granola mixture.

FOUR

Line a baking tray with baking paper then spread the granola over evenly. Place in the oven for 10 minutes, stir the mixture then bake for another 5–10 minutes or until golden.

MAKES 4 CUPS

Chocolate Banana Granola

1 cup rolled oats

1 banana, mashed

½ cup raw almonds

¼ cup coconut flakes

2 tbsp raw cacao powder

2–3 tbsp raw honey

⅓ cup virgin organic coconut oil, melted

¼ tsp vanilla powder

a pinch of Himalayan pink rock salt

1 tsp ground cinnamon

Paleo Granola

2 cups coconut flakes

¼– ⅓ cup virgin organic coconut oil, melted

2 cups mixed raw nuts, roughly chopped

½ cup sunflower seeds and pumpkin seeds

2 tbsp rice malt syrup or maple syrup

1 tsp ground cinnamon

Orange & Coconut Granola

This is my mum's best friend, Orit's, favourite!

1 cup almonds, roughly chopped

1 cup walnuts, roughly chopped

½ cup sunflower seeds

½ cup rolled oats

¼ cup coconut flakes

¼ cup pumpkin seeds

1 tsp ground cinnamon

2 tbsp orange zest

2 tbsp maple syrup

⅓ cup virgin organic coconut oil, melted

Almond & Coconut Granola

1 cup rolled oats

⅓ cup virgin organic coconut oil, melted

½ cup coconut flakes

½ cup raw almonds

2 tbsp maple syrup

1 tsp ground cinnamon

½ tsp grated nutmeg

Almond and Rosemary Paleo Loaf

Paleo, grain-free, gluten-free, dairy-free and so nutritious.
Just about the healthiest and tastiest loaf ever.

2 cups almond meal

¼ cup psyllium husk

¼ cup chia seeds

¼ cup ground flaxseed

¼ cup raw walnuts, roughly chopped + 2 tbsp extra to decorate

2 tbsp rosemary leaves, roughly chopped + extra sprigs to decorate

1 tsp Celtic sea salt

1½ tsp baking powder

1 clove garlic, crushed

3 eggs, lightly beaten

¼ cup Almond Milk (see page 306)

1 tbsp olive oil

1. Preheat the oven to 190°C (170°C fan-forced).
2. Combine all the ingredients in a large bowl (except the loaf decorations) and mix well using a wooden spoon.
3. Spoon into a lightly oiled and lined standard loaf tin (approximately 21 cm x 11 cm), gently smooth the top, and decorate with the extra walnuts and rosemary.
4. Bake in the oven for 30 minutes, or until the loaf is cooked. To check if it's cooked, insert a skewer into the middle of the loaf. If the skewer comes out dry, it's done. Cover with foil if the top is browning too much.
5. Cool, and serve the loaf sliced.

SERVES 8
PREP TIME: 45 MINUTES, INCLUDING COOKING

Stuffed Mushrooms

4 large portobello mushrooms

4 eggs

2 tbsp roughly chopped fresh herbs (I use thyme and rosemary)

3 tbsp ricotta or goat's cheese (optional)

Himalayan salt and ground pepper

2 tbsp cold-pressed extra-virgin olive oil or olive oil spray

2 tbsp Homemade Walnut Pesto (see page 252, to serve)

mixed leaf salad (to serve)

1. Preheat the oven to 180°C (160°C fan-forced). Line a baking tray with baking paper.

2. Clean the mushrooms and remove the stalks. Place the mushrooms cap-side down on the tray. Carefully crack an egg into the centre of each mushroom, sprinkle with the herbs and top with the cheese, if using. Season with salt and pepper, and drizzle with olive oil.

3. Cook for 15–20 minutes, or until the eggs are cooked to your liking.

4. Serve with the Homemade Walnut Pesto and mixed salad leaves.

SERVES 4

PREP TIME: 35 MINUTES, INCLUDING COOKING

Healthy Vegetable Bread

This has become a staple in the JSHealth kitchen. I was inspired by my visit to Hu Kitchen in New York and had to recreate it. If you're a bread lover, this is a must bake!

2 cups almond meal

½ cup psyllium husk

¼ cup pumpkin seeds

1 carrot, grated

1 zucchini, grated

1 onion, grated

1 clove garlic, crushed

1 tbsp yeast (optional)

fresh basil and rosemary

½ tsp paprika

½ tsp cumin

1 tsp Celtic sea salt or rock salt

1 tsp baking powder

2 eggs, beaten

2 tbsp olive oil

1. Preheat the oven to 180°C. Lightly oil a standard loaf tin (approximately 21 cm x 11 cm).

2. Grate zucchini, then salt and squeeze to remove all liquid. Combine all the dry ingredients in a bowl, then add the eggs and olive oil and mix.

3. Pour into the tin and bake for about 50 minutes or until the top is just golden.

4. Serve warm with avocado, fresh tomato and rocket.

SERVES 8

PREP TIME: 60 MINUTES, INCLUDING COOKING

Breakfast on the Run

While it's ideal to sit down to a nutritious breakfast, sometimes that's just not possible. Go for these options when you're time poor:

Bircher Muesli (see page 146)
or 3-Step Overnight Pudding (see page 158)

Boiled eggs and a handful of nuts

My Breakfast Protein Balls (see page 162)

Plain yoghurt with nuts, seeds and berries

JSHealth Protein Smoothie (see page 132)

GOING OUT FOR BREKKIE?

Choose one of these options:

- **poached or boiled eggs** with avocado, mushrooms, spinach or smoked salmon on the side. If you are having toast, choose 1 piece of rye, spelt or sourdough
- **gluten-free toast** with avocado smash, grilled mushrooms and goat's cheese
- **porridge** made with water or milk of choice and topped with nuts, berries or natural yoghurt
- **scrambled pesto eggs** with a side of grilled mushrooms
- **omelette** filled with veggies
- **buckwheat pancakes.**

TOP TIP

Avoid the granola when eating out – it's usually laden with sugar.

More Brekkie Ideas

- **Smashed avo with goat's cheese and tomato on good quality wholegrain or gluten-free toast.** For the perfect flavour combination, use ½ avocado (smashed with lemon juice), Himalayan salt, mixed seeds, 2 tbsp goat's cheese and sliced tomatoes.

- **Pan-fried mushrooms in virgin organic coconut oil with thyme.** Serve with goat's cheese and herbs on toast. Try with my Almond and Rosemary Paleo Loaf (see page 167).

- **Scoop out the seeds of half a papaya and fill the cavity with Greek-style yoghurt or coyo.** Sprinkle ground cinnamon, mixed seeds and nuts or 4-Step Granola (see page 164) on top.

- **Brekkie Salad:** 1 cup rocket or baby spinach leaves, ¼ sliced avocado, 1 sliced tomato, a handful of sprouts and 1 sliced boiled egg. Add a drizzle of lemon juice and serve with Himalayan salt and ground pepper.

- **Pesto Eggs:** Scramble 2 eggs with a dollop of fresh Homemade Walnut Pesto (see page 252). Amp up your breakfast with baby spinach and avocado. Place the eggs and avocado on 2 brown rice cakes.

- **Simple Eggs:** Boil, poach or scramble 1 or 2 eggs and add sautéed spinach, onion, zucchini, tomatoes (or whatever veggies you have in the fridge). Serve with a drizzle of lemon juice, ¼ avocado, rocket and sweet potato, quinoa or 2 brown rice cakes. Roll your boiled eggs in herbs or spices – turmeric, dukkah or zaatar are great. You can thank me later!

- **Shakshuka or baked eggs.** Simply bake eggs with veggies of your choice. These are an excellent option when you're eating out.

- **Sweet Egg Scramble:** Combine 2 eggs with 1 tbsp ricotta, 1 tbsp flaxseed, ½ mashed banana, raw honey, stevia powder and ground cinnamon. Fry in virgin organic coconut oil. Sprinkle with nuts and seeds.

- **Power Omelette:** Whisk 2 eggs or 3 egg whites with some fresh chopped spinach and veggies of your choice. Enjoy with ¼ avocado on gluten-free grain bread or my Signature Gluten-free Loaf (see page 141).

- **Healthy Yoghurt:** Top 100–200 g natural yoghurt with 2 tbsp LSA, berries and ground cinnamon. Sprinkle with stevia powder or raw honey to sweeten. Freeze for homemade froyo.

- **Gluten-free Muesli:** Make your own by throwing together coconut flakes, pumpkin seeds, sunflower seeds, raw nuts, goji berries and puffed quinoa or buckwheat. Serve with 200 g Greek-style yoghurt, stevia powder, ground cinnamon or nut milk.

- **Baked Oatmeal:** Mix slow-cooked oats with ground cinnamon, berries, mashed banana, coconut butter, nut butter and Almond Milk (see page 306). Bake in the oven, and top with nuts and berries.

Main Meals

Healthy food does not need to be complicated. My rule of thumb is some lean protein grilled with veggies that have been jazzed up with herbs, spices and good oils. Choose a dish from the Side Dishes, Soups and Salads section on page 215 and you'll have a complete, nutritionally balanced main meal. Simple is delicious!

Japanese-inspired Salmon

An absolute family favourite. I make this dish often, and they love it. It's incredibly quick to prepare, which makes it a perfect mid-week dinner option.

4 x 180 g salmon fillets, bones removed and skin on

¼ cup spring onions, thinly sliced (to serve)

MARINADE

1 tbsp sesame oil

½ cup tamari

1 tsp grated fresh ginger

1 tbsp Dijon mustard

¼ cup sesame seeds, white or black

1 tbsp honey or 1 tsp stevia powder (optional)

1. Preheat the oven to 200°C (180°C fan-forced). Line a baking tray with baking paper.
2. In a large bowl, whisk together the marinade ingredients. Marinate the salmon for up to 30 minutes in a covered bowl or in a large snap-lock bag.
3. Remove the salmon from the marinade. Reserve the marinade.
4. Lay the salmon, skin-side down, on the lined tray. Bake for 15–20 minutes, or until cooked to your liking.
5. Remove from the oven. Pour over the reserved marinade and scatter over the spring onions.
6. This is good with some bok choy stir-fried in a hot wok or frying pan with tamari, sesame oil and freshly grated ginger.

SERVES 4
PREP TIME: 50 MINUTES, INCLUDING MARINATING AND COOKING

Herb-crusted Salmon

Juicy and flavourful, this is guaranteed to become a regular in your dinner rotation.

2 x 180 g salmon fillets, bones removed and skin on

2 tbsp each roughly chopped dill, parsley and coriander

2 tbsp cold-pressed extra-virgin olive oil

Himalayan pink rock salt and ground pepper

1 tbsp tamari

juice of 1 lemon

1. Preheat the oven to 200°C (180°C fan-forced). Line a baking tray with baking paper.
2. In a bowl, mix the herbs with the oil, salt and pepper.
3. Place the salmon fillets on the tray, skin-side down. Spread the herbs over the salmon and sprinkle over the tamari.
4. Bake for 15 minutes or until cooked through. Remove from the oven and drizzle with the lemon juice to serve.

SERVES 2
PREP TIME: 25 MINUTES, INCLUDING COOKING

Crisp-skin Salmon with Tahini Lemon Dressing

Crisp salmon is perfectly paired with creamy hummus,
giving an incredible combination of textures.

2½ tbsp olive oil

4 x 180 g salmon fillets, bones removed and skin on

1 tsp fennel seeds, lightly crushed

Himalayan salt and ground pepper

Tahini Lemon Dressing (see page 258)

1 clove garlic, crushed

½ tsp chilli flakes

1 eschalot, finely chopped

1 bunch English spinach, trimmed and roughly chopped

1 tbsp slivered almonds, toasted

lemon wedges (to serve)

1. Rub the salmon flesh with ½ tbsp of the olive oil and sprinkle with fennel seeds. Season the skin with salt and pepper.
2. Prepare ¼ cup Tahini Lemon Dressing.
3. Heat another 1 tbsp of the olive oil in a large non-stick frying pan over a medium–high heat. Cook the salmon, skin-side down, for 4–5 minutes or until the skin is golden and crisp. Turn and cook for 3–4 minutes on the other side or until done to your liking. Transfer and rest on a plate for 5 minutes, covered loosely with foil.
4. Meanwhile, heat the remaining olive oil on medium heat and cook the garlic and chilli flakes for 1 minute. Add the eschalot and cook for 3–4 minutes or until softened. Add the spinach and cook for 2–3 minutes, or until wilted. Season to taste. Sprinkle with almonds.
5. Serve the salmon with the spinach, dressing and lemon wedges.

SERVES 4
PREP TIME: 20 MINUTES, INCLUDING COOKING

Herb and Almond–crusted Snapper

Delicate, flaky snapper is a great way to introduce your family to seafood. The blend of herbs pairs perfectly with this mild fish. This herb mixture freezes very well; I often make a big batch and freeze in single-serve containers. This comes in handy on those nights when I'm running short on time.

½ cup raw or toasted almonds

¼ cup parsley

¼ cup basil + extra leaves (to serve)

¼ cup coriander

1 tbsp lemon juice

1 tbsp cold-pressed extra-virgin olive oil

1 tbsp grated parmesan (optional)

Himalayan salt and ground pepper

4 x 180 g snapper fillets or other firm white fish fillets such as barramundi, skin off

olive oil (to serve, optional)

1. Preheat the oven to 200°C (180°C fan-forced). Line a large baking tray with baking paper.
2. Place the almonds, parsley, basil, coriander, lemon juice, olive oil and parmesan, if using, in a food processor and process until finely chopped. Season with Himalayan salt and pepper.
3. Place the fish on a large plate. Coat the fish with the herb and almond mixture, pressing firmly into the flesh.
4. Place the fish, herb-side up, on the tray and bake for 12 minutes or until the fish flakes easily when tested with a fork. Serve drizzled with extra olive oil, if desired.

SERVES 4
PREP TIME: 25 MINUTES, INCLUDING COOKING

Asian-style Snapper

4 x 180 g snapper fillets, skin on

sliced red chilli, coriander leaves and lime wedges (to serve)

MARINADE

½ cup tamari

1 tbsp sesame oil

1 tbsp grated fresh ginger

1 tbsp Dijon mustard

¼ cup sliced spring onions

juice of 1 lemon

1 tbsp raw honey (optional)

1. In a large bowl, whisk together the marinade ingredients. Marinate the fish for up to 30 minutes in a covered bowl or in a large snap-lock bag.
2. Preheat the oven to 200°C (180°C fan-forced). Line a baking tray with baking paper.
3. Remove the fillets from the marinade. Reserve the marinade.
4. Lay the fish, skin-side down, on the lined tray and bake for 15–20 minutes or until cooked to your liking.
5. Drizzle the fish with the remaining marinade and serve with chilli, coriander and lime wedges.

SERVES 4
PREP TIME: 50 MINUTES, INCLUDING MARINATING AND COOKING

Curried Barramundi with Cavolo Nero

Looks and tastes exotic, but so simple to create. I love making this unique fish recipe and Dean loves it too!

1 tbsp Madras curry powder or any mild curry powder

¼ tsp turmeric

¼ tsp ground cinnamon

4 x 200 g barramundi fillets, skin on

Himalayan sea salt and ground pepper

1 tbsp virgin organic coconut oil

1 tbsp olive oil

1 clove garlic, crushed

1 tsp chilli flakes

1 leek, pale part only, thinly sliced

1 bunch cavolo nero, roughly chopped

2 tbsp water

⅓ cup Greek-style yoghurt

1 tbsp chopped mint

lemon wedges (to serve)

1. Preheat the oven to 180°C (160°C fan-forced). Line a baking tray with baking paper.

2. In a small bowl combine the curry powder, turmeric and cinnamon. Coat the whole barramundi fillets in the spice mix, and season.

3. Heat the coconut oil in a large non-stick frying pan over a medium–high heat. Cook the barramundi for 2 minutes on each side, or until lightly browned. Place the fillets on the lined tray and cook for 8 minutes, or until the fish is done to your liking.

4. Meanwhile, heat the olive oil in the cleaned frying pan and cook the garlic and chilli flakes for 1 minute. Add the leek and cook for 3–4 minutes or until softened. Add the cavolo nero and water and cook for 2–3 minutes or until wilted.

5. Combine the yoghurt and mint in a small bowl. Season.

6. Serve the barramundi with the leek and cavolo nero, the mint yoghurt and lemon wedges.

SERVES 4
PREP TIME: 25 MINUTES, INCLUDING COOKING

Prawn and Zucchini Noodles

A tasty, low-carb spin on seafood pasta. People are always amazed that you can make noodles out of veggies! You could also try konjac noodles instead of zucchini.

2 zucchini

2 cloves garlic, crushed

1 tbsp sesame oil

1 tbsp tamari

1 red chilli, seeded and thinly sliced (or to taste)

juice of 1 lime

1 capsicum, thinly sliced

2 spring onions, thinly sliced

300 g peeled tiger or king prawns, tails on (about 700 g unpeeled)

1 tbsp fish sauce (optional)

3 tbsp cashews

lime wedges and coriander sprigs (to serve)

1. To make the zucchini pasta, leave the skin on and, using a vegetable spiraliser or peeler, make noodle-like strips.
2. To a large frying pan or wok over a medium–low heat, add the garlic, sesame oil, tamari, chilli and lime juice. Cook for 1 minute.
3. Add the capsicum and spring onions and cook for 5 minutes or until tender. Add the zucchini and toss through well.
4. Add the prawns and fish sauce, if using, and continue to cook for another 3 minutes, stirring until the prawns are cooked through. Taste, and add extra sesame oil and tamari if needed.
5. Scatter over the cashews and serve with lime wedges and coriander.

SERVES 4
PREP TIME: 25 MINUTES, INCLUDING COOKING

Lemon and Herb Chicken

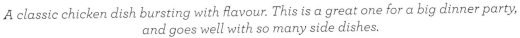

A classic chicken dish bursting with flavour. This is a great one for a big dinner party, and goes well with so many side dishes.

⅓ cup extra-virgin olive oil

juice and zest of 2 lemons

1 tbsp crushed garlic

2 tbsp rosemary, chopped + extra sprigs (to serve)

Himalayan pink rock salt and ground pepper

4 chicken breast fillets, beaten thin

lemon cheeks (to serve)

1. Preheat the oven to 200°C (180°C fan-forced). Line a large baking dish with baking paper.
2. In a large mixing bowl, combine all the ingredients except the chicken.
3. Place the chicken in the baking dish and pour over the marinade. Turn to coat well.
4. Bake in the oven for 20–25 minutes, turning frequently until cooked through.
5. Serve with extra rosemary and lemon cheeks.

SERVES 4
PREP TIME: 35 MINUTES, INCLUDING COOKING

Teriyaki Chicken

Most restaurant teriyaki dishes are high in sugar – this is a healthy, sugar-free alternative.

6 chicken thighs, fat trimmed, cut into 4 cm pieces

1 tbsp virgin organic coconut oil

1 clove garlic, crushed

1 tbsp finely grated fresh ginger

1 head broccoli, cut into florets

¼ small Chinese cabbage, finely shredded

2 spring onions, thinly sliced diagonally + extra (to serve)

1 tsp sesame seeds, toasted

⅓ cup Teriyaki Sauce (see page 259)

1. Make the Teriyaki Sauce in a shallow bowl or large snap-lock bag. Season and add the chicken, coating in the marinade. Refrigerate for 30 minutes. Drain the chicken from the marinade.
2. Melt the coconut oil in a large non-stick frying pan or wok over a medium–high heat. Add the garlic and ginger and cook for 1 minute, or until fragrant.
3. Add the chicken and stir-fry for 3–4 minutes or until the chicken is browned. Add the broccoli and cook for a further 3 minutes, or until the broccoli is tender. Add the cabbage and spring onions and cook for 1 minute, or until the cabbage is wilted and the chicken is cooked through.
4. Serve sprinkled with sesame seeds and the extra spring onions. Brown rice is a good accompaniment.

SERVES 4
PREP TIME: 50 MINUTES, INCLUDING MARINATING AND COOKING

Nicky's Herb-crusted Roast Chicken

A family favourite from my mummy, Nicky Sepel. Mum makes her famous roast chicken every Monday after family yoga and it's the best roast chicken you could ever eat.

1 whole organic chicken, washed and dried

juice of 1 lemon (reserve the shells to use for stuffing)

8 baby carrots, trimmed

1 red onion, quartered

1 cauliflower, cut into small florets

½ cup finely chopped mixed herbs (sage, rosemary and thyme)

1 clove garlic, crushed

1 tsp chilli flakes

1 tbsp cold-pressed extra-virgin olive oil

Himalayan salt and ground pepper

1 tbsp chopped parsley (to serve)

1. Preheat the oven to 200°C (180°C fan-forced).
2. Place the chicken in the middle of a large roasting pan.
3. Cut the juiced lemon into quarters and place inside the chicken cavity. Add the carrots, onion and cauliflower to the pan.
4. In a small bowl, mix the herbs, garlic, chilli flakes, olive oil, salt, pepper and lemon juice. Rub over the chicken.
5. Spray the veggies with olive oil.
6. Roast for 1½ hours, rotating the pan so the chicken browns evenly.
7. Remove the pan from the oven, cover loosely with foil and leave to rest for 10 minutes before carving. Sprinkle over the parsley and serve the chicken with the roast vegetables.

SERVES 6
PREP TIME: 1 HOUR 50 MINUTES, INCLUDING COOKING

Lettuce Burger and Eggplant Chips

Love a good burger and chips? Once again, you don't have to feel deprived when you embrace healthy living – you just need to swap out a few ingredients for a deeply delicious meal. My family and I go nuts for this one. You can use zucchini instead of eggplant to make the chips.

PATTIES

1 clove garlic, crushed

½ brown onion, finely chopped

500 g organic minced beef

2 tbsp almond meal

½ tsp ground cumin

½ tsp ground coriander

½ tsp chilli flakes

2 spring onions, finely chopped

1 egg, lightly beaten

1 tbsp olive oil

Himalayan salt and ground pepper

EGGPLANT CHIPS

1 eggplant, thinly sliced

1 tsp Himalayan sea salt

1 tsp spice blend of your choice

2 tbsp virgin organic coconut oil

1 clove garlic, crushed

butter lettuce leaves, sliced truss tomatoes, sliced pickles and organic tomato sauce (to serve)

1. To make the patties, combine all the ingredients, except the olive oil, in a large bowl. Season to taste and using your hands divide the mixture into 4 patties.
2. Heat the olive oil in a large non-stick frying pan over a medium–high heat, and cook the patties for 4–5 minutes on each side, or until cooked to your liking. Place on a plate and cover with foil to keep warm.
3. To make the eggplant chips, sprinkle the eggplant slices with the salt and spice blend. Heat the coconut oil in a large non-stick frying pan over a medium–high heat. Cook the garlic for 1 minute then cook the eggplant, in batches, for 2–3 minutes on each side, or until golden.
4. Place the eggplant on a plate lined with kitchen paper to drain.
5. To serve, lay a lettuce leaf on a plate, top with a meat patty, tomato and pickle slices and tomato sauce. Top with another lettuce leaf. Repeat with the remaining patties, and serve with eggplant chippies.

SERVES 4
PREP TIME: 30 MINUTES, INCLUDING COOKING

Slow-cooked Lamb Shoulder

A healthy take on Jamie Oliver's famous lamb shoulder. My last meal would be a slow-cooked lamb shoulder with cauliflower mash and a glass of Shiraz! Heaven. Can you tell I've thought about this?

2 kg organic lamb shoulder, bone in

1 bulb garlic, halved crossways + a few extra cloves, thinly sliced

a handful of rosemary sprigs

a handful of thyme sprigs

olive oil spray

Himalayan salt and ground pepper

½ tsp lemon zest

2 red onions, cut into wedges

2 small bulbs fennel, trimmed and quartered

3 carrots, roughly chopped

2 sticks celery, cut into pieces

1 large leek, pale part only, trimmed and cut into 4 cm pieces

2 tbsp tamari

cold-pressed extra-virgin olive oil spray

1. Preheat the oven to 200°C (180°C fan-forced).
2. Using a sharp knife, make 2 cm incisions over the lamb and insert the sliced garlic, rosemary and half the thyme. Spray the lamb with olive oil, season with salt, pepper and lemon zest and put it into a roasting pan.
3. Add the garlic, onions, fennel, carrots, celery and leek, then lay the remaining thyme over the vegetables. Spray the vegetables with olive oil and season. Drizzle the tamari over the meat.
4. Cover the pan tightly with two layers of foil and place in the oven. Reduce the temperature to 175°C (155°C fan-forced) and cook for 3½–4 hours, or until the lamb is tender and falling off the bone.
5. Gently break up the meat and pull out the bones then drizzle with extra tamari, if desired. Serve the lamb with the roasted garlic and vegetables.

SERVES 6
PREP TIME: 4 HOURS, 20 MINUTES, INCLUDING COOKING

Cauliflower Cottage Pie

Classic comfort food at its finest – my family loves this dish on cosy winter evenings.

1 tbsp extra-virgin olive oil

2 cloves garlic, crushed

1 red onion, finely chopped

500 g organic beef mince

1 carrot, finely diced

1 zucchini, finely diced

150 g green beans, trimmed and cut into 3 cm lengths

1 small head broccoli, cut into small florets

700 mL organic tomato passata

1 tbsp thyme

½ head cauliflower, cut into florets, steamed

¼ cup milk of choice

Himalayan salt and ground pepper

2 tbsp finely grated parmesan

2 tbsp chopped parsley (to serve)

1. Preheat the oven grill to medium–high. Lightly grease a baking dish (about 6-cup capacity).
2. In a large frying pan, heat the olive oil over a medium–high heat. Cook the garlic and onion for 5 minutes or until softened. Add the mince and cook for 5 minutes or until browned.
3. Add the carrot, zucchini, beans and broccoli to the pan, and cook for 3–4 minutes. Add the tomato passata and thyme, stir and cook for 10 minutes or until the vegetables are tender.
4. Season and spoon the mince mixture into the baking dish.
5. Place the cauliflower and milk in a large bowl and roughly mash. Season and spoon over the mince. Sprinkle with the parmesan and lightly spray the top with olive oil.
6. Grill for 5 minutes, or until lightly browned.
7. Serve sprinkled with chopped parsley.

SERVES 4
PREP TIME: 45 MINUTES, INCLUDING COOKING

Quinoa Sushi

A healthier take on traditional sushi. So nutritious and packed with flavour.
It's a total crowd-pleaser as a starter for a dinner party.

1 cup quinoa (red, white or mixed)

nori (seaweed) sheets

2 tbsp hummus or Dijon mustard

1 avocado, sliced

2 Lebanese cucumbers, thinly sliced

¼ red or white cabbage, shredded

cos lettuce, shredded

2 carrots, thinly sliced

150 g tuna, chicken breast, lean meat or egg (optional)

DRESSING

1 tbsp tahini

1 tbsp rice vinegar or apple cider vinegar

1 tsp maple syrup

juice of ½ lemon

SIDES

pickled ginger

tamari

wasabi

sweet chilli sauce

1. Cook the quinoa according to the packet instructions. Drain and set aside to cool.

2. In a small bowl, mix together all the dressing ingredients and stir through the quinoa.

3. Place a sushi mat on a chopping board (it's okay if you don't have a mat – do this manually with cling wrap). Top with a sheet of seaweed, shiny-side down, and spread the hummus onto the seaweed.

4. Dip your hands in water and spread some quinoa evenly over the nori, leaving a 1 cm border along the edge furthest from you.

5. Arrange the vegetables in a row across the nori. Be careful not to overfill to avoid the rolls bursting. Add a protein, if desired.

6. Holding the edge of the mat with your thumb, lift it along with the filling and roll away from you. Hold the filling as you roll and gently pull the mat as you continue rolling. Once you have a neat roll, fold your hands over the mat to tighten the roll. Moisten the edge of the nori with water to seal.

7. Slide the roll off the mat and use a very sharp knife to cut it into individual pieces.

8. Serve with your choice of sides such as pickled ginger, tamari, wasabi and sweet chilli sauce.

SERVES 4
PREP TIME: 50 MINUTES, INCLUDING COOKING

Grass-fed Eye Fillet with Sautéed Garlic and Thyme Mushrooms

Absolutely decadent! My go-to recipe when I'm craving iron. If you're a non-vegetarian remember to eat approximately two serves of red meat a week.

⅓ cup olive oil

4 cloves garlic, crushed

⅓ cup basil leaves, finely chopped

Himalayan salt and ground pepper

4 x 180 g beef eye-fillet steaks, fat trimmed

400 g brown mushrooms, sliced

2 tbsp thyme

baby spinach leaves

1. Make a basil oil by combining ¼ cup of the olive oil, half of the crushed garlic, the basil, salt and pepper in a small bowl. Set aside.

2. Heat a lightly greased chargrill pan or barbecue to a medium–high heat. Season the steaks, and cook to your liking, 4–5 minutes each side for medium-rare. Set the steaks aside on a plate, cover with foil and rest for 10 minutes.

3. Meanwhile, heat the remaining olive oil in a large non-stick frying pan and cook the remaining garlic for 1 minute. Add the mushrooms and cook for 3–4 minutes, or until tender and golden brown. Toss the thyme through the mushrooms and season.

4. Top the steaks with the basil oil, and serve with the garlic mushrooms and baby spinach leaves.

SERVES 4
PREP TIME: 20 MINUTES, INCLUDING COOKING

Herbed Chicken Schnitzel

Another favourite comfort food, but the traditional version is not the healthiest. This 'healthified' version tastes just as delicious.

1 cup almond meal

zest of 1 lemon

⅓ cup finely chopped mixed herbs (sage, parsley and thyme)

2 tbsp finely grated parmesan

2 free-range or organic eggs, lightly beaten

1 tbsp milk of choice

1 clove garlic, crushed

Himalayan salt and ground pepper

2 organic chicken breast fillets, sliced in half lengthways

1 tbsp olive oil

lemon wedges (to serve)

1. In a large shallow bowl, combine the almond meal, lemon zest, herbs and parmesan.
2. In a separate large shallow bowl, whisk the egg, milk and garlic, and season with salt and pepper.
3. Dip the chicken into the egg mixture, then coat evenly in the almond mix.
4. Heat the olive oil in a large non-stick frying pan over a medium heat and cook for 3–4 minutes on each side or until the chicken is lightly golden and cooked through.
5. Serve with lemon wedges and Cauliflower Rice below.

SERVES 4
PREP TIME: 25 MINUTES, INCLUDING COOKING

Cauliflower Rice

A unique preparation of cauliflower that is a deceptively easy replacement for standard rice when you're looking to pack more of a veggie punch into a meal.

1 head cauliflower, cut into florets

2 tbsp olive or virgin organic coconut oil

1 leek, thinly sliced

1 clove garlic, crushed

2 tsp mild curry powder

1 tsp Cajun spice mix

1 tsp turmeric

½ tsp ground cinnamon

1 tsp Celtic sea salt

ground pepper

¼ cup chopped walnuts

¼ cup chopped parsley leaves

1. Process the cauliflower florets until they reach a rice-like consistency, about 20 seconds depending on your machine.
2. Heat the olive oil in a large non-stick frying pan over a medium heat.
3. Add the leek and garlic, and cook for 3–4 minutes.
4. Add the cauliflower, spices and seasoning and cook for a further 5 minutes or until lightly golden.
5. Scatter the cauliflower with walnuts and parsley to serve.

SERVES 4
PREP TIME: 20 MINUTES, INCLUDING COOKING

Cauliflower Pizza

Who doesn't love Friday-night pizza with the family? My family and I make our own cauliflower-pizza variations. I top my personal pizza with leek, mushroom, parmesan and rocket.

½ head cauliflower, cut into florets

1 free-range or organic egg, lightly beaten

1 onion, finely chopped

1 tsp ground cumin

1 tsp ground coriander

1 tsp finely chopped rosemary

1 tsp finely chopped sage

1 tsp cold-pressed extra-virgin olive oil

Himalayan salt and ground pepper

toppings of your choice

1. Preheat the oven to 180°C (160°C fan-forced). Line a large baking tray with baking paper.
2. In a food processor, pulse the cauliflower until it's the consistency of fine crumbs. You can either steam the cauliflower first or use it raw; it works both ways.
3. Place the cauliflower in a clean tea towel and squeeze out as much moisture as possible. The key is to make a crisp pizza base.
4. To a mixing bowl, add the cauliflower and combine with the egg, onion, spices, herbs, olive oil, salt and pepper.
5. Place the cauliflower mixture in the centre of the tray. Lay a second sheet of baking paper on top and use your palms or a rolling pin to flatten into a circle.
6. Bake for 20–25 minutes or until the base is firm and slightly browned.
7. Remove from the oven and top with your favourite ingredients. You may also want to add more seasoning, plus some extra olive oil.
8. Return the pizza to the oven for another 10–15 minutes.
9. Take the pizza out of the oven and cool for a few minutes before slicing.

SERVES 2
PREP TIME: 55 MINUTES, INCLUDING COOKING

CAULIFLOWER PIZZA VARIATIONS

- Leek, parmesan and mushroom
- Goat's cheese, Homemade Walnut Pesto (see page 252) and tomato
- Eggplant, basil and mozzarella

I also love broccoli, beans, sliced zucchini, onion and avocado.

Tomato and Basil Zucchini Pasta

I grew up LOVING pasta – especially pesto pasta. This is the healthy version.
It tastes just as good and won't leave you feeling bloated.

6 zucchini

2 tbsp olive oil

1 clove garlic, crushed

1 long red chilli, seeded and finely chopped

1 200 g punnet cherry tomatoes, halved

400 g tin baby Roma tomatoes

¼ cup basil, roughly chopped + small basil leaves to garnish

Himalayan salt and ground pepper

2 tbsp Homemade Walnut Pesto (see page 252)

4 tbsp ricotta (optional)

parmesan shavings (to serve, optional)

1. Using a vegetable spiraliser, vegetable peeler or knife, shave the zucchini into thin, noodle-like strips. If you want a fettuccine-like pasta, use the vegetable peeler.

2. Heat the olive oil in a large non-stick frying pan over a medium heat. Cook the garlic and chilli for 1–2 minutes or until fragrant.

3. Add the cherry tomatoes and cook for 2–3 minutes, or until slightly softened. Add the tinned tomatoes and cook for 10 minutes, or until slightly reduced.

4. Add the zucchini to the pan and cook for 5 minutes. Stir through the chopped basil and season.

5. Serve the zucchini pasta topped with the pesto, ricotta, parmesan, if using, and whole basil leaves.

SERVES 4
PREP TIME: 30 MINUTES, INCLUDING COOKING

Burnt Sage and Parmesan Pasta

A delicious gluten-free vegetarian dish – rich and so satisfying. We cooked this dish on a family holiday in Byron Bay and all agreed it had to be in this book!

200 g mung bean pasta

¼ cup olive oil + extra (to serve, optional)

2 cloves garlic, finely chopped

⅓ cup sage leaves

2 tsp grated lemon zest

1½ cups baby rocket

Himalayan salt and ground pepper

shaved parmesan (to serve)

1. Cook the pasta in a large saucepan of boiling salted water according to the packet instructions. Drain and set aside.
2. Meanwhile, heat the olive oil in a large non-stick frying pan over a medium–high heat and cook the garlic and sage until the sage is crisp.
3. Add the pasta to the pan with the lemon zest and baby rocket. Season and toss to combine.
4. Serve the pasta topped with shaved parmesan and a drizzle of olive oil, if desired.

SERVES 4 AS AN ENTRÉE
PREP TIME: 20 MINUTES, INCLUDING COOKING

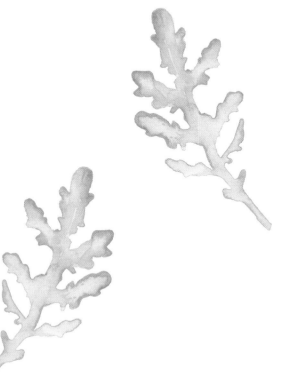

Chicken Teriyaki Bowl

1 tbsp Teriyaki Sauce (see page 259)

½ cup cooked brown rice

150 g chicken breast fillet, grilled, poached or steamed

1 cup broccoli florets, steamed

½ avocado, sliced

1 tsp sesame seeds, toasted

1 spring onion, thinly sliced

1. Prepare the Teriyaki Sauce.
2. Place the rice, sliced chicken, broccoli and avocado in a bowl. Sprinkle with sesame seeds and spring onions and drizzle with the sauce to serve.

SERVES 1
PREP TIME: 20 MINUTES, INCLUDING COOKING

Crunchy Lettuce Cups

2 cups cooked quinoa

1 head broccoli, cut into florets, steamed and cooled

1 zucchini, coarsely grated

1 carrot, coarsely grated

¼ cabbage, finely shredded

100 g snowpeas, trimmed and thinly sliced

1 tomato, diced

2 spring onions, thinly sliced

¼ cup coriander leaves

Himalayan salt and ground pepper

1 avocado, mashed

juice of ½ lemon

½ tsp Moroccan spice

12 lettuce leaves

¼ cup walnuts, chopped

1 tbsp sunflower seeds

Tahini Lemon Dressing (see page 258)

1. In a large bowl combine the quinoa, broccoli, zucchini, carrot, cabbage, snowpeas, tomato, spring onions and coriander. Season and gently toss together.
2. Combine the avocado, lemon juice and Moroccan spice in a small bowl. Season.
3. Prepare the Tahini Lemon Dressing in a small bowl and season to taste.
4. To serve, lay the lettuce leaves on a platter, spoon some of the quinoa mix into the leaf, and drizzle with the dressing. Serve with the walnuts and seeds scattered over, and a dollop of avocado.
5. Optional: Add 1 serve of your choice of protein. Try chicken, tuna, egg or lean meat.

SERVES 4
PREP TIME: 35 MINUTES, INCLUDING COOKING

Step-by-Step Stir-Fry

Quick, simple, versatile and so delicious – stir-fries are my go-to meal when I'm pressed for time or need to use up a fridge full of veggies.

ONE

Choose your protein. Try chicken breast strips, turkey breast strips, tempeh, grass-fed beef strips, lean lamb strips, salmon, white fish, prawns, seafood or 1–2 eggs. Allow 150 g per person, or about the size of your palm. Melt 1 tbsp coconut oil or olive oil in a wok and stir-fry until it's slightly undercooked. Remove from wok and set aside.

TWO

In a clean wok, melt 1 tbsp coconut oil or olive oil and stir-fry your choice of the following:
- 1 clove garlic, thinly sliced
- ginger, thinly sliced or grated
- ½ leek, pale part only, sliced
- 1 red or brown onion
- 2 spring onions, sliced

THREE

Now add at least 2 cups of vegetables with as many greens as possible. Stir-fry for about 3–4 minutes or until cooked. Choose from the following:
- green beans
- broccolini or broccoli
- Brussels sprouts, shredded
- carrots
- cauliflower florets
- celery
- fresh organic baby corn
- eggplant
- mushrooms
- snowpeas
- yellow squash
- zucchini

FOUR

Place the protein back in the wok and add your choice of leafy greens and/or noodles. Cook for another 3 minutes. Choose from:

Leafy greens
- beansprouts
- bok choy
- cabbage
- kale
- silverbeet
- spinach

Noodles
- black bean noodles
- kelp noodles
- konjac noodles
- mung bean noodles
- soba noodles
- zucchini noodles

FIVE

Add extra flavour from the following list and stir-fry for 2 minutes:
- 1 tsp chopped fresh chilli or chilli flakes
- a handful of coriander, basil, parsley or mint leaves
- 3 tbsp lemon or lime zest or juice
- 1 tbsp tamari

SIX

Serve topped with your choice of:
- a handful of raw cashews
- chopped coriander, thinly sliced spring onions or other herbs of choice
- beansprouts
- snowpea sprouts
- a handful of toasted sesame seeds

More Main Meal Ideas

Think lean protein and greens, greens, greens.

- **Lean grass-fed beef** with roast vegetables and a side salad.
- **Quinoa or brown rice sushi with salad.** Enjoy 2 big rolls with extra sashimi, but no more than twice a week due to the mercury content.
- **Spinach and mushroom omelette** with a side of avocado and a green salad.
- **Vegetable stir-fry with protein**, using tamari instead of soy sauce.
- **Stir-fried bok choy with chicken breast fillet.**
- **Baked mushrooms** stuffed with ricotta and herbs plus a poached egg.
- **Grilled salmon or snapper** with Cauliflower Mash or Broccoli Mash (see page 229).
- **Vegetarian lasagne with salad.**
- **Slice of pumpernickel/Ezekiel bread** topped with hummus, rocket and a sliced boiled egg.
- **Lentil and vegetable soup.** It doesn't get more nutritious than that!
- **Chicken tenderloins** marinated in rosemary, cold-pressed extra-virgin olive oil, 1 crushed clove garlic and lemon juice. Serve with baked sweet potato and a green salad.
- **Lamb backstraps.** Serve with pesto, green beans and a side salad and/or sautéed kale (cooked in virgin organic coconut oil and seasoned with rock salt, chilli and ground pepper).

- **Sesame salmon fillet.** Marinate in tamari, ginger, sesame seeds and lemon juice, and serve with steamed asparagus, green beans and broccoli.
- **Steamed fish** with ginger, shallots, bok choy and broccolini. Super healthy and easy to make, this is a winner on a weekday night.
- **Beef fillet** with sautéed mushrooms, leeks, onion and spinach.
- **Cajun-spiced Dory** with roasted fennel and cauliflower. Serve with a green salad.
- **Grilled chicken breast** or thigh fillet on top of a green salad with a dressing of natural yoghurt, cold-pressed extra-virgin olive oil, lemon juice, salt and pepper.
- **Egg salad** with asparagus, spinach, pumpkin seeds and quinoa. Add Tahini Lemon Dressing (see page 258).
- **Zucchini 'bolognese'** with lean beef or chicken mince. Like pasta, only loaded with nutritional value!

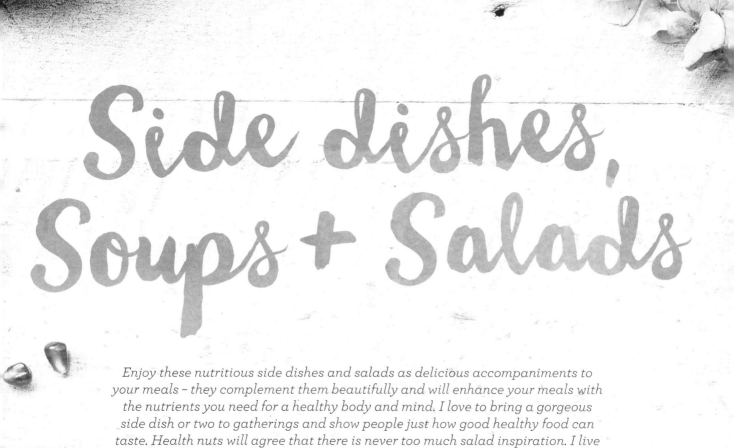

Side dishes, Soups + Salads

Enjoy these nutritious side dishes and salads as delicious accompaniments to your meals – they complement them beautifully and will enhance your meals with the nutrients you need for a healthy body and mind. I love to bring a gorgeous side dish or two to gatherings and show people just how good healthy food can taste. Health nuts will agree that there is never too much salad inspiration. I live on salads – they do beautiful things for my culinary creativity, my senses and my energy. Enjoy these salads – they keep me happy all day and they'll be life-changing for you too. And remember never be afraid to eat more greens!

Salad Basics

STEP 1

Choose the base. Put 2 cups of any of the following in a large bowl:
- mixed lettuce
- spinach
- rocket
- kale
- cos or iceberg lettuce

STEP 2

Add your favourite vegetables. I like to add leftover roast vegetables. Try to make your mix as colourful as possible! Go for any of the following:
- carrots
- cucumber
- tomato
- celery
- red onion or spring onions
- mushrooms
- red or white cabbage
- zucchini shavings
- green beans or snowpeas
- red or green capsicum
- steamed cauliflower
- steamed broccoli
- fennel

STEP 3

Throw in your choice of protein:
- 150 g chicken
- 150–200 g fish
- 150 g lean meat
- 2 eggs
- 120 g tempeh
- 3–4 tbsp cheese (e.g. cottage cheese, fetta, goat's cheese or ricotta)
- ½ cup cooked lentils or quinoa + ½ cup beans (e.g. chickpeas, or kidney, lima or cannellini beans)

STEP 4

Include a fat source:
- 1 tbsp tahini
- ¼ avocado
- 1 tbsp hummus
- a handful of nuts or seeds
- 1 tbsp Homemade Walnut Pesto (see page 252)

STEP 5

Add your choice of complex carbohydrates or starchy veggies:
- ½ cup cooked sweet potato
- ½ cup cooked pumpkin
- ½ cup cooked beetroot or raw shredded beetroot
- ⅓ cup cooked quinoa
- ½ cup cooked brown rice

STEP 6

See salad dressing ideas on page 258 or make your own dressing with these ingredients:
- cold-pressed extra-virgin olive oil
- cold-pressed flaxseed oil
- sesame oil
- lemon or lime juice
- crushed garlic
- grated fresh ginger
- tahini
- balsamic vinegar
- apple cider vinegar
- wholegrain or Dijon mustard
- miso paste
- tamari
- almond butter
- Himalayan pink rock salt
- ground pepper
- add sprouts or herbs to your salad for an extra nutrient hit, e.g. parsley, mint, dill or coriander and either mung beans, bean sprouts or green salad sprouts.

My Super Clean Dressing

My go-to daily salad dressing – it perfectly highlights any veggie combo. I often triple the ingredients and keep it in the fridge – it lasts the whole week!

⅓ cup apple cider vinegar or white wine vinegar

1 tbsp Dijon mustard

1 tbsp cold-pressed extra-virgin olive oil

juice of ½ lemon

1 tbsp tahini

a pinch of Himalayan salt and ground pepper

1 tsp maple syrup or stevia powder (optional)

1. Combine all the ingredients and whisk well.

SERVES 1
PREP TIME: 5 MINUTES

Cauliflower and Pomegranate Salad

This is a salad my mum taught me to make, inspired by Yotam Ottolenghi. We love making this for lunch and typically add about 100 g goat's cheese too.

1 head cauliflower, cut into small florets

1 tbsp each: cumin seeds, coriander seeds and fennel seeds, pounded using a pestle and mortar

1 clove garlic, crushed

2 tbsp cold-pressed extra-virgin olive oil

chilli flakes

Himalayan salt and ground pepper

½ cup mixed coriander and parsley leaves, roughly chopped

½ cup pomegranate seeds

½ cup toasted hazelnuts or almonds, roughly chopped

1 tbsp pomegranate molasses

1. Preheat the oven to 200°C (180°C fan-forced).
2. Place the cauliflower in a baking dish and sprinkle with the spices, garlic, 1 tbsp of the olive oil and chilli flakes to taste. Season with salt and pepper. Toss well to coat and place in the oven for 20 minutes or until tender and lightly golden. Set aside to cool for 10 minutes.
3. Place the cauliflower in a large salad bowl and add the chopped herbs, pomegranate seeds and roasted hazelnuts or almonds.
4. Toss together, and drizzle with the pomegranate molasses and remaining olive oil before serving.

SERVES 6
PREP TIME: 40 MINUTES, INCLUDING COOKING

Kale, Fennel, Avocado and Almond Salad

A total superfood bowl – and just wait until you try the green garlic dressing.
This salad tastes lovely when heavily dressed and is inspired by the wholefood website 101
Cookbooks. Try adding a poached egg for an appetising variation.

SALAD

½ bunch kale, stems removed and leaves torn

1 small bulb fennel, thinly sliced, fronds reserved for garnish

1 avocado, sliced

½ cup roasted almonds, roughly chopped

GREEN DRESSING

2 spring onions, thinly sliced

juice of 1 lemon

1 clove garlic, roughly chopped

⅓ cup cold-pressed extra-virgin olive oil

½ avocado, chopped

1 tsp raw honey or maple syrup

¼ cup basil, roughly chopped

Himalayan salt and ground pepper

1. To make the green dressing, purée all the ingredients together with a stick blender or in a food processor. Taste and adjust with more seasoning, honey or lemon juice.

2. Combine the kale with about half of the dressing in a large bowl. Use your hands to work the dressing into the kale – it will soften slightly.

3. Add the fennel, more dressing, a couple of pinches of salt, then toss again.

4. Add the avocado and almonds, and toss gently one last time. Drizzle the salad with the remaining dressing and garnish with the fennel fronds.

SERVES 4
PREP TIME: 20 MINUTES

Mixed Bean, Hazelnut and Goat's Cheese Salad

This vegetarian salad is packed with protein and healthy fats from beans, nuts and cheese – perfect for a vegetarian meal.

4 cups green beans, topped and tailed, halved lengthways

2 cups cooked or tinned beans (mix of lima, chickpeas, kidney and/or cannellini)

½ cup hazelnuts or almonds, chopped

100 g goat's cheese or fetta

a handful of fresh mint and parsley leaves

Himalayan salt and ground pepper

DRESSING

1 tbsp tahini

juice of ½ lemon

2 tbsp apple cider vinegar

1 tsp wholegrain mustard

1. To make the dressing, whisk all the ingredients together and set aside.
2. Steam the green beans for 3–4 minutes or until tender. When cooked, remove from the heat and rinse under cold water.
3. Combine the green beans, mixed beans, hazelnuts, goat's cheese and herbs in a large bowl. Add the dressing and season to taste with salt and pepper.

SERVES 6
PREP TIME: 20 MINUTES, INCLUDING COOKING

Parmesan Asparagus

Such an easy side dish that takes no time to make and goes with absolutely everything.

2 bunches asparagus, trimmed

1½ tbsp olive oil

½ tsp ground cumin

½ tsp ground coriander

Himalayan salt and ground pepper

¼ cup finely grated parmesan

2 tbsp finely chopped parsley

lemon wedges (to serve)

1. In a large bowl toss together the asparagus, olive oil, cumin, coriander, salt and pepper.
2. Heat a chargrill pan or barbecue to a medium–high heat, and cook the asparagus for 6–8 minutes or until tender, turning regularly.
3. Sprinkle with parmesan and parsley and serve with lemon wedges.

SERVES 4
PREP TIME: 20 MINUTES, INCLUDING COOKING

Green Bean and Roast Beetroot Salad

My aunty Cathy makes this salad, and it's so delicious I have to share it. Cath is a huge inspiration to me in the kitchen. She is vegetarian, so she really knows how to use vegetables. She has a talent for putting wholefoods together and creating magical dishes that are both tasty and nutritious.
I am so grateful for all your inspiration, Cath.
Beetroot is a delicious superfood – comment on nutritional benefits

4 whole beetroot, peeled and diced into small cubes

olive oil

Himalayan salt and ground pepper

200 g green beans, topped and tailed, halved lengthways

1 orange capsicum, halved and seeded

1 red capsicum, halved and seeded

1 yellow capsicum, halved and seeded

2 large handfuls of mixed lettuce leaves

100 g goat's cheese or fetta, crumbled

2 tbsp cold-pressed extra-virgin olive oil

2 tbsp balsamic vinegar

½ cup roughly chopped roasted walnuts

a handful of fresh mint leaves, roughly chopped

1. Preheat the oven to 190°C (170°C fan-forced).
2. Toss the beetroot in the olive oil and season well with salt and pepper. Roast for 45 minutes or until tender.
3. Roast the capsicums on a baking tray until the skins shrink. When they are ready, cool and rinse under water to peel.
4. Steam the beans for 4–5 minutes or until tender.
5. Place the mixed lettuce leaves on a large platter. Top with the beans, beetroot and sliced roasted capsicum, followed by the cheese. Drizzle the extra-virgin olive oil and balsamic vinegar over the salad and scatter over the walnuts and mint leaves to serve.

SERVES 6
PREP TIME: 1 HOUR, INCLUDING COOKING

Detox Salad

My go-to salad during a seasonal cleanse. It's the perfect way to detox your liver without sacrificing your tastebuds. This salad also works well if topped with a portion of your favourite protein.

⅛ red cabbage, shredded

⅛ white cabbage, shredded

1 carrot, grated

1 cup broccoli florets, steamed

½ cup baby spinach or rocket

¼ cup walnuts

¼ cup chopped spring onions

½ avocado, sliced

½ cup sliced fennel

¼ cup roughly chopped parsley

2 tbsp mixed raw seeds

½ pear, cored and sliced (optional)

DRESSING

1 tsp ground turmeric

juice of ½ lemon

1 tbsp Dijon mustard

1 clove garlic, crushed

2 tbsp apple cider vinegar

1 tsp tahini

1 tsp raw honey or stevia powder

Himalayan salt and ground pepper

1. Combine all the salad ingredients in a large salad bowl and mix well.
2. In a separate bowl, whisk the dressing ingredients together and season to taste. Drizzle the salad with the dressing and serve.

SERVES 2
PREP TIME: 15 MINUTES

Eggplant with Tahini Dressing and Pomegranate

A creamy tahini dressing enhances eggplant's smoky flavour, and the pop of pomegranate is out of this world. A recipe inspired by Yotam Ottolenghi.

2 large, long eggplants

⅓ cup cold-pressed extra-virgin olive oil + extra (to serve)

1 tbsp lemon thyme + extra whole sprigs to garnish

Himalayan salt and ground pepper

1 pomegranate

1 tbsp zaatar

TAHINI DRESSING

4 tbsp tahini

½ cup Greek-style yoghurt

juice of 1 lemon

2 tbsp cold-pressed extra-virgin olive oil

1 small clove garlic, crushed

a pinch of salt

1. Preheat the oven to 200°C (180°C fan-forced).
2. Cut the eggplants in half lengthways. Use a small sharp knife to make 4–5 parallel incisions in the cut side of each eggplant half, without cutting through to the skin. Repeat at a 90-degree angle to get a diamond-shaped pattern.
3. Place the eggplant halves, cut-side up, on a baking tray lined with baking paper. Brush the eggplant with the olive oil until all of the oil is absorbed. Sprinkle with the lemon thyme and season with salt and pepper. Roast for 35–40 minutes, until the flesh is tender and golden.
4. Meanwhile cut the pomegranate in half. Hold one half over a bowl, with the cut side against your palm, and use the back of a wooden spoon or a rolling pin to gently knock on the pomegranate shell. Continue beating until the seeds start falling between your fingers into the bowl. Sift through them to remove any bits of membrane.
5. To make the tahini dressing, whisk together all the ingredients. Refrigerate until needed.
6. To serve, drizzle the eggplant with the dressing. Sprinkle the zaatar and pomegranate seeds on top and garnish with lemon thyme. Finish with a drizzle of olive oil.

SERVES 4
PREP TIME: 55 MINUTES, INCLUDING COOKING

Cauliflower Mash

Love, love, love! The smooth, creamy texture makes this mash such a winner – your family will honestly not know the difference between this and mashed potato. It goes so well with protein and it's very low in carbs, which is a good thing at dinnertime, in my opinion. Cauliflower is a real superfood – packed with vitamin C, antioxidants and it's a great liver cleanser.

1 head cauliflower, cut into florets

⅓ cup milk of choice

1 tbsp virgin organic coconut oil or organic butter

3 tbsp crushed walnuts

Himalayan salt and ground pepper

1 tsp paprika (to serve)

1. Steam the cauliflower until cooked, approximately 10–15 minutes. Let it cool.
2. Add the milk, coconut oil or butter, and walnuts to the cauliflower, then purée the mixture with a food processor or stick blender until smooth. If it's too thick, add a little water. Season with salt and pepper, and serve sprinkled with the paprika.

Broccoli Mash

Who knew broccoli could be so versatile? This simple side perfectly accompanies any dinner.

2 heads broccoli, roughly chopped

⅓ cup milk of choice

1 tbsp cold-pressed extra-virgin olive oil

1 tbsp lemon juice

Himalayan salt and ground pepper

1 tbsp grated parmesan

1. Steam or boil the broccoli until cooked. Let it cool.
2. Using a food processor, process until the broccoli reaches a mash consistency. Add the milk, olive oil and lemon juice. Season and process until blended. Or you can use a potato masher or stick blender. Sprinkle with parmesan to serve.

Sweet Potato Mash

Sweet potatoes are chock full of vitamins and carotenoids – you'll love this nutrient-packed spin on classic mashed potato. Delicious with my Slow-cooked Lamb Shoulder (see page 193).

2 large orange sweet potatoes, peeled and cut into small cubes

⅓ cup milk of choice

1 tbsp organic butter or cold-pressed extra-virgin olive oil

1 tsp ground cinnamon + extra (to serve)

Himalayan salt and ground pepper

1. Place the sweet potatoes in a large saucepan, add enough water to cover and bring to the boil.
2. Reduce the heat to medium, cover and simmer for 10–12 minutes or until the sweet potatoes are tender. Or you can steam them.
3. When the sweet potatoes are soft and tender, drain and return to the saucepan. Add the milk, butter or olive oil, cinnamon, salt and pepper and mash together using either a potato masher or stick blender. Serve sprinkled with a little extra cinnamon.

SERVES 4
PREP TIME: 25 MINUTES, INCLUDING COOKING

Mediterranean Roasted Eggplant

2 eggplants

Himalayan salt and ground pepper

6 ripe tomatoes, roughly chopped

¼ cup basil leaves, chopped + small leaves (to garnish)

½ tsp chilli flakes

2 tbsp cold-pressed extra-virgin olive oil

shaved parmesan cheese (to serve)

1. Cut the eggplants in half and sprinkle with salt, then leave for 1 hour. Rinse off the salt and dry. Cut the eggplants in half again lengthways, and score into squares with a knife.

2. Preheat the oven to 175°C (155°C fan-forced).

3. Combine the tomatoes, chopped basil and chilli flakes in a large bowl, using the back of a wooden spoon to lightly crush the tomatoes.

4. Coat the eggplants generously with olive oil and season with salt and pepper. Bake for 45 minutes.

5. Take the eggplants out of the oven and spoon over the tomato mixture. Bake again for 15 minutes or until golden brown.

6. Serve with the extra basil leaves and parmesan.

SERVES 4
PREP TIME: 2 HOURS, INCLUDING RESTING AND COOKING

Tomato and Basil-Stuffed Capsicum

*Simple and a classic – a great vegetarian meal. Or add minced
chicken or turkey to boost the protein factor.*

4 red capsicums

1½ 200 g punnets cherry tomatoes, roughly chopped

1 small red onion, finely chopped

1 clove garlic, finely chopped

1 rosemary sprig, chopped

a handful of basil leaves, roughly chopped + small leaves (to serve)

Himalayan salt and ground pepper

2 tbsp cold-pressed extra-virgin olive oil

2 tbsp ricotta

1. Preheat the oven to 180°C (160°C fan-forced).
2. Cut the tops off the capsicums, leaving the stems attached (these will be your lids). Remove the seeds and membranes and discard.
3. Mix together the tomatoes, onion, garlic, rosemary and chopped basil.
4. Fill the capsicums with the vegetable mixture. Season with salt and pepper.
5. Place the 'lids' on top, drizzle with the olive oil and bake for 20–25 minutes or until cooked through.
6. Serve topped with the ricotta and basil leaves.

SERVES 4
PREP TIME: 35 MINUTES, INCLUDING COOKING

Roast Eggplant with Sage and Goat's Cheese

Inspired and taught to me by my biggest cooking inspo, my mum, Nicky Sepel.

2 eggplants

1 tbsp Himalayan salt and ground pepper

2 tbsp olive oil

¼ cup finely chopped sage

¼ tsp chilli flakes

60 g goat's cheese, crumbled

¼ cup roughly chopped parsley

lemon wedges (to serve)

1. Preheat the oven to 200°C (180°C fan-forced).
2. Slice the eggplants in half lenghways, sprinkle with salt and leave to stand for 1 hour.
3. Rinse off the salt and pat the eggplants dry with paper towels. Score the flesh in a diamond pattern. Put the eggplants on a baking tray lined with baking paper.
4. In a small bowl, mix together the olive oil, sage and chilli flakes. Season with salt and pepper.
5. Spoon the mixture over the eggplants and bake for 35–40 minutes or until tender and browned.
6. Remove from the oven, scatter over the goat's cheese and parsley and serve with lemon wedges, if desired.

SERVES 4
PREP TIME: 1 HOUR 50 MINUTES, INCLUDING RESTING AND COOKING

Zucchini and Mint Soup

This warming soup gets a pop of flavour from the mint.

¼ cup cold-pressed extra-virgin olive oil + extra (to drizzle, optional)

2 cloves garlic, crushed

2 leeks, pale part only, sliced

6 zucchini, sliced

½ tsp chilli flakes

½ tsp ground coriander

½ tsp ground cumin

Himalayan salt and ground pepper

4 cups organic chicken stock

⅓ cup mint leaves, finely chopped + extra leaves (to serve)

2 tbsp goat's cheese, crumbled (to serve)

2 tbsp roughly chopped almonds (to serve)

1. Heat the olive oil in a large saucepan over a medium heat and cook the garlic and leeks for 5 minutes, or until softened. Add the zucchini, chilli flakes, coriander, cumin, salt and pepper and cook for about 5 minutes.
2. Add the chicken stock and enough water to cover the vegetables, then bring to the boil.
3. Reduce the heat to a simmer and cook for 30 minutes or until the zucchini is tender.
4. Using either a stick blender or food processor, blend the soup until smooth. Stir through the chopped mint.
5. To serve, scatter the extra mint leaves, goat's cheese and almonds over the soup. Season and drizzle the soup with olive oil, if desired.

SERVES 4
PREP TIME: 50 MINUTES, INCLUDING COOKING

Broccoli Soup

A healthy twist on the creamy, comforting classic. Recipe by Robyn Kaufman.

⅓ cup virgin organic coconut oil

1 leek, pale part only, finely chopped

1 chilli, seeded and finely chopped or use chilli flakes

Himalayan salt and ground pepper

2 heads broccoli, chopped coarsely (including stems)

4–5 cups vegetable stock

cold-pressed extra-virgin olive oil (to serve)

parmesan (to serve)

crushed walnuts (optional)

1. Melt the coconut oil in a large soup pot and lightly fry the leek, chilli and 1 tsp salt.
2. Once the leek is golden (after about 10 minutes), add the broccoli and the stock, and bring to the boil. Cover and simmer for about 20 minutes.
3. Once the soup is ready, use a stick blender to finely purée the mixture. Add extra salt and pepper to taste.
4. Serve drizzled with the olive oil and parmesan. Top with crushed walnuts, if desired.

SERVES 6
PREP TIME: 35 MINUTES, INCLUDING COOKING

Japanese Broccolini and Green Bean Salad

1 head broccoli, cut into florets

2 bunches broccolini, halved

250 g green beans

2 tbsp olive oil

juice of ½ lemon

2 tbsp roughly chopped Brazil nuts

½ tsp chilli flakes

DRESSING

⅓ cup rice wine vinegar

1 tbsp rice malt syrup

1 tbsp sesame oil

1 tbsp tamari

1 tbsp grated fresh ginger

1 tbsp sesame seeds

1. Steam the broccoli, broccolini and green beans until tender. Drain and set aside to cool slightly.
2. Place the vegetables in a large bowl, and drizzle with the olive oil and lemon juice. Season and toss to combine.
3. Whisk the dressing ingredients in a small bowl and pour over the vegetables. Scatter over the Brazil nuts and chilli flakes to serve.

SERVES 6
PREP TIME: 25 MINUTES, INCLUDING COOKING

Broccoli Rice

A twist on my classic Cauliflower Rice (see page 201). This is the perfect base for your protein of choice and is an absolute nutrient powerhouse.

2 heads broccoli, cut into florets

1 tbsp virgin organic coconut oil

2 cloves garlic, crushed

1 onion, thinly sliced

1 tsp ground cumin

1 tsp ground coriander

a good handful of parsley, roughly chopped

¼ tsp cayenne pepper

Himalayan salt and ground pepper

1. Steam the broccoli for just under 5 minutes. Once cooked, add half of the steamed broccoli to a food processor. Pulse until it resembles crumbs or rice – don't let it become too fine – then transfer to a bowl. Repeat with the remaining broccoli. Set aside until ready to use.
2. Once the broccoli rice is ready, melt the coconut oil in a frying pan over a medium heat, then add the garlic and onion and sauté until soft.
3. Add all the remaining ingredients, including the broccoli, and stir for a further 4 minutes or until the rice mixture has softened and cooked well. Adjust the seasoning and serve.

SERVES 4
PREP TIME: 25 MINUTES, INCLUDING COOKING

Spiced Cauliflower, Pumpkin Seed and Carrot Salad with Tahini Lemon Dressing

This salad can easily be made into a delicious meal by adding chicken, lamb, fish, tempeh or egg.

1 head cauliflower, cut into small florets

1 tsp Celtic sea salt

1 heaped tbsp sumac

1 tsp chilli flakes

ground pepper

¼ cup olive oil

Tahini Lemon Dressing (see page 258)

¼ cup dried cranberries

½ cup pumpkin seeds

2–3 large carrots, peeled into thin ribbons

2 cups baby spinach

parsley leaves

1. Preheat the oven to 200°C (180°C fan-forced). Line a large baking tray with baking paper.
2. In a large bowl toss together the cauliflower, salt, sumac, chilli flakes, pepper and olive oil. Spread onto the prepared tray and bake for 40 minutes, or until golden and roasted.
3. Make one serve of Tahini Lemon Dressing.
4. Toss the roasted cauliflower, cranberries, pumpkin seeds, carrots and spinach leaves together, drizzle the salad with the dressing and scatter over the parsley.

SERVES 6
PREP TIME: 50 MINUTES, INCLUDING COOKING

Crispy Brussels Sprouts

One of my all-time favourite veggies! I cannot get enough crispy brussels sprouts, caramelised to perfection. Definitely the recipe to use when introducing someone to this cruciferous veg.

20 brussels sprouts

¼ cup virgin organic coconut oil, melted

1 tsp Himalayan pink rock salt

½ tsp chilli flakes

1 tsp ground cumin

1 tsp sumac

1. Preheat the oven to 200°C (180°C fan-forced).
2. In a large bowl, mix together the brussels sprouts, coconut oil, salt, chilli flakes, cumin and sumac. Use your hands to mix thoroughly. Spread the brussels sprouts in a single layer in a large baking dish.
3. Roast for 20–25 minutes, turning every 10 minutes, until tender and caramelised around the edges.
4. Remove from the oven and serve warm or at room temperature.

SERVES 4
PREP TIME: 35 MINUTES, INCLUDING COOKING

Crisp Cauliflower with Sage

1 head cauliflower, washed

¼ cup sage leaves, roughly chopped

¼ cup olive oil

2 cloves garlic, crushed

Himalayan sea salt and ground pepper

2 tbsp finely grated parmesan

1. Preheat the oven to 200°C (180°C fan-forced). Place the cauliflower in a large baking dish.
2. In a small bowl combine the sage, olive oil and garlic. Rub the mixture all over the cauliflower. Season with salt and pepper.
3. Bake for 1½ hours, or until tender and golden brown. Sprinkle with parmesan before the end of the 15 minutes' cooking time.

SERVES 4

PREP TIME: 1 HOUR 45 MINUTES, INCLUDING COOKING

Crunchy Baked Cauliflower with Sumac

*Oh, Mum, you are such an inspiration. My mum makes this most nights
for the family as a side dish. It's incredibly tasty. I now make it for Dean and me in our new home.*

1 head cauliflower, trimmed and cut into small florets

¼ cup olive oil

1 tbsp sumac

1 tsp chilli flakes

Himalayan salt and ground pepper

¼ cup finely chopped parsley

60 g goat's fetta, crumbled

2 tbsp pomegranate seeds

1. Preheat the oven to 200°C (180°C fan-forced). Line a large baking tray with baking paper.
2. Spread the cauliflower on the tray, drizzle with the olive oil and toss to coat. Sprinkle with the sumac, chilli flakes, salt and pepper.
3. Bake for 50–60 minutes until tender and golden brown, checking to ensure the cauliflower does not burn.
4. To serve, sprinkle the cauliflower with the parsley, and scatter over the fetta and pomegranate seeds.

SERVES 4

PREP TIME: 1 HOUR 10 MINUTES, INCLUDING COOKING

Roasted Cinnamon and Almond Carrots

So warm and nourishing, and one of my favourite side dishes.

1 large bunch orange and purple carrots, cut in half lengthways

¼ cup cold-pressed extra-virgin olive oil

1 tbsp Moroccan spice mix

Himalayan salt and ground pepper

1 tbsp ground cinnamon

1 cup raw almonds, roughly chopped in a food processor

1 tsp lemon zest

1 tbsp thyme

1 tbsp roughly chopped rosemary

1. Preheat the oven to 180°C (160°C fan-forced). Line a baking tray with baking paper.
2. Place the carrot halves on the tray, pour over 2 tbsp of the olive oil and sprinkle with the Moroccan spice mix, salt, pepper and cinnamon.
3. In a bowl, mix together the almonds, lemon zest and thyme. Bind with the remaining 1 tbsp olive oil.
4. Evenly spoon the almond mixture on top of the carrots and bake for 40 minutes or until the topping is golden and the carrots are cooked.
5. Place the carrots on a serving platter and sprinkle with the rosemary.

SERVES 6
PREP TIME: 55 MINUTES, INCLUDING COOKING

Carrot and Leek Bake

6 small carrots, quartered lengthways

2 leeks, pale part only, thinly sliced

2 tbsp olive oil

2 tbsp white wine vinegar

1 tbsp thyme leaves

½ tsp chilli flakes

Himalayan salt and ground pepper

¼ cup finely chopped parsley

1 tsp sesame seeds, toasted

1. Preheat the oven to 200°C (180°C fan-forced).
2. Place the carrots in a baking dish and scatter over the leeks. Drizzle with the olive oil and vinegar. Sprinkle with the thyme, chilli flakes, salt and pepper. Gently toss to coat.
3. Cook for 50–55 minutes or until tender and golden.
4. Serve sprinkled with the parsley and sesame seeds.

SERVES 4
PREP TIME: 1 HOUR 5 MINUTES, INCLUDING COOKING

Cinnamon Sweet Potato Fries

I LOVE fries – I prefer savoury over sweet. Hot chips with tomato sauce used to be a childhood favourite. Since embracing a healthy lifestyle I have tuned to sweet potato chips – and I have never looked back.

3 sweet potatoes, scrubbed and cut into wedges

2 tbsp cold-pressed extra-virgin olive oil or coconut oil

1 tsp ground cinnamon

1 tsp maple syrup

½ tsp chilli flakes

Himalayan salt and ground pepper

⅓ cup Greek-style yoghurt

2 tbsp finely chopped mint leaves

1 clove garlic, crushed

lime wedges (to serve)

1. Preheat the oven to 200°C (180°C fan-forced). Line a large baking tray with baking paper.
2. In a large bowl combine the sweet potato with the olive oil, cinnamon, maple syrup, chilli flakes, salt and pepper, tossing well to coat.
3. Arrange the sweet potato wedges in a single layer on the tray and bake for 40 minutes or until tender and golden.
4. In a small bowl combine the yoghurt, mint and garlic. Season. Serve the fries with the mint yoghurt and lime wedges.

SERVES 4
PREP TIME: 55 MINUTES, INCLUDING COOKING

Brussels Sprout Skewers with Parmesan

This is an amazing starter at dinner parties. A spicy twist on one of my favourite green veggies – chillies pack a little heat to any dish. You will need to pre-soak 8 long bamboo skewers for this.

16 brussels sprouts, trimmed and halved

2 tbsp virgin organic coconut oil, melted

½ tsp chilli flakes

Himalayan salt and ground pepper

¼ cup finely chopped coriander leaves

¼ cup finely grated parmesan

olive oil, to drizzle

lemon wedges (to serve)

1. Thread 4 brussels sprout halves onto each skewer. Brush with coconut oil, sprinkle with chilli flakes and season with salt and pepper.
2. Heat a chargrill pan or barbecue to a medium–high heat and cook the skewers for 4–5 minutes on each side, turning often, until tender and browned.
3. Sprinkle the skewers with the coriander and parmesan, drizzle with a little olive oil, and serve with lemon wedges.

SERVES 4
PREP TIME: 25 MINUTES, INCLUDING COOKING

Cleansing Chopped Salad

A blog hit and working-lunch staple. Most lunchtimes I throw all the veggies I can find in the fridge into my food processor to make a chopped salad. Chopping the veggies brings out the flavour. I then add a protein for a quick and easy meal.

a portion of your choice of protein

1 cup baby spinach

1 small cucumber, chopped

1 cup shredded red cabbage

a handful of raw almonds, roughly chopped

1 carrot, grated

a handful of basil leaves

a handful of mint leaves

½ head broccoli, steamed and chopped into florets

½ avocado, sliced

DRESSING

1 tbsp olive oil

juice of ½ lemon

2 tbsp apple cider vinegar

1 tsp tahini

1 tsp honey

Himalayan salt and ground pepper

1. Layer all the salad ingredients in a large glass jar or bowl, finishing with the avocado.
2. Whisk together the dressing ingredients, season and drizzle over the salad. Serve.

SERVES 1
PREP TIME: 15 MINUTES

Shredded Vietnamese Salad

3 small carrots, cut into matchsticks

2 Lebanese cucumbers, peeled into ribbons

¼ white cabbage, finely shredded

¼ red cabbage, finely shredded

2 zucchini, peeled into ribbons

1 cup beansprouts

½ cup mint leaves, torn

½ cup coriander leaves

2 tbsp sunflower seeds

1 tsp sesame seeds, toasted

½ red chilli, thinly sliced

DRESSING

¼ cup lime juice

2 tbsp fish sauce

1 tablespoon rice wine vinegar

2 teaspoons tamari

½ tsp sesame oil

2 tbsp rice malt syrup

1 clove garlic, crushed

1 tsp finely grated fresh ginger

½ long red chilli, seeded and finely chopped (optional)

1. In a large bowl, combine all the salad ingredients and toss to combine.
2. In a jar, combine all the dressing ingredients and shake well.
3. Serve the salad drizzled with the dressing and topped with extra chilli, if desired.

SERVES 4
PREP TIME: 20 MINUTES

Sautéed Kale with Parmesan

This is an easy side dish that goes with pretty much anything!

1 bunch kale

1 tbsp virgin organic coconut oil

Himalayan salt and ground pepper

juice of ½ lemon

2 tbsp shaved parmesan

1. Remove the stems from the kale so you are left with only the leaves. You can discard the stalks, as they are tough to digest and quite bitter. Wash the leaves thoroughly, pat dry and roughly chop.
2. Melt the coconut oil in a non-stick frying pan over a medium heat. Add the kale and sauté for 5–6 minutes until soft. Turn the heat off, season to taste, add the lemon juice and stir.
3. Serve with the shaved parmesan.

SERVES 4
PREP TIME: 15 MINUTES, INCLUDING COOKING

Roasted Fennel

Crispy and so savoury – I add it to salads and to enhance the flavour of any protein dish. Fennel is amazing for digestion.

⅓ cup cold-pressed extra-virgin olive oil

4 bulbs fennel, cut horizontally into 5 mm thick slices, fronds reserved

Himalayan salt and ground pepper

1 clove garlic, crushed

½ tsp chilli flakes

2 tbsp ground fennel seeds

⅓ cup shaved parmesan (optional)

1. Preheat the oven to 190°C (170°C fan-forced). Lightly oil a large baking dish.
2. Arrange the fennel in the dish and sprinkle with the salt and pepper, garlic, chilli flakes and fennel seeds.
3. Finally, drizzle with the remaining olive oil and bake until the fennel is tender and the top is golden; this should take about 45 minutes.
4. Chop enough of the fennel fronds to get 2 tsp and sprinkle it over the roasted fennel.
5. Serve hot or, if you want to add the parmesan, allow it to cool first for about 10 minutes.

SERVES 3–4
PREP TIME: 50 MINUTES, INCLUDING COOKING

Dips, Dressings + Marinades

One of the best things about homemade dressings and marinades is that you know exactly what is in them. Unlike so many bottled and packaged versions on the market, these are free from nasties like sugar, transfats, excess sodium and preservatives. Not only are they better for your body, they are so much more delicious! I make a batch of a few different ones at the beginning of the week, store it in a sealed container in the fridge, and add it to meals as needed.

Zucchini Hummus

There is absolutely nothing wrong with chickpeas. They are incredibly nutritious. But some people really struggle to digest legumes, so this is an alternative to chickpea-based hummus. Try it – it's a total crowd-pleaser and great as a dip, pasta sauce or spread for toast.

2 zucchini, chopped

½ cup tahini

juice of 1 lemon

2 tbsp cold-pressed extra-virgin olive oil + extra to drizzle

2 tbsp filtered water

1 clove garlic, crushed

½ tsp ground cumin

½ tsp turmeric

Himalayan salt and ground pepper

1. Combine all the ingredients in a food processor and blend until smooth. If it's too thick, add more olive oil or some water.
2. Drizzle with extra olive oil to serve, if desired.

MAKES ABOUT 2 CUPS
PREP TIME: 15 MINUTES

Broccoli Pesto

One of my staples, you will always find a container of this in my fridge. More cruciferous veggies add a unique flavour to this pesto, which is perfect dolloped on your favourite seafood. Did you know that cruciferous veggies are great for liver detoxing?

1 cup basil leaves

1 cup chopped silverbeet or spinach

1 head broccoli, steamed and roughly chopped

2 spring onions, roughly chopped

½ cup walnuts

1 clove garlic

juice of ½ lemon

2 tbsp cold-pressed extra-virgin olive oil

1 tbsp filtered water

Himalayan salt and ground pepper

1. Process all the ingredients in a food processor until well combined and smooth.
2. To serve, sprinkle Almond Dukkah (see page 256) on top and use for pasta, pizzas, in salads or as a dip with vegetables.

SERVES 6
PREP TIME: 10 MINUTES

Homemade Walnut Pesto

This twist on a classic pesto uses walnuts in place of pine nuts, which are absolutely packed with omegas and healthy fats.

1 cup roughly chopped walnuts

2 heaped cups basil

2 cloves garlic, chopped

juice of 1 lemon

¼ cup cold-pressed extra-virgin olive oil + extra (to drizzle, optional)

¼ cup grated parmesan (optional)

Himalayan salt and ground pepper

2 tbsp filtered water

1. In a food processor, combine the walnuts with the basil. Process until the nuts are well ground and the basil is incorporated.
2. Add the garlic, lemon juice, olive oil and parmesan, if using, and season with salt and pepper.
3. With the food processor running, pour in the water. Keep adding until the pesto is smooth and creamy. Drizzle with extra olive oil, to serve, if desired.
4. Store in an airtight container in the fridge. This pesto will keep for 5–6 days.

MAKES ABOUT 2 CUPS
PREP TIME: 15 MINUTES

Carrot and Rosemary Dip

This is my new favourite. I've been adding this to everything, especially the Crisp Cauliflower with Sage (see page 240).

2 large carrots, steamed until very soft

1 capsicum, seeded and roughly chopped

3 rosemary sprigs, leaves picked + extra (to serve)

1 tsp sea salt

2 tbsp tahini

½ tsp ground cinnamon + extra (to serve)

ground pepper

2 tbsp olive oil + extra (to serve)

celery sticks (to serve)

1. Place all the ingredients, except the olive oil, in a food processor and blend to combine.
2. With the motor running, slowly add the olive oil and blend until well combined. Transfer the dip to a bowl.
3. Drizzle the dip with the extra olive oil and sprinkle with the extra cinnamon and rosemary sprigs to serve.
4. Serve with celery sticks.

MAKES ABOUT 2 CUPS
PREP TIME: 30 MINUTES, INCLUDING COOKING

Avocado Smash

Who doesn't love avo smash with poached eggs on some homemade gluten-free toast? Avocado just makes everything better.

2 large ripe avocados, peeled and stoned

2 spring onions, thinly sliced

juice of 1 lime

¼ cup finely chopped basil

Himalayan salt and ground pepper

6 cherry tomatoes, diced

40 g goat's cheese, crumbled (optional)

1 tbsp olive oil

1. Place the avocado in a medium-sized bowl and mash with a fork until almost smooth.
2. Add the spring onions, lime juice and basil to the bowl and mix well.
3. Season to taste with salt and pepper.
4. Top with the tomatoes and goat's cheese, if using, and drizzle with the olive oil to serve.

SERVES 4
PREP TIME: 10 MINUTES

Almond Dukkah

An incredible combo of nuts and seeds that lends the perfect crunch to salads and sides, and can be used as a rub for chicken, fish and other meats. I like it on hard-boiled eggs, too.

½ cup almonds

¼ cup coriander seeds

3 tbsp sesame seeds

2 tbsp cumin seeds

1 tsp black peppercorns

1 tsp fennel seeds

1 tsp dried mint or oregano

1 tsp Himalayan pink rock salt

1. Heat a heavy-based frying pan over a high heat. Add the almonds and dry-roast until slightly browned and fragrant. Be careful they don't burn. Remove from the heat and cool completely.
2. Repeat for the spices, allowing each to cool completely.
3. Place the almonds, spices, mint or oregano and salt into a mortar, and pound until the mixture is crushed. Alternatively, you can use a food processor and pulse the ingredients until they are roughly chopped. Do not allow the mixture to become a paste.
4. Store the mixture in an airtight container for up to 1 month.

MAKES 1 CUP
PREP TIME: 20 MINUTES, INCLUDING COOKING

Herb Rub

Best for fish and chicken and amazing with grass-fed beef steak.

½ cup chopped basil

½ cup chopped parsley

2 tbsp cold-pressed extra-virgin olive oil

1 tbsp balsamic vinegar

¼ tsp chilli flakes

Himalayan salt and ground pepper

1. Whisk together all the ingredients and season to taste.

MAKES ABOUT ½ CUP
PREP TIME: 10 MINUTES

Simple Salad Dressings

TAHINI LEMON DRESSING

Consider adding a protein of choice – chicken, lamb, fish, tempeh and egg are all delicious options.

⅓ cup cold-pressed extra-virgin olive oil

⅓ cup white wine vinegar

1 clove garlic, crushed

1 tbsp tahini

juice of 1 lemon

2 tbsp Dijon mustard

1 tsp poppy seeds (optional)

1 tbsp maple syrup (optional)

1 tbsp finely chopped chives (optional)

Himalayan salt and ground pepper

Whisk all the ingredients together until smooth and combined. Serve drizzled over your salad or protein of choice. Alternatively, this can be used as a marinade.

MAKES ½ CUP
PREP TIME: 5 MINUTES

ALL DRESSINGS SERVE 2

LEMON MUSTARD Whisk together 2 tbsp cold-pressed extra-virgin olive oil, juice of ½ lemon, 1 tbsp Dijon mustard, crushed clove/s garlic and 1 tsp tamari.

HERB AND YOGHURT Whisk together ⅓ cup white wine balsamic, the juice of ½ lemon, 1 tsp pomegranate molasses, 2 tbsp natural yoghurt, 1 tbsp tahini, chopped fresh parsley, crushed clove/s garlic, sea salt and ground pepper.

SLIM DOWN Whisk together ⅓ cup apple cider vinegar, 1 tbsp Dijon mustard, 1 tsp cold-pressed extra-virgin olive oil and juice of ½ lemon.

My Favourite Marinades and Rubs

I never use bottled marinades as they're loaded with bad fats, salt, sugar and preservatives. I also stick to 1 tbsp of marinade per person so adjust ingredients below to change serves.

ASIAN Whisk together 1 tbsp sesame oil, 1 tbsp tamari, juice and zest of 1 lemon, 1 crushed clove garlic, grated fresh ginger, chilli flakes (optional), ground pepper, chopped fresh parsley, dill and coriander. Best for: fish and chicken.

SERVES 4
MAKES ¼ CUP

LEMON MUSTARD Whisk together the juice of 1 lemon, 2 tbsp cold-pressed extra-virgin olive oil, 1 tbsp Dijon mustard, 1 crushed clove garlic, finely chopped rosemary, salt and pepper. Best for: chicken.

SERVES 4
MAKES ¼ CUP

MISO

Tangy and just a little salty, miso is a favourite on roast veggies — especially eggplant!

¼ cup flaxseed oil

1 tbsp miso paste

1 tsp raw honey

2 tbsp tamari

1 tsp finely grated fresh ginger

1 clove garlic, crushed

1 spring onion, thinly sliced

1 tsp sesame seeds, toasted

Whisk all the ingredients together until combined. This can be used as a marinade or a dressing.

MAKES ½ CUP
PREP TIME: 10 MINUTES

TERIYAKI Whisk together ¼ cup tamari, 2 tsp sesame oil, 2 tsp stevia powder, 1 tsp grated fresh ginger, Dijon mustard, Himalayan sea salt and ground pepper. Best for: fish, or chicken and beef strips for a stir-fry.

SERVES 4
MAKES ⅓ CUP

VEGETABLE SPICE RUB Using a mortar and pestle, pound together 1 tbsp dried coriander, 1 tbsp dried oregano, 1 tbsp dried thyme, 1 tbsp ground cumin, 1 tbsp fennel seeds, 1 clove garlic, ½ tsp chilli flakes, 2 tbsp cold-pressed extra-virgin olive oil, sea salt and ground pepper. Best for: cauliflower, pumpkin, fennel or sweet potato.

ZAATAR: 3 tbsp zaatar spice. This can be found at most health-food stores. Best for: chicken, fish or coating eggs.

Healthy Snacks

Making healthy snacks is absolutely crucial for healthy living. In this section you will find a variety of options so you won't ever need to seek a vending machine. I encourage you to put together a few different snacks on Sunday and keep them in the fridge or pantry for the week ahead. These recipes are also packed with nutrients, fibre and protein that will keep you feeling full until your next meal – healthy snacking at its finest!

Banana, Date and Walnut Muffins

These muffins have been the biggest hit on the blog. They make a perfect snack or on-the-go breakfast option, and are packed with fibre, good fats and protein to keep you feeling satisfied.

DRY

2 cups almond meal

¾ cup roughly chopped walnuts

2 tsp baking powder

1 tsp ground cinnamon

a pinch of sea salt

WET

1 cup fresh dates, pitted and chopped

3 free-range or organic eggs

2 large bananas + 1 extra, thinly sliced

¼ cup virgin organic coconut oil, melted

1 tsp chia seeds

1 tbsp maple syrup (to drizzle, optional)

1. Preheat the oven to 180°C (160°C fan-forced).
2. In a large bowl, combine all the dry ingredients.
3. In a food processor, combine the dates, eggs, 2 large bananas and coconut oil.
4. Add the wet mixture to the dry, and combine well. Divide the mixture among 8 paper-lined muffin-tin holes and top with the chia seeds and sliced banana.
5. Bake for 35–40 minutes or until the muffins are golden brown.
6. Drizzle with maple syrup to serve, if desired.

MAKES 8 LARGE MUFFINS
PREP TIME: 50 MINUTES, INCLUDING BAKING

Healthy Muesli Bars

Most packaged muesli bars have a lot of refined sugar. These are packed with all sorts of good things.

½ cup almonds

½ cup pistachios

1 cup pumpkin seeds

½ cup white quinoa

1 cup shredded coconut

½ cup sunflower seeds

¼ cup chia seeds

20 fresh Medjool dates, pitted

6 tbsp coconut oil, melted

4 tbsp raw cacao powder

1 tsp vanilla extract

2 tbsp raw honey

½ cup rolled oats

⅓ cup dried cranberries

2 tbsp raw cacao nibs

1. To a food processor or high-power blender, add the almonds, pistachios, pumpkin seeds, quinoa, shredded coconut, sunflower seeds and chia seeds and pulse a couple of times to roughly chop. Set aside in a mixing bowl.
2. Add the dates to the food processor, along with the coconut oil, cacao powder, vanilla and honey. Blend until it reaches a smooth consistency. You may need to stop a couple of times to scrape down the side and add a little extra coconut oil (or water).
3. Add the date mixture to the mixing bowl with the other ingredients. Stir through the rolled oats, cranberries and cacao nibs until well combined.
4. Press the mixture firmly into a lightly greased and lined 28 cm x 18 cm baking pan and refrigerate for 30 minutes.
5. Cut into thick bars and store in an airtight container. They will keep for a week in the fridge.

MAKES 12 BARS
PREP TIME: 50 MINUTES, INCLUDING REFRIGERATION

Flaxseed Crackers

1 cup ground flaxseed

½ cup sunflower seeds, ground

½ cup pumpkin seeds, ground

2 tbsp chia seeds

2 tbsp sesame seeds

1 clove garlic, crushed

2 tbsp finely chopped rosemary

2 tbsp thyme

2 tbsp finely grated parmesan

juice and zest of ½ lemon

¼ cup olive oil

¼ cup filtered water

Himalayan rock salt and ground pepper

1. Preheat the oven to 180°C (160°C fan-forced). Line a large baking tray with baking paper.
2. In a medium-sized bowl, combine the dry ingredients and season.
3. In a jug combine the lemon juice and zest, olive oil and water. Slowly whisk the wet ingredients into the dry. The mixture should be sticky but not too wet, and spreadable.
4. Spread the mixture evenly and thinly on the prepared tray. Place the tray in the oven and bake for 20 minutes. Remove from the oven and, using a knife, cut the crackers into rectangles. Turn the crackers over and cook for another 15–20 minutes, or until crisp.
5. Cool crackers on the tray. Store in an airtight container.

MAKES ABOUT 20 CRACKERS
PREP TIME: 55 MINUTES, INCLUDING COOKING

Chocolate Frozen Yoghurt

200 g Greek-style yoghurt or coyo

½ tsp ground cinnamon

½ tsp vanilla powder

1 tsp stevia powder or raw honey

1 tbsp chocolate protein powder or LSA (optional)

½ banana, mashed (optional)

1 tsp raw cacao powder + extra (to serve)

raw cacao nibs (to serve)

1. Mix together all the ingredients until smooth. Freeze for 40 minutes.

2. Sprinkle with extra raw cacao powder and raw cacao nibs to serve.

SERVES 1
PREP TIME: 50 MINUTES, INLUDING FREEZING

FROYO VARIATIONS

Berry Vanilla Blend the following ingredients and freeze for 30 minutes: 1 cup frozen berries, ½ frozen banana, ¼ cup milk, 2 tbsp Greek-style yoghurt, 2 tbsp LSA, 1 tbsp almond butter, 1 tsp ground cinnamon, 1 tsp stevia powder or raw honey and ¼ tsp vanilla powder or extract.

Banana and Hazelnut Blend the following ingredients and freeze for 30 minutes: 2 frozen bananas, 2 tbsp natural yoghurt, 1 tsp ground cinnamon, 1 tsp stevia powder, 2 tbsp hazelnut butter, 2 tbsp whole hazelnuts, ¼ tsp vanilla powder and 2 tbsp milk.

Chocolate and Peanut Butter Mix these ingredients in a bowl and freeze for 45 minutes: 200 g Greek-style yoghurt, 2–3 drops vanilla stevia or 1 tsp stevia powder, 1 tbsp raw cacao powder, 1 tbsp peanut butter, ½ tsp ground cinnamon.

Toasted Chai-spiced Nuts

My sister Olivia makes these nuts to add to her Greek-style yoghurt and berries most mornings.

1 tbsp virgin organic coconut oil

1 cup mixed raw nuts

1 tsp ground cinnamon

¼ tsp grated nutmeg

1 tsp maple syrup or stevia drops

1. Melt the coconut oil in a non-stick frying pan over a medium heat.
2. Add the nuts, cinnamon, nutmeg and maple syrup, and fry until golden brown, taking care not to let the nuts burn. Cool and serve.

SERVES 4
PREP TIME: 10 MINUTES, INCLUDING COOKING

JSHealth Sugar-free Protein Balls

These are life-savers, my clients tell me. In my nutrition clinic I often advise to make them at the beginning of the week and keep in the fridge. I carry them in my bag and take them to work. The protein will keep you feeling full and the stevia will help keep the sugar cravings at bay.

4 heaped tbsp LSA or chocolate protein powder

2 tbsp mixed seeds (I like pumpkin and sunflower seeds)

1 heaped tbsp raw cacao powder

2 heaped tbsp almond butter or peanut butter

1 tsp ground cinnamon

1 tbsp chia seeds or psyllium husk

2 tbsp stevia powder or 3–4 drops stevia liquid

¼ cup warm filtered water

1. Combine all the ingredients in a high-powered blender or food processor and blend until smooth.
2. If the mixture is too wet, add more LSA; if the mixture is too dry, add a splash of warm water.
3. Roll into balls of your desired size and refrigerate in an airtight container for up to 7 days.

MAKES 10 BALLS
PREP TIME: 5 MINUTES

Kale Chips

Who needs crisps when you can have this healthy snack? They're a healthy-eating game-changer!
Make a big batch and use them as a crunchy topping for soups and salads.

1 bunch kale

1 tbsp virgin organic coconut oil, melted

½ tsp ground turmeric, cumin or spice of your choice

Himalayan rock salt and ground pepper

1. Preheat the oven to 200°C (180°C fan-forced). Line a baking tray with baking paper.
2. Tear the kale leaves into bite-size pieces (discard the stems). Wash and dry the leaves using a salad spinner. The leaves should be extremely dry.
3. Mix the kale with the melted coconut oil, spices, salt and pepper.
4. Spread the kale in a single layer on the baking tray and bake for about 12 minutes or until they are crisp.
5. Serve with a tahini and lemon dipping sauce: whisk together 1 tbsp tahini, juice of ½ lemon, 1 tsp maple syrup, and season with Himalayan salt and ground pepper.

SERVES 3
PREP TIME: 15 MINUTES, INCLUDING COOKING

LOVE KALE CHIPS?

Why not be creative and use other veggies too? I like sweet potato, beetroot, Brussels sprouts and parsnip.

Cut the vegetable using a mandolin so it's wafer-thin, and lay out on a baking tray lined with baking paper. Drizzle with virgin organic coconut oil, and sprinkle over cumin, salt and pepper.

Cook for 20 minutes or until brown. Be sure to turn them over halfway through the cooking time.

Natural Banana Protein Bars

Practically non-existent on supermarket shelves. It is so hard to find a protein bar that is free from artificial junk, so I make my own from real ingredients. They are high in fibre and protein to keep you full and satisfied. A perfect recipe to make each week and keep in the fridge for a healthy snack option.

DRY

½ cup rolled organic oats (gluten-free option: quinoa flakes)

½ cup LSA or protein powder

¼ cup mixed seeds

3 tbsp chia seeds

½ cup chopped raw walnuts and/or almonds

¼ cup shredded coconut

¼ cup psyllium husk

1 tsp ground cinnamon

½ tsp baking soda

¼ tsp sea salt

1 tsp vanilla powder

WET

1 banana, mashed

2 tbsp nut butter

¼ cup maple syrup or rice malt syrup

1 tbsp milk

1. Preheat the oven to 180°C (160°C fan-forced). Line a standard loaf tin (approximately 21 cm × 11 cm) with baking paper (you can grease with olive oil as well).
2. Combine the dry ingredients in a large mixing bowl.
3. In a separate bowl, whisk the wet ingredients together.
4. Add the dry ingredients to the wet ingredients and combine well with a wooden spoon.
5. Pour the batter into the tin and press down firmly. Bake for 20–25 minutes or until cooked through and the top is golden brown.
6. Allow to cool in the tin then slice into bars. These can be kept in an airtight container in the fridge for a week.

MAKES ABOUT 10 SLICES
PREP TIME: 35 MINUTES, INCLUDING COOKING

Skin Glow Balls

Beauty from the inside out, these balls contain ingredients that will make your skin glow.
Gluten-free, dairy-free, sugar-free.

½ cup almond meal

¼ cup ground flaxseed

½ cup desiccated coconut

¼ cup sunflower seeds

2 tbsp goji berries

2 tbsp almond or any other nut butter

½ tsp ground cinnamon

½ tsp vanilla powder

2 tbsp stevia powder or raw honey

a pinch of sea salt

a squeeze of lemon juice

¼ cup water

1. To a high-powered blender or food processor, add all the ingredients, except the water, and blend until the mixture is smooth. Slowly add the water, but only pour enough to make the mixture sticky and not too wet. You may not need all of it, just use enough to achieve the desired consistency.
2. Using damp hands, roll 1½ tablespoons of the mixture into balls.
3. Refrigerate for up to 7 days in an airtight container.

MAKES 10
PREP TIME: 10 MINUTES

Choc Protein Truffles

Chocoholic? You're in good company! These creamy truffles taste just
like the classic but without the refined sugar.

2 servings chocolate protein powder

2 heaped tbsp almond butter

½ cup Brazil nuts

½ cup almond meal

2 tbsp raw cacao powder

4 tbsp sunflower seeds

2 tbsp raw honey

2 tsp ground cinnamon + extra to sprinkle

a couple of drops of filtered water

1. Place all the ingredients in a food processor and blend until smooth.
2. Using damp hands, roll heaped tablespoons of the mixture into balls. Sprinkle with extra cinnamon and place in the freezer for 30 minutes.
3. Refrigerate for up to 5 days in an airtight container.

MAKES 12 BALLS
PREP TIME: 40 MINUTES, INCLUDING FREEZING

More Snack Suggestions

- **1 cup blueberries with a handful of walnuts.** Or try ½ cup mixed berries with a sprinkle of ground cinnamon and desiccated coconut.

- **2–3 pieces of 70 or 85 per cent cocoa dark chocolate.** Perfect for those with a sweet tooth! You can't beat Lindt.

- **1–2 protein or bliss balls.**

- **Slice of my Gluten-free Banana Bread** (see page 152) with 1 tbsp nut butter.

- **Protein Shake.** In a blender, mix natural protein powder (e.g. NuZest, Sunwarrior, Vital Pea, Tony Sfeir) or LSA, a handful of berries, stevia, any seeds or nuts, milk and ground cinnamon.

- **Antioxidant Berry Smoothie.** In a blender, mix ½ cup frozen berries, 1 tsp maqui berry powder, ½ frozen banana, spinach leaves, 2 tbsp vanilla protein powder or LSA, 1 tbsp Greek-style yoghurt, a squeeze of lemon, 1 tsp stevia, ½ tsp ground cinnamon, ½ cup Almond Milk (see page 306) and ½ cup ice cubes.

- **Healthy Banana Boat.** In a blender mix ½ banana with 2 tbsp Greek yoghurt, a drizzle of maple syrup, ground cinnamon and 1 tbsp seeds or crushed walnuts.

- **Cleansing Smoothie.** In a blender, mix spinach leaves, grated carrot, ½ frozen banana, ¼ avocado, a handful of goji berries or blueberries, 1 tsp chia seeds, 1 tbsp coyo or natural yoghurt, 1 tbsp psyllium husk, 1 tsp ground cinnamon, a handful of ice and Almond Milk (see page 306).

- **Homemade Trail Mix.** I prefer to make my own mix rather than buy one. You can put in anything you like or what you have on hand. Mix all or some sort of the following in a bowl: almonds, walnuts, sunflower seeds, pumpkin seeds, raw cacao nibs, goji berries and mulberries. Make a big batch and divide into snap-lock bags.

- **Almond Dream Smoothie.** In a blender, mix a handful of almonds (about 10), 1 cup Almond Milk (see page 306), 1 fresh pitted date, ½ frozen banana, 1 tsp almond butter, 1 tsp chia seeds, 3–4 ice cubes, 1 tsp ground cinnamon and 1 tsp vanilla powder.

- **A handful (¼ cup) of raw, activated nuts and seeds.**

- **2 fresh pitted dates** stuffed with almond butter, raw seeds or 4–5 raw almonds.

- **Chopped vegetables** like carrots, celery or cucumber with 2–3 tbsp of either hummus, tahini, guacamole or cottage cheese.

- **Sweet Ricotta.** 4 tbsp ricotta mixed with 1 tsp ground cinnamon, 1 tsp raw honey and some raw nuts or seeds.

- **1 boiled egg.** Add chopped veggies if you're still hungry.

- **1 low-GI fruit.** Green apples, berries, citrus fruits and nectarines are all great choices. Add a handful of nuts to this option for an extra protein boost.

- **Nori sheets** with hummus and chopped veggies, avocado and a drizzle of tamari.

- **Apple slices** spread with 1 tbsp almond butter and a sprinkle of ground cinnamon.

- **Grated carrot** with a drizzle of lemon juice and Himalayan salt.

- **2 brown rice cakes** with 1 tbsp almond butter, ground cinnamon and a drizzle of raw honey. If you're craving something savoury, go with a smear of tahini or avocado.

- **Veggie Juice.** Throw kale, cucumber, celery, carrot, ginger and lemon in a blender – or ask your local juice bar to make one for you. The fresher, the better!

- **Steamed broccoli** with sea salt, lemon juice and cold-pressed extra-virgin olive oil. Sprinkle with mixed seeds.

Sweet Treats

What I have learnt about healthy eating is that you can ALWAYS make a healthy alternative to your favourite treat. The following recipes will inspire you to make the healthy swap – you will not feel deprived after tasting some of these wholesome sugar-free treats.

Chocolate Paleo Soufflé

Oh my, this incredible treat is packed with rich chocolate and fudgey texture,
it tastes absolutely sinful – but it's not!

1 egg, lightly beaten

1 banana, mashed

2 heaped tbsp raw cacao powder

2 tbsp almond butter

½ tsp baking powder

1 tsp ground cinnamon

1 tsp stevia powder

a pinch of grated nutmeg (optional)

goji berries and chopped nuts (to serve)

1. Mix the ingredients together in a bowl until combined. Spoon into two small lightly greased cups or ramekins (for microwave) or lined muffin tins for the oven.
2. For the microwave, cook on high for 1–2 minutes, or until risen and cooked but still gooey in the middle.
3. For the oven, cook for 15 minutes on 180°C (160°C fan-forced) or until the muffins are still a little soft.
4. Top with goji berries and chopped nuts to serve.

SERVES 2
PREP TIME: 25 MINUTES, INCLUDING COOKING

Almond and Vanilla Protein Cookies

I love a warm cookie with tea, don't you? You will be so excited about this incredibly easy and delicious recipe. The cookies are gluten-free, sugar-free, paleo and dairy-free, and quite possibly the healthiest cookies ever! If you are a raw foodie you can make a raw version too.

2 tbsp almond butter

¼ cup raw almonds or Brazil nuts

2 tbsp LSA or almond meal

¼ cup desiccated coconut

2 tbsp vanilla protein powder

¼ tsp Celtic sea salt

1 tsp ground cinnamon

1 tbsp raw honey or maple syrup

4–5 drops vanilla stevia liquid

2–3 tbsp filtered water

1. Blend all the ingredients in a food processor until smooth.
2. Using damp hands, roll heaped tablespoons of the mixture into balls. Place in the freezer for 30 minutes for a raw version, or flatten balls onto a lined baking tray and bake in a preheated oven at 160°C (140°C fan-forced) for 20–25 minutes or until golden and cooked through.
3. Refrigerate the raw balls for up to 5 days in an airtight container.

MAKES 12
PREP TIME: 30 MINUTES, INCLUDING COOKING

Banana Hazelnut Nice-cream

1 frozen banana

½ cup Greek-style yoghurt

2 tbsp whole hazelnuts

2 tbsp hazelnut butter or any other nut butter

1 tsp ground cinnamon

1 tsp vanilla powder

1 tsp stevia powder

2 tbsp milk of choice

sliced banana and chopped hazelnuts (to serve)

1. Combine all the ingredients in a blender or food processor and blend until smooth. Freeze for 1½–2 hours before serving.

SERVES 1

PREP TIME: 1 HOUR, 40 MINUTES TO 2 HOURS, 10 MINUTES, INCLUDING FREEZING

NICE-CREAM VARIATIONS

Salted Caramel Blend in a food processor: 1 frozen banana, 1 tbsp almond butter, 1 tsp mesquite powder, 2–3 tbsp Almond Milk (see page 306), ¼ tsp Celtic sea salt and 1 tbsp maple syrup, rice malt or stevia powder. Freeze for 1½–2 hours before serving.

Chai Coconut Blend in a food processor: 1 frozen banana, ½ cup desiccated coconut, 1 tsp chai spice, 1 tsp ground cinnamon, 2–3 tbsp Almond Milk (see page 306), 1 tbsp maple syrup, rice malt or stevia powder. Freeze for 1½–2 hours before serving.

My favourite finishing touches Goji berries, coconut chips, raw nuts (almonds, macadamias, Brazil nuts or walnuts), almond butter, raspberries, blueberries, raw seeds (chia , pumpkin or sunflower), vanilla powder or essence, ground cinnamon, raw cacao nibs, spice, mint, chilli or Himalayan pink rock salt.

Raw Chocolate Almond Tart

NUT CRUST

1 cup almonds

½ cup shredded coconut

⅓ cup melted coconut oil

1 cup fresh dates, pitted

a pinch of Himalayan salt

CHOCOLATE FILLING

¼ cup virgin organic coconut oil

1 tsp ground cinnamon

⅓ cup rice malt syrup

2 tbsp shredded coconut, toasted (to serve)

½ cup cacao powder

1 tbsp tahini

1. To make the nut crust, soak the almonds for 4–6 hours beforehand (optional). Process all the ingredients in a high-powered blender or food processor until well mixed.

2. Spoon the crust mixture into a paper-case lined 6-hole muffin tray or 20 cm lightly greased fluted tart tin with removable base. Press down firmly using the back of a spoon and place in the freezer.

3. To make the chocolate filling, melt the coconut oil over a low heat and then turn off the heat. Add the remaining ingredients and whisk until smooth.

4. Remove the tart crust/s from the freezer and spoon in the filling. Refrigerate for at least 1 hour.

5. When ready to serve, remove from the fridge and sprinkle the top with coconut. You can add toppings such as goji berries, walnuts or fresh berries.

MAKES 6 MINI TARTS OR 1 LARGE TART
PREP TIME: 1½ HOURS, INCLUDING CHILLING

Raw Carrot Mini-cake with Cashew and Coconut Icing

This is hands down one of my favourite desserts. I could eat carrot cake every day, and this is my version when the craving strikes.

CAKE

2 carrots, peeled and roughly grated

1⅔ cups almond meal

2 cups Medjool dates, pitted

2 tbsp psyllium husk

⅔ cup desiccated coconut

1 tsp ground cinnamon

ICING

2 cups raw cashews, soaked in water for 2 hours

2 tbsp lemon juice

¼ cup maple syrup

2 tbsp virgin organic coconut oil, melted

½ cup filtered water

toasted shredded coconut and toasted chopped hazelnuts (to serve)

1. To make the cake, place all the ingredients in a blender or food processor and pulse until combined and sticking together.

2. Line a standard muffin tin with 12 paper cases and divide the cake mixture evenly between the cases, gently pressing down with a spoon. Freeze while you make the icing.

3. To make the icing, blend all the ingredients in a blender or food processor until smooth, adding water gradually as required.

4. Spoon the icing evenly over the cakes, sprinkle with coconut and hazelnuts, and return to the freezer for 30 minutes, or until the icing sets.

MAKES 12
PREP TIME: 50 MINUTES, INCLUDING FREEZING

Banoffee Tarts

TART BASE

1 cup fresh dates, pitted

1 cup almonds

½ tsp Celtic sea salt

1 tbsp filtered water

FILLING

1 cup raw cashews

1 tsp ground cinnamon

¼ cup coconut milk

1 banana

2 tbsp coconut flakes

1 tbsp virgin organic coconut oil

1 tsp raw honey

torn dates

raw cacao powder (to serve)

1. Line a muffin tray with six paper cases.
2. To make the tart base, place all the ingredients in a food processor and pulse until combined.
3. Divide the mixture between the paper cases, pressing down with the back of a teaspoon. Place in the freezer while you make the filling.
4. To make the filling, blend all the ingredients in a food processor until smooth. Spoon into the tart shells, top with a torn date and freeze for an hour. Sprinkle with raw cacao powder to serve, if desired.

MAKES 6
PREP TIME: 1 HOUR 20 MINUTES, INCLUDING FREEZING

Chocolate Walnut and Tahini Brownies

Rich, gooey AND healthy – the perfect brownies!

1 cup walnuts

1 cup fresh dates, pitted

4 heaped tbsp raw cacao powder + 1 tbsp for icing

1 tsp ground cinnamon

pinch Celtic sea salt

¼ cup desiccated coconut

½ tsp vanilla powder

2 tbsp virgin organic coconut oil, melted

2 tbsp raw honey

¼ cup hulled tahini

a few drops of filtered water

1. Grind the walnuts to a fine crumb in a food processor. Add the dates, raw cacao powder, cinnamon, salt, coconut and vanilla and process until sticky.
2. Line a small square dish (or loaf tin) with baking paper. Press the mixture in firmly.
3. To make the icing, place the coconut oil, honey, tahini and 1 tbsp raw cacao powder in the processor. Process until the mixture is firm and smooth in texture. If it is too thick, add a few drops of water.
4. Spread the icing evenly over the brownies with a spatula.
5. Put into the fridge for at least 30 minutes to set.
6. Serve with a dollop of yoghurt or coconut ice-cream and crushed berries.

MAKES 15 SQUARES
PREP TIME: 50 MINUTES, INCLUDING REFRIGERATION

Lemon and Cream Bars

Saturday-morning rain makes me want to eat lemon and cream bars with tea, a childhood treat. I grew up in South Africa absolutely loving lemon and cream biscuits. As a little girl my cousins and I would wake up every morning in our holiday house in Plett and make tea with these biscuits. Here is a far more adult version.

1 cup cashews

1 cup almond meal

2 tbsp psyllium husk

2 heaped tbsp almond butter

⅓ cup desiccated coconut

1 tsp ground cinnamon

2 tbsp rice malt syrup

4 drops of vanilla stevia liquid

juice and zest of 1 lemon

¼ cup filtered water

shredded coconut and extra lemon zest (to decorate)

1. Line a lightly greased 20 cm square baking tin with baking paper.
2. Blend all the ingredients in a food processor until combined. Using a spoon, press the mixture evenly into the tin. Sprinkle with the lemon zest and shredded coconut, lightly pressing them into the top of the mixture.
3. Freeze for about 2 hours, or until firm, cut into bars and serve.

MAKES 12
PREP TIME: 2 HOURS 15 MINUTES, INCLUDING FREEZING

Chocolate Pudding

A dessert classic with a healthy twist. So rich and creamy, and utterly delicious.

DRY

3 tbsp almond meal

2 tbsp raw cacao powder

1 tsp ground cinnamon

a pinch of sea salt

½ tsp gluten-free baking powder

WET

1 free-range or organic egg

2 tbsp stevia powder or maple syrup

2 tbsp Almond Milk (see page 306)

1 tbsp virgin organic coconut oil, melted

1. Preheat the oven to 160°C (140°C fan-forced).
2. In a mixing bowl, combine the dry ingredients. Combine the wet ingredients in a separate bowl.
3. Add the dry ingredients to the wet. Mix together well using a spatula, ensuring there are no lumps.
4. Pour the mixture into a greased ovenproof bowl or a ramekin. Bake for 30 minutes or until the pudding starts to rise. Allow to cool before serving.
5. Serve topped with spiced cinnamon nuts, a dollop of natural yoghurt or coconut cream.

SERVES 1
PREP TIME: 40 MINUTES, INCLUDING COOKING

Chocolate Peanut Butter Nice-cream

1 frozen banana, chopped

1½ tbsp natural peanut butter

1 tbsp raw cacao powder

1 tsp ground cinnamon

¼ cup Almond Milk (see page 306)

1 tbsp stevia powder

2 tbsp desiccated coconut

crushed peanuts (to serve)

1. Combine all the ingredients in a blender or food processor and blend until smooth. Freeze for an hour before serving. Serve topped with crushed peanuts.

SERVES 1
PREP TIME: 1 HOUR 5 MINUTES, INCLUDING FREEZING

Apple Crumble

One of my favourite indulgences is a warm apple crumble with coyo ice-cream or Greek-style yoghurt. This one is good for the soul.

5 large apples (any kind), cored and chopped into small pieces

juice of 1 lemon

1 tsp vanilla bean powder

2 tsp ground cinnamon

CRUMBLE

½ cup rolled oats or quinoa flakes

1 cup LSA or 1 cup ground flaxseed and almond meal or 1 cup almond meal

¼ cup coconut flakes or desiccated + extra (to serve)

¼ cup mixed seeds

½ cup flaked almonds + extra (to serve)

½ cup chopped walnuts

¼ cup fresh dates, pitted and chopped

2 tbsp stevia powder, coconut sugar or maple syrup

½ tsp grated nutmeg

¼ cup virgin organic coconut oil, melted

1. Preheat the oven to 180°C (160°C fan-forced).
2. Place the apples in a pie dish. Add the lemon juice, vanilla and 1 tsp of the cinnamon and mix well.
3. To make the crumble, combine the ingredients in a bowl and mix well until it reaches a sandy texture.
4. Spread the crumble over the apples and place in the oven.
5. Bake for 40 minutes or until the apples are tender and the topping is golden.
6. Once cooled, sprinkle with the extra coconut and almonds.
7. Serve with a scoop of organic coconut ice-cream or Greek-yoghurt with the remaining cinnamon and some coconut sugar.

SERVES 6
PREP TIME: 50 MINUTES, INCLUDING COOKING

Kady's Coconut and Orange Macaroons

My lovely graphic designer, Kady, made these for me one morning and I just adore them.

2 egg whites

1 tbsp virgin organic coconut oil, melted

½ cup maple syrup

1 tbsp grated orange zest + extra (to serve)

½ tsp vanilla bean paste

½ tsp sea salt

200 g desiccated coconut

shredded coconut and extra orange zest (to serve)

1. Preheat the oven to 160°C (140°C fan-forced). Line a large baking tray with baking paper and grease with the melted coconut oil.
2. Beat the egg whites and maple syrup using an electric mixer for 5–7 minutes until thick and pale. Stir in the orange zest, vanilla bean paste, salt and coconut.
3. Spoon heaped tablespoons of the mixture onto the lined tray, leaving at least 3 cm between the biscuits.
4. Bake for 25–30 minutes or until lightly golden.
5. Decorate with shredded coconut and orange zest.

MAKES 16
PREP TIME: 40 MINUTES, INCLUDING COOKING

Raw Chocolate Crackles

I love this simple recipe for a classic chocolate treat. It's a great one for the kids to have as a special snack.

⅓ cup LSA

⅓ cup mixed seeds

¼ cup raw almonds or walnuts (or a mixture of both)

1 heaped tbsp raw cacao powder

1 heaped tbsp nut butter (I use almond)

5 fresh dates, pitted and roughly chopped

1 tsp ground cinnamon

¼ tsp Celtic sea salt

1 tsp virgin organic coconut oil, melted

¼ cup filtered water

1 tsp raw honey or stevia powder (optional)

1. Blend all the ingredients together in a high-powered food processor. The mixture should have a gooey texture, so adjust by using more or less water.
2. Roll into balls and then place in mini paper cupcake cases. Refrigerate for 30 minutes before serving.
3. These can be refrigerated for up to 7 days in an airtight container.

MAKES 10
PREP TIME: 45 MINUTES, INCLUDING REFRIGERATION

Chocolate Almond Mousse

1 banana or mashed pumpkin

½ avocado

2 tbsp raw cacao powder

3 fresh dates, pitted and roughly chopped

2 tbsp almond butter

a handful of raw almonds

1 tsp stevia powder, raw honey or maple syrup

⅓ cup filtered water

1 tsp ground cinnamon

a pinch of sea salt

1. In a high-powered blender, blitz all the ingredients until smooth and creamy.
2. Refrigerate for 30 minutes. Serve chilled topped with blueberries, almonds and mint leaves, if desired.

SERVES 2
PREP TIME: 40 MINUTES, INCLUDING REFRIGERATION

Raspberry and Coconut Sweet Loaf

DRY

2 cups almond meal

½ cup ground flaxseed

¼ cup psyllium husk

½ cup desiccated coconut + 1 tbsp for decoration

2 tsp ground cinnamon

1 tsp vanilla powder (optional)

1½ tsp baking powder

WET

3 eggs, lightly beaten

6 fresh dates, pitted and chopped

2 tbsp maple syrup, raw honey or stevia powder

¼ cup Almond Milk (see page 306)

2 tbsp virgin organic coconut oil, melted

¼ cup Greek-style yoghurt

1 cup raspberries, fresh or frozen

1. Preheat the oven to 180°C (160°C fan-forced).
2. Combine all the dry ingredients in a large mixing bowl. Then separately in a large jug, whisk all the wet ingredients together, except the raspberries.
3. Add the wet mixture to the dry, mixing gently until well combined. Fold the raspberries through the mixture. If the batter is too wet, add extra almond meal; if it is too dry, add extra almond milk.
4. Lightly spray coconut oil in a standard loaf tin (21 cm x 11 cm). Spoon the batter into the tin. Top the loaf with extra desiccated coconut, if desired.
5. Bake for 45–50 minutes. To check if it's cooked, insert a skewer into the middle of the loaf. If the skewer comes out clean, it's done. If the top is starting to brown, cover with foil and continue baking the loaf.
6. When cooked, remove from the oven and cool in the tin. Remove the loaf and slice. Serve with almond butter, tahini or Greek yoghurt. If kept covered in the fridge, it will keep up to 1 week.

MAKES 1 LOAF
PREP TIME: 1 HOUR 5 MINUTES, INCLUDING COOKING

Berry, Fig and Almond Crumble

Fresh figs are such a treat when in season. I love this combination, but you can switch out other berries in this classic crumble recipe.

700 g frozen mixed berries

3 fresh figs, sliced (dried figs if not in season)

juice of 1 lemon

1 tsp vanilla extract

1 tbsp ground cinnamon

CRUMBLE

½ cup almond meal

½ cup coconut flakes

½ cup roughly chopped almonds

½ cup mixed seeds (pumpkin, sesame and sunflower)

2 tbsp chia seeds

2 tbsp psyllium husk

1 tsp grated nutmeg

2 tbsp maple syrup

2 tbsp virgin organic coconut oil, melted

½ cup Greek-style yoghurt (to serve)

1. Preheat the oven to 180°C (160°C fan-forced).
2. Place the berries and figs in a pie dish. Add the lemon juice, vanilla and 2 tsp of the cinnamon and gently stir to combine.
3. To make the crumble, combine all remaining ingredients in a large bowl and mix until it reaches a sandy texture.
4. Sprinkle the crumble mixture over the berries and figs and place in the oven.
5. Bake for 30 minutes or until the fruit is tender and the topping is golden.
6. Serve with a dollop of Greek-style yoghurt.

SERVES 6
PREP TIME: 50 MINUTES, INCLUDING COOKING

Homemade Chocolate Nutella

1 cup hazelnuts, soaked beforehand for 2 hours

4 tbsp raw cacao powder

1 tsp ground cinnamon

½ tsp vanilla extract

½ cup maple syrup, raw honey or rice malt syrup

2 tbsp virgin organic coconut oil

1. Grind the hazelnuts to a powder form using a high-powered blender or food processor.
2. Add the rest of the ingredients and combine until smooth.
3. Serve with fresh strawberries, sliced banana and/or shredded coconut.

SERVES 4
PREP TIME: 2 HOURS 10 MINUTES, INCLUDING SOAKING

Salty Cinnamon and Almond Chocolate Bark

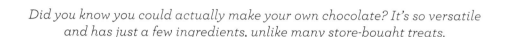

Did you know you could actually make your own chocolate? It's so versatile and has just a few ingredients, unlike many store-bought treats.

½ cup virgin organic coconut oil

⅔ cup raw cacao powder

1 tbsp tahini

3 tbsp raw honey, coconut sugar, maple syrup or rice malt syrup

Celtic sea salt

½ tsp ground cinnamon

½ cup raw almonds, whole, crushed or flaked

1. Melt the coconut oil in a saucepan over a medium heat. Lower the heat and whisk in the raw cacao powder, tahini and sweetener of your choice – my favourite is rice malt syrup. Continually mixing to avoid lumps then add a pinch or two of salt and the cinnamon. Take off the heat. Allow to sit for approximately 5 minutes so the mixture doesn't spread too thin on the baking pan.
2. Line a small baking pan with baking paper and pour the mixture onto the baking pan. The baking pan should be 1–2 cm deep. Top the mixture with almonds and add more cinnamon if you wish.
3. Cover with cling wrap and freeze flat for 30–40 minutes or until the chocolate is set. You can then break apart the chocolate and store in the fridge or freezer.

SERVES 6
PREP TIME: 50 MINUTES, INCLUDING FREEZING

CHOCOLATE BARK VARIATIONS

Try mixing your favourite flavours. I recommend coconut flakes, goji berries, orange zest or oil, coffee, hazelnuts or pistachios.

Satisfying Your Sweet Tooth

Before you scan this list, try some herbal tea with a drop of stevia and cinnamon. If that still doesn't hit the spot, go ahead and savour one of the following options.

- **2–3 squares of 85 per cent cocoa dark chocolate.**
- **150–200 g Greek-style yoghurt** mixed with stevia, raw cacao powder and ground cinnamon. Freeze for 30 minutes to make chocolate frozen yoghurt.
- **1–2 fresh dates** filled with almond butter and raw nuts.
- **1 bliss ball.**
- **'Chai latte':** I love to sip on rooibos chai or Bengal spice tea with warm Almond Milk (see page 306), ground cinnamon and vanilla-flavoured stevia – it satisfies the sweet cravings!
- **Cinnamon Bananas:** Sauté ½ sliced banana with ground cinnamon, maple syrup or stevia and virgin organic coconut oil in a pan. Top with mixed nuts, raw cacao nibs or shredded coconut.
- **Ayurveda Hot Chocolate** with raw cacao powder (see page 301).
- **5 cut-up strawberries** with 1 tbsp Homemade Nutella (on previous page).
- **Raw walnuts or almonds** sprinkled with ground cinnamon and coconut.
- **1 cup of berries** sprinkled with ground cinnamon and coconut.

Drinks

Water is the perfect beverage for ultimate hydration – but sometimes you want some liquid that tantalises your tastebuds too. It's easy to craft healthy, flavourful drinks with fresh fruits, vegetables, herbs and spices – no processed sugar necessary. I hope this section will inspire you to get creative with your hydration!

Ayurveda Hot Chocolate

*An Ayurvedic winter warmer, sleepy-time aphrodisiac and healing hot drink in one.
So many of us experience that nagging sweet tooth after dinner. This drink is the perfect sweet
treat to aid inner calm and sleep. Warmed milk and nutmeg are natural sedatives.*

1 cup milk, Almond Milk (see page 306) or coconut milk

¼ cup almonds

1 tbsp maca powder

1 tbsp raw cacao powder + extra (to serve, optional)

2 fresh dates, pitted

½ tsp grated nutmeg

½ tsp ground cinnamon + extra (to serve, optional)

¼ tsp ground cardamom

a pinch of sea salt

1 tbsp virgin organic coconut oil

1. Bring the milk to the boil in a stainless steel saucepan over a medium heat. Once boiled, reduce to a simmer for 3 minutes. Turn the heat off, add the remaining ingredients and stir well.
2. Add this warm mixture to your high-powered blender and blend.
3. Pour into your favourite mug, sprinkle with a little extra cinnamon or raw cacao powder and sip away!

SERVES 1
PREP TIME: 10 MINUTES, INCLUDING COOKING

Meta-boost Drink

This drink will kickstart your metabolism and digestion in the morning.

½ tsp finely grated fresh ginger

½ tsp ground cinnamon

a pinch of cayenne pepper

1 tsp Manuka honey or stevia powder

1 tbsp apple cider vinegar

juice of ½ lemon

1 cup filtered water

1. Combine all the ingredients in a shaker cup with a lid, and shake to combine. Or warm the water, add all the other ingredients and mix with a spoon.

SERVES 1
PREP TIME: 5 MINUTES

Healthy Freezochino

Oh, you'll know I am South African now – SA gals love their Freezochinos! They're delicious, but usually packed with sugar and preservatives. Now you can enjoy an all-natural version.

1 tsp instant organic coffee or 1 espresso shot

1 tbsp stevia powder

¼ tsp Celtic sea salt

½ tsp ground cinnamon + extra to sprinkle

1 tbsp raw cacao powder

1 cup Almond Milk (see page 306) or coconut milk

1½ cups ice cubes

1 tbsp nut butter (optional)

1. Place all the ingredients in a blender and process until the ice is crushed. Sprinkle with a little extra cinnamon to serve, if desired.

SERVES 2
PREP TIME: 10 MINUTES

Chocolate Cinnamon Thickshake

¼ avocado

½–1 frozen banana

2 heaped tbsp raw cacao powder

1 tsp ground cinnamon + extra (to serve)

a pinch of grated nutmeg

a pinch of sea salt

1 heaped tbsp raw honey, maple syrup or stevia powder

1 cup ice cubes

1 cup milk of choice

2 tbsp Greek-style yoghurt (optional)

walnuts, crushed

1. Process all the ingredients together in a blender. If it's too thick for your taste, add some filtered water to thin it out. Serve with crushed walnuts and extra ground cinnamon.

SERVES 1
PREP TIME: 5 MINUTES

Beetroot and Carrot Juice

A delicious blend, especially for those who are new to juicing since the combination is naturally sweet and it gives a great energy boost.

2 raw beetroot, peeled and chopped

2 carrots, peeled and chopped

a handful of parsley

½ tsp ground turmeric

1 tsp stevia powder

3–4 ice cubes

juice of 1 lemon

½ cup coconut water

1. Blend all the ingredients together in a blender or juicer. If the juice is quite thick, thin it with some coconut water or filtered water.

SERVES 2
PREP TIME: 5 MINUTES

JSHealth Green Juice

Get in a huge dose of vitamins and minerals with this nutrient-rich blend of greens.

1 cup spinach and/or kale leaves

½ cucumber

4 sticks celery

a small knob of ginger, peeled

½ green apple

juice of 1 lemon

½ cup filtered water or coconut water

3–4 ice cubes

parsley, mint, aloe vera juice and/or apple cider vinegar (optional)

1. Blend all the ingredients together in a blender or juicer. If the juice is quite thick, thin it with some filtered water or extra ice cubes.

SERVES 1
PREP TIME: 5 MINUTES

Homemade Almond Milk

Once you've tried this recipe, you'll never go back to the store-bought version.
Save the almond pulp for baking. Recipe inspired by Dr Libby's Real Food Chef.

1 cup raw almonds, soaked in water for 12 hours

a pinch of Himalayan pink rock salt

½ tsp ground cinnamon

¼ tsp vanilla extract

3 cups filtered water

1. Combine the soaked almonds with the salt, cinnamon and vanilla in the bowl of a food processor or blender. Process until coarsely chopped. With the motor running, add the water until the ingredients are very well ground.

2. Strain the mixture through a piece of muslin into a bowl or jar. Add the almond meal if you don't mind a coarse texture to the milk.

3. Use the almond milk as you would any other, keeping it refrigerated until ready to use.

4. Once you have made the milk, dry off the almonds to make almond meal. In a food processor, add the almonds and pulse until they are crumbs. Store in the fridge.

MAKES 1 LITRE
PREP TIME: 15 MINUTES + OVERNIGHT SOAKING

Strawberry and Coconut Thickshake

Just like the strawberry milkshakes you loved as a child – but this one is packed
with good-for-you ingredients and has no added sugar.

1 cup strawberries + extra slice (to serve, optional)

1 serving vanilla pea protein powder

2 tbsp desiccated coconut + extra (to serve)

1 tbsp coyo or Greek yoghurt

a handful of walnuts

a squeeze of lemon juice

1 tsp ground cinnamon

1 tsp raw honey

1 cup Almond Milk (see above)

1 cup ice cubes

1. Place all the ingredients in a high-powered blender and blitz until thick and creamy. Top with desiccated coconut and strawberry slices, if desired.

SERVES 2
PREP TIME: 10 MINUTES

ICY POLES THAT HIT THE SPOT

Pour any of these into your icy-pole container:
- Fave juice or smoothie
- Coconut water, mint and frozen or fresh berries

Healthy Vitamin Water

A delicious way to boost your hydration AND vitamin intake. I love prepping several versions in the summertime with whatever fresh fruit I have on hand. They work well at parties too.

½ grapefruit, sliced

½ Lebanese cucumber, sliced

½ lemon, sliced

½ lime, sliced

½ cup mint leaves

a pinch of Himalayan pink rock salt

3 cups filtered water or coconut water

1. In a serving jug or bottle, combine everything and stir well. Don't feel like you need to add everything – just use whatever you've got.

MAKES 1 JUG
PREP TIME: 5 MINUTES

MY FAVOURITE VARIATIONS:

Basic Citrus 1 sliced orange, ½ sliced grapefruit, 1 sliced lemon

Peach and Vanilla 1 sliced peach, 2 vanilla pods, a pinch of stevia powder

Mint, Cucumber and Lime a handful of mint leaves, 1 sliced Lebanese cucumber, 1 sliced lime

Grapefruit and Citrus: ½ sliced grapefruit, ½ sliced Lebanese cucumber, ½ sliced lemon, ½ sliced lime, ½ cup mint leaves, a pinch of Himalayan pink rock salt

Cleansing Tonic Shot

Perfect if you're detoxing!

a small knob of ginger, peeled and finely grated

½ tsp cayenne pepper

½ tsp stevia powder or raw honey

juice of 1 lemon

1. Mix together all the ingredients and drink as a shot. Or mix with ½ cup filtered water. It will taste spicy and zesty, and it is incredible for your digestive system.

SERVES 1
PREP TIME: 5 MINUTES

Amazing Resources for a Healthier Life

Health is a wonderful, fascinating thing, and there's always something new to learn. It doesn't matter where you are on your health journey, there are plenty of resources to help you take the next step. Here you'll find my favourite blogs, websites, apps, films, books and Instagram accounts.

Food and recipe blogs

101 Cookbooks
100 Days of Real Food
A Healthy Passion
Alkaline Sisters
Deliciously Ella
Elana's Pantry
Fig and Fork
Gluten-Free Diva
Gluten-Free Girl
Gluten-Free Goddess
Green Kitchen Stories
Kale with Love
Kibby's Blended Life
Lola Berry
My New Roots
Nourished Living
   Network
Nutrition Stripped
Oh My Veggies
Oh She Glows
One Part Plant
Petite Kitchen
Pure Posana
Roost
Scandi Foodie
So Good and Tasty
Sprouted Kitchen
Supercharged Food
The Healthy Chef
The Holistic Ingredient
The Holy Kale
The Nourishing
   Gourmet
Vegan Easy
Veggie Wedgie
Vegie Head
Whole Promise

Health and educational websites

Chris Kesser
Danielle LaPorte
David Wolfe
Dr Hyman
Dr Marilyn Glenville
Dr Mercola
Elevate Vitality
en*theos
Harvard School of Public Health Institute
   for Integrative Nutrition
Lissa Rankin MD
Mark's Daily Apple
MindBodyGreen
Mindd Foundation
Natural Society
Sara Gottfried MD
Sarah Wilson
The Psychology of Eating
Well + Good NYC

Awesome apps

Buddhify2
Chemical Maze
ESCOP Herb Reference
Heart Meditation with Deepak Chopra
My Pilates Guru
Period Tracker Lite
Seafood Watch
Sleep Stream
Spirit Junkie
Yoga 101

Inspirational Instagram accounts

@_sarahwilson_
@aconsciouscollection
@basebodybabes
@cocohealth
@consciousfoodie
@cookeatrunrepeat

@deliciouslyella
@elsas_wholesomelife
@feltbyheart
@flowathletic
@gabbybernstein
@hannahbronfman
@health_and_me
@holistichealing
@jesscoxnutritionist
@joyoushealth
@Julia&Libby
@katiedalebout
@keriglassman
@leesupercharged
@lornajaneactive
@nourishandbalance
@peteevanschef
@sammiwallis
@sproutedkitchen
@theholisticingredient
@theholykale
@veggie_moments
@yummololaberry

Online fitness classes

Barre3
BeFIT
Daily Burn
Do Yoga With Me
Tara Stiles
YogaGlo

How to deep belly breathe

It's amazing how breathing through your diaphragm can make you feel so much better. Check out Dr Elisha Goldstein's instructional video www.youtube.com/watch?v=ceoXgjVpbOI

Food-related films

Fat, Sick and Nearly Dead
Food Matters
Forks Over Knives
Supersize Me
That Sugar Film

Brilliant books

Accidentally Overweight – Dr Libby Weaver
Balance Your Hormones, Balance Your Life – Dr Claudia Welch
Breaking Free from Emotional Eating – Geneen Roth
Diet No More – Judith and Jenny McFadden
Food Rules – Michael Pollan
Food: The Good Girl's Drug. How to Stop Using Food to Control Your Feelings – Sunny Sea Gold
In Defense of Food – Michael Pollan
Living Foods Lifestyle – Dr Ann Wigmore
Natural Health, Natural Medicine – Andrew Weil, MD
REVIVE – Dr Frank Lipman
Rushing Woman's Syndrome – Dr Libby Weaver
Superfoods: The Food and Medicine of the Future – David Wolfe
Sweet Poison – David Gillepsie
The Beauty Detox Solution – Kimberly Snyder
The Body Ecology Diet – Donna Gates
The Calorie Myth: How to Eat More, Exercise Less, Lose Weight and Live Better – Jonathan Bailor
The Conscious Kitchen – Alexandra Zissu
The Gabriel Method – Jon Gabriel
The Optimum Nutrition Bible – Patrick Holford
The Pill – Jane Bennett and Alexandra Pope
The Ultramind Solution – Mark Hyman, MD
Thrive – Arianna Huffington
Wheat Belly – Dr William David, M.D.
When Food is Love – Geneen Roth
Women, Food and God – Geneen Roth
You Can Heal Your Life – Louise Hay

Before I let you go ...

My health journey has been an unforgettable ride, filled with learning and a lot of love.

I completed a Bachelor of Health at Macquarie University, Sydney. In this three-year course, I learnt a great deal about human biology and how to promote health in the body. I wanted to be a clinical nutritionist, so I followed up my degree with a two-year course in Nutritional Medicine at a private college. During that time, I observed an integrative GP in clinic, and devoted my life to reading books, attending seminars and retreats, and talking to health experts around the world. I also earned a Certificate IV in Food Coaching.

In my fourth year of study, I felt this incredible urge to release all the knowledge I was gaining. Deep down, I knew I wanted to clear up the confusion, mixed messages and propaganda about health, and help women heal their relationships with their bodies. I started my blog, www.jessicasepel.com, as a creative outlet. I worked on the blog for around five months before I made it public. Why? I was nervous! But my gorgeous partner, Dean, convinced me I had something special to share. So I took the plunge, began publishing my posts ... and the rest, as they say, is history.

People responded instantly, and I soon realised I wasn't the only one battling with loving my body and myself – far from it. I opened my eyes and saw so many tired, unhappy, exhausted, anxious and overweight people looking for answers. I don't pretend to have all the answers. But I do know we need to start tuning in to our bodies to figure out what they really need. Though I'm a few years wiser, I still don't understand why – and when – women became so disconnected from their own bodies. It breaks my heart. That's why I tell people I'm still on a health journey. I'm still learning, and I really hope my blog – and now this book – plays a part in enhancing the quality of life of my readers.

I'm often asked how I built up my health brand. The truth is, it grew organically. But if I had to pinpoint the reason why my blog has been so successful, it would be its honesty. I don't hold back – you shouldn't either.

Being real means being relatable. There are so many people out there who need to hear they're not alone; they will learn and benefit from your journey. We underestimate the power of our own voices and the beautiful ways we can help each other. The human connection is so powerful, and it needs to be harnessed more.

I want to empower women to support each other, not tear each other down. That's why I do what I do.

Jess xo

Big thanks

The Healthy Life is the first of hopefully many books! It's the product of years of research, tapping away at the computer, and tons of passion and support. I have so many people in my life to be grateful for, but there are a special few that I can't thank enough.

Dean, my darling partner. You are my rock and so much more. I could never have written this book without your support and absolute devotion to helping me make my dreams come true. You believed in me from the start, and I never would have predicted we'd end up here! You make me the happiest girl in the world. I love you.

Nicky, my gorgeous mother and mentor. Thank you for your guidance and patience over the years. You steered my love and appreciation for healthy food, and you're my biggest cooking inspiration. Oh – and thank you for letting me use your kitchen for all of my crazy experiments!

Glenn, my lovely father and role model. I appreciate how you instilled the importance of healthy living in me from a young age. Thank you for your ongoing support and business acumen, and for always being there to offer sage advice and make me smile. You've shown me what really matters in life.

Gabrielle and Olivia, my beautiful sisters. I am so lucky to call you family. Thank you for the constant love, support and encouragement. I'm proud of you both, and that will never change. I can't wait to see what you have in store for the world.

Barbie, my incredible grandmother. I always remember you glowed with health and happiness from the inside out. Thank you for taking me to health spas from a young age, letting me raid your supplements cupboard, and teaching me the importance of meditation.

Layla, my best friend, soul sister and second mum. You have taught me such valuable life lessons for which I'll be forever grateful. You are one of my biggest health mentors and influences, and best friends for life!

Dr Jeff Jankelson, my integrative GP and mentor. Your guidance and encouragement throughout my studies was invaluable. Thank you for believing in me and for pushing me to start my own business.

Cathy and Jane, my inspirational aunties. You have both had such a positive influence on my life, and have always encouraged me to cook with love. Your Friday-night feasts are a highlight of my week.

Hannah, Sam, Cara and Julia, my fantastic cousins. Thank you for your unwavering support, and for spreading my message to all of your equally cute friends.

Kira, Cayley, Montarna, Steph, Vicky, Alexa and Britt, my best friends. I could never do what I do without you. You're my biggest fans, always there to chat and offer advice. You may not realise it, but so much of my inspiration comes from you.

Dr Libby Weaver, for being a huge mentor to me. Your research, books and nutritional philosophy approach have really inspired my own work in this field as well as my own personal journey of healing – thank you. Words cannot describe my gratitude.

Carli Freiberg, for being such a special friend to me. You have always inspired me with your quest for an honest and wholesome life. You are not afraid to be real and vulnerable. You are living a holistic life in every sense. Thank you for your wisdom.

Ingrid Ohlsson, my publisher. You helped me make this huge dream into a reality. Thank you for believing in me and my message. Thank you for your constant support, encouragement and dedication to making this beautiful book possible. I have such admiration for you, both personally and professionally.

Charlotte Ree, my publicist. It is because of your faith that I could make this dream happen. You believed in me from the get-go. You are a true superstar in every sense. Thank you so much for your constant care and guidance. Your support blows me away.

Danielle Walker, my editor. I am beyond grateful for your hard work as we brought this book to life. Your TLC comes through in everything you do. It has been such a pleasure going through this labour of love with you!

Kate Summers, Olivia Templeman and Alex Solomon, my team! You girls are superstars. I count my blessings to have found such a dynamic group of women who believe in the JSHealth message. You have such love and passion for wellness and supporting others, and thank you for helping make my work so enjoyable. I couldn't do it without you.

First published in 2015 by Pan Macmillan Australia Pty Limited
1 Market Street, Sydney, New South Wales, Australia 2000
Text copyright © Jessica Sepel 2015
Photography copyright © Rob Palmer 2015
Additional photography © Jeremy Simons 2015
The moral right of the author has been asserted.

Cataloguing-in-Publication entry is available from the
National Library of Australia
http://catalogue.nla.gov.au

Design by Kirby Armstrong
Editing by Foong Ling Kong
Index by Frances Patterson, Olive Grove Indexing Services
Typesetting by Kirby Jones and Post Pre-press Group
Photography by Rob Palmer
Additional photography by Jeremy Simons
Photography on pages 29 and 61 by Tal Gilead
Prop and food styling by Bernadette Smithies
Food preparation and recipe testing by Sarah Mayoh
Illustrations by Juliet Sulejmani

The publishers and their respective employees or agents will not accept
responsibility for injuries or damage occasioned to any person as a result
of participation in the activities described in this book. It is recommended
that individually tailored advice is sought from your healthcare
professional.

Colour and reproduction by Splitting Image Colour Studio,
Clayton, Victoria
Printed and bound by 1010 Printing